TRUE CRIME

Key Themes and Perspectives

Ian Cummins, Martin King and Louise Wattis

Guest contributor
Katerina Gachevska

First published in Great Britain in 2025 by

Bristol University Press
University of Bristol
1–9 Old Park Hill
Bristol
BS2 8BB
UK
t: +44 (0)117 374 6645
e: bup-info@bristol.ac.uk

Details of international sales and distribution partners are available at bristoluniversitypress.co.uk

© Bristol University Press 2025

DOI: 10.51952/9781529238204

British Library Cataloguing in Publication Data
A catalogue record for this book is available from the British Library

ISBN 978-1-5292-3815-0 hardcover
ISBN 978-1-5292-3819-8 paperback
ISBN 978-1-5292-3821-1 ePub
ISBN 978-1-5292-3820-4 ePdf

The right of Ian Cummins, Martin King and Louise Wattis to be identified as authors of this work has been asserted them in accordance with the Copyright, Designs and Patents Act 1988.

All rights reserved: no part of this publication may be reproduced, stored in a retrieval system, or transmitted in any form or by any means, electronic, mechanical, photocopying, recording, or otherwise without the prior permission of Bristol University Press.

Every reasonable effort has been made to obtain permission to reproduce copyrighted material. If, however, anyone knows of an oversight, please contact the publisher.

The statements and opinions contained within this publication are solely those of the authors and contributor and not of the University of Bristol or Bristol University Press. The University of Bristol and Bristol University Press disclaim responsibility for any injury to persons or property resulting from any material published in this publication.

Bristol University Press works to counter discrimination on grounds of gender, race, disability, age and sexuality.

Cover design: Qube Design
Front cover image: iStock/GeorgePeters

Contents

| 1 | Introduction | 1 |

PART I Exploring True Crime
2	A Short History of True Crime	11
3	Ethics and True Crime	24
4	True Crime and Punishment	38

PART II Case Studies
5	Norman Mailer's *The Executioner's Song*	53
6	British Serial Killers on Screen	65
7	Darkness Doubled: The Bundy Myth	81
8	Fear of Masks: The Crimes of Peter Sutcliffe	93
9	True Crime/*True Detective*	108
10	True Crime and News Representations of a Femicide in Bulgaria: Narratives of Conspiracy and State Corruption *Katerina Gachevska*	121
11	Lucy Letby: The Vanilla Killer	136
12	Conclusion	148

| References | 159 |
| Index | 186 |

1

Introduction

In November 1959, Truman Capote read a brief news report in the *New York Times*. The report was a short account of a murder in Kansas of wealthy farmer. The story was a brief factual account of the brutal attack and murders of Mr Hebert Clutter, his wife and two teenage children. The family lived on a wheat and cattle ranch in a remote part of Kansas. Capote was a well-known, awarding winning author and literary figure. In a later interview with the *New York Times*, Capote stated that he had been seeking to write a non-fiction novel. He explained:

> after reading the story it suddenly struck me that a crime, the study of one such, might provide the broad scope I needed to write the kind of book I wanted to write. Moreover, the human heart being what it is, murder was a theme not likely to darken and yellow with time. (Plimpton, 1966)

The final result of Capote's research was the true crime classic *In Cold Blood* (1966). Capote's work can be viewed as one of the starting points of the modern true crime genre. *In Cold Blood* (1966) provided a template, which many writers have followed. This template includes the central positioning of the author, a focus on the motivations of the perpetrators and the marginalization of the suffering of victims and families. The development of true crime and the recent explosion in the genre that are examined in this volume have seen shifts in the balance between these features. The fundamental framework is still visible. In the intervening years true crime has witnessed a boom in popularity, in print, on screen and, more recently, via the development of new techniques, such as podcasts, streaming services and social media. It is only relatively recently that it has become the subject of academic analysis and critical study. This volume will examine in detail examples of true crime texts old and new. This will be achieved by examining the texts through the lenses of a range of disciplines including criminology, sociology, psychology, media studies and cultural analysis. In doing so, the goal of this volume is to apply these academic perspectives to better understand the genre's cultural impact.

This cultural impact can take many forms. Haggerty's (2009) work in the serial killing industry in which he argues that serial killing is essentially a phenomenon of modernity, with a particular focus on the role of the mass media, now of course expanded to include new platforms, and the rise of celebrity, is a key concept that will be explored within this volume. Similarly, Greer's (2004) work on mediatized murder and the relationship between the media and its audience within the true crime genre is also a key text.

The increased public consumption of true crime is another key area examined within this volume. Wattis (2024) argues that true crime offers the thrill of confronting brutality in a safe environment. Seltzer (1998) has suggested that we now live in a culture 'in which addiction to violence has become not merely a collective spectacle' but 'one of the crucial sites when private desire and public fantasy cross'.

Within these broad theoretical frameworks, true crime will also be examined in relation to class, race and gender, and we feel that the multi-disciplinary of approaches taken within the volume is one of its strengths.

Taking a variety of critical academic lenses to true crime is vital in seeking to understand how the portrayal of particular types of crime and offenders influence wider public understandings. This becomes even more significant in an environment where the boundaries between fact and fiction have been blurred and there is such a symbiotic relationship between crime reporting and other cultural forms. Sensationalism has been a feature of the coverage of crime since the invention of print media. It is open to debate whether modern social media has taken this to new levels as the prurient interest in true crime expands into new forms and forums. Sensationalized media coverage can lead to the perception that crime is increasing when it is actually falling (Ditton et al, 2004). This can drive increased public anxiety and lead to a focus on crimes such as serial murder that are, thankfully, comparatively rare (Cohen, 2011). True crime makes claims for authenticity and validity. It can skew public perceptions of what constitutes a 'typical' crime or rates of violent offending. This can increase public fear but also put pressures on policy makers.

Another key area that this volume explores is the ethical questions raised by the production and consumption of true crime. The overarching ethical concern is that true crime exploits the suffering of victims and families for commercial gain. True crime content is based on the real-life experiences of individuals, families and communities who have been forced into the media spotlight. The curious form of fame or celebrity, which is attached to those caught up in crimes that become the subject of intense media scrutiny, is not one that has been actively sought. Wattis (2024b) highlights the potential retraumatizing impact that this commercialization can have.

The other ethical question that follows from the production of true crime is 'what are the implications of consuming it?' There is a danger that true crime becomes a respectable form of voyeurism rather than a sober reflection on the nature of crime and punishment. True crime texts also raise questions about the boundaries between fact and fiction. True crime is part of the broader entertainment industry so will construct a narrative and frame events in such a way as to engage consumers and increase dramatic impact.

True crime has adopted many of the conventions and the narrative arc of crime fiction and drama. This includes the construction of moral dichotomies that position the perpetrator as 'other'. In addition, populist ideas, for example, that liberal attitudes and policies mean that criminal justice system (CJS) agencies are hampered in the fight against crime, are often deeply embedded within the true crime discourse. True crime's focus on individuals ignores the social, economic and political construction of crime and criminal behaviour (Carlen, 1992).

Popular representations of law-and-order echo themes in crime fiction where detection is a battle of wits between criminals and police officers. More recent developments have seen the production of a now cliched portrayal of the loner detective who is both obsessed with the job and broken by it. True crime has incorporated some long-standing tropes within cultural representations of law and order. These include an uncritical representation of the police as the thin blue line protecting society. One of the questions considered in this volume is whether the genre can become a space where some of the key arguments that have shifted law and order to the right can be challenged.

Since *In Cold Blood* (1966), the gonzo journalist perspective, in which the reporter or podcaster places themselves at the centre of the action, has become a key trait in true crime, and this will be examined in later chapters.

New technological developments have led to emergence of new types of true crime texts, the podcast being a particularly popular new phenomenon. One interesting development in this area has been the use of new media as a forum for the examination of miscarriages of justice. One of the case studies in the volume, an examination of the podcast *Serial*, explores the ethical issues that exist in this area, where the law, justice and media representation intersect.

The structure of this volume

This volume is divided into two sections. The first section includes a brief history of true crime, followed by an examination of the ethics of true crime and a final chapter which discusses the potential impact of the true crime boom on attitudes to penal policy. Chapter 2 is a short history of true crime that acts as an introduction to the genre. In discussing the history of true crime, this section notes that depictions of violence and brutality are not products of the modern media age. What is significantly different is the commodification of human suffering. This chapter argues that true crime has become a key element of what Seltzer (1998: 1) termed modern 'wound culture'. Seltzer (1998) defined wound culture as the ongoing public fascination with the physical and psychological impact of violence and trauma. Within wound culture, Seltzer argues, there is an obsession with sexual violence and serial killing. This will be explored in more detail in later chapters.

Throughout the volume the authors use the term true crime in a flexible way. This means that we include discussions of works of fiction as well as TV and film dramatizations of high-profile cases. This reflects the porous nature of the boundaries between 'fact' and 'fiction' in true crime. This broad definition provides a way of discussing the symbiotic relationship between the media and crime. Chapter 3 is a discussion of the ethical dilemmas that true crime creates. True crime is inextricably linked to arguments about the impact of violent content. Like crime fiction, true crime focuses on the most violent crimes, which are the rarest. Hence the domination of the serial killer as a focus for the genre. The debates about the impact of the consumption of violent content is linked to the long-standing argument that it leads individuals committing acts of violence. This is a consistent feature of tabloid coverage of high-profile cases. For example, the judge in the trial of the boys found guilty of murdering James Bulger, felt that their exposure to violent videos was a factor in their committing the crime. The fact that there are repeated moral panics about the issue should not obscure the potential impact of violent content. The development of mass media has seen a huge growth in the availability of violent media that is easily accessible. True crime fundamentally takes the suffering of individuals, families and communities, and monetizes it. It is a genre that is particularly suited to the digital age. One of the long-standing criticisms of true crime has been the focus on male serial killers and the marginalization or exploitation of victims. This chapter examines this issue. It then goes on question the claim that new forms of true crime represent a progressive, ethical shift in the genre. New approaches to true crime, most notably *Serial*, represent a commitment to exposing injustice and to highlights organizational and institutional failures in the CJS.

Part I concludes with a discussion of the development of the politics of law and order since the Thatcher and Reagan revolutions of the early 1980s. This period has seen an expansion of the penal state. The USA and the UK have seen expansions in the use of imprisonment alongside new forms of more punitive sentencing. Critical criminology has highlighted key areas including the framing of debates about crime rates, the focus on violent crime, racist discourses, a lack of scrutiny of white collar and corporate crime, and ongoing institutional failings.

Part II of the volume comprises a series of case studies. These case studies explore key texts in true crime through a variety of multi-disciplinary academic lenses.

Issues and debates around ethics, crime and punishment and the role of the death penalty are explored in relation to the case of Gary Gilmore via Norman Mailer's work.

Chapter 6, British Serial Killers on Screen, discusses the way in which the representation of British serial killers has a lot in common with the British kitchen-sink dramas of the 1950s/60s and, as such, provides a sharp contrast to the often glamourous portrayal seen in US crime texts.

The creation of the serial killer as celebrity is examined through an exploration of the myth of Ted Bundy, using a number of true crime texts which do, we would argue, glamorize Bundy. This is contrasted with the psycho-geographical approach that underpins Gordon Burn's portrayal of the crimes of Peter Sutcliffe, the so-called Yorkshire Ripper. The role of the citizen detective is examined in relation to emerging new media formats for true crime. We are grateful to Dr Katerina Gachevska for her contribution, a discussion of the way in which true crime texts have approached a case of murder linked to political corruption. During the writing of this volume, the trials of Lucy Letby, the British nurse labelled 'The Vanilla Killer' by the media, took place. Chapter 11 is a case study analysis of the media coverage of the case.

A note on method: bricolage and true crime

The authors argue that bricolage is a research method that is ideally suited to the analysis of true crime. It is a method that has become increasingly popular particularly in sociology and cultural studies. Bricolage is flexible and adaptive. It allows researchers to use a range of tools and methods to construct a comprehensive understanding of an area. In this volume, it is used to explore individual cases as well as the wider true crime phenomenon.

Bricolage as an approach is supported by Levi Strauss' (1972) ideas on the complexity and unpredictability of the cultural domain. Lincoln (2001) sees the bricoleur as anthropologist. Wibberley (2012: 6) argues 'bricolage brings together in some form, different sources of data'. It is important to consider the process by which the bricolage is built. It forms a reflexive commentary (Wibberley, 2012). Using bricolage as a research method allows, in fact requires, the researcher to draw on a wide range of texts and sources. The attraction of bricolage is that there is not necessarily a hierarchy of the significance of texts that need to be observed. This volume, then, considers academic texts on psychology, sociology, criminology and penal theory, alongside media texts. Bricolage is an inclusive not an exclusionary approach. We, therefore, consider a wide range of texts from a number of sources, both academic and populist. Kincheloe (2005) argues that bricolage allows researchers to construct a method from the tools that are at hand. He suggests that it is a fundamentally radical approach that challenges the notion that there are 'correct' methodologies that are universally applicable. Bricoleurs creates a new hybrid method for each new project. In this work, bricolage is the overall approach, but it has been developed or used differently for the themes that we explore. This involves a slightly different focus or concentration on sources or texts. Bricolage can be viewed as a toolbox approach. Denzin and Lincoln (2000) regard bricolage as an eclectic approach that allows the researcher to draw on methods from a range of disciplines and employ them as appropriate.

Kincheloe (2005) emphasizes that bricolage requires researchers to move beyond their own disciplines. He argues that researchers become too narrow in their focus and concerns. This process of engaging with new methods and conceptual paradigms is a vital one in that it leads to new disciplinary approaches and should, in Kincheloe's (2005) view, lead to creative, dynamic and critical forms of research. Bricolage has its roots in philosophical perspectives that form the basis of critical theory. It requires the analysis of power relationships and the way that they are embedded within particular modes of discourse. Roberts (2018) notes that bricolage as an approach can put researchers, who seek to use it, at odds with the more instrumentalist paradigms that dominate the neoliberal academy. He notes such researchers often face huge challenges to gain ethical approval to conduct direct field work. Kincheloe (2001) suggests that there is an implicit assumption in the criticism of inter-disciplinary approaches that means that the research is somehow superficial. This is, of course, linked to the notion that there is purity and rigour in particular methods that need to be maintained. This can be manifested in a range of often dismissive reactions to bricolage and the products of its use. This is partly because bricoleurs as researchers are stepping into new spaces.

Conclusion

In putting together this volume we produced a list of questions which we think are pertinent for students of true crime to consider:

- Why does true crime fascinate us?
- What are the ethical implications of the production and consumption of true crime?
- What does true crime reveal about the nature of society and its values?
- How does true crime affect wider public attitudes to law and order?
- How can the conventions of true crime be used to highlight critical organizational and institutional failings within the CJS?

It is our hope that this volume, with its overall aim of applying critical academic lenses to a range of true crime texts to better understand the genre's cultural impact, will have provided at least some of the answers to these questions and, hopefully, will stimulate further debate about a genre which continues to grow in popularity.

PART I

Exploring True Crime

2

A Short History of True Crime

True crime is everywhere. Seltzer (2007) suggests that true crime is the reporting of 'crime fact' that is presented in forms that have more in common with crime fiction. Punnett (2018) suggests that it is a form of entertainment that uses nonfiction narratives of criminal events that actually took place. Novelists and dramatists have always used real-life events as inspiration for their work. This continues. The long-running series *Law and Order* (Wolf, 1993–present) rips stories from the headlines. True crime is different in that it attempts to give a definitive account of a crime and its aftermath. True crime can be distinguished from journalism by the fact that it includes the addition and fictionalization of events (Punnett, 2018). True crime raises many similar ethical issues to crime fiction and drama. These include the exploitation and commodification of pain and suffering, and the representation of women and people from minority backgrounds. Alongside these, questions are raised about the politics of true crime and its relationship to wider debates about penal policy. For example, LaChance and Kaplan (2019) see much of the policing reality TV as 'crimesploitation'. They argue that these programmes are exploitative but also inherently reactionary. The framing of the programmes presents police officers battling the legal system and liberal elites as well as the offenders.

True crime is not just a genre, it is a hugely successful industry. It is a form that has spread across all modern media formats. It creates stars and fans. Crimecon UK 2024 took place in London. It advertised itself as the ultimate true crime event: 'We bring newsmakers, experts, podcasters, content creators, personalities, and the best professionals together and then we mix in enthusiasts to create a community interested in true crime' (Crimecon, 2024).

A platinum ticket for the two-day event costs over £750 – payment options are available. An ordinary day ticket for the Saturday is over £160. There was a similar event in Nashville. There was even a five-day true crime Caribbean Crimecon organized for November 2024. These events are really fan conventions with a programme that allows 'members of the true crime community' to meet the stars of the true crime podcast world, listen to guest speakers and, most importantly, buy merchandise.

True crime is a rapidly evolving genre. It is a form that is not only consumed by but often co-created with fans. The subject matter of true crime, like wider media reporting, focuses on violent and sexual crimes. These cases remain dominant. There is a cathartic element to exploring such horrific events. The evolution of true crime has seen it develop to encompass the retelling of cases alongside ongoing investigations including cold cases. True crime as a form is used to challenge miscarriages of justices and highlight issues such as domestic violence. One of the huge attractions of true crime is that allows the audience to occupy the same space as the professionals or, in the case of citizen detectives, take on aspects of the role (Seltzer, 2007). The solving of the mystery or puzzle is one of the attractions of detective fiction. This remains the case in some examples of true crime. True crime allows a return to the scene of the crime. It is part recreation and part representation (Seltzer, 2007). True crime loops back on itself. The genre has become a mixture of spectacle, information and entertainment (Seltzer, 2007). The market for true crime appears to be still expanding. The arrival of the true crime podcast has been a significant boost. Examples, including *Serial* are discussed in later chapters. There is one huge advantage that producers have, there is a continuous supply of new cases. Alongside these cases, drawn from the news headlines, there is an almost limitless supply of historical cases.

It is possible to trace a pattern in the media response to cases that become part of the true crime genre. It is important to recognize most crimes do not make it to the media. This is true of even violent and sexual offences, including murder and rape. Even in this area, many cases are given the most perfunctory media coverage. News coverage is followed by a longer documentary outlining the investigation. Then a true crime programme focusing on the case is produced. These are often followed by a crime drama or fictionalized version of the crime. This is not necessarily a linear progression. It highlights the interconnectedness of media formats and representations.

True crime: a history

The biblical story of Cain demonstrates that true crime narratives were part of cultural discourse long before Truman Capote read a newspaper report of the murder of the Clutterbuck family in Kansas. The biblical account of Cain follows or creates a murder narrative that can be seen to this day. A murder is committed, there is a motive. There is an attempt to conceal the crime. The crime is solved, and the perpetrator then brought to justice. True crime is not a product of the modern media age. In Elizabethan and

Stuart England, pamphlets were published recounting recent murders (Lake, 1990). These pamphlets included descriptions of violence and cruelty that would match the most exploitative modern TV series. The stories in these pamphlets were grounded in Christian notions of sin, divine providence and redemption. The stories are also concerned with the transgression of community values. The perpetrator has, at some point, rejected Christian values. This leads to a dissolute life and eventually crime. The only way for the murderer to be redeemed is to embrace the Christian values that they had previously rejected. These narratives contrast with the modern concerns of true crime – individual motivation and the social factors that create crime. In colonial New England, 'execution sermons' were a form of murder narrative (Gottlieb, 2005). These sermons were a public attempt to make sense of the crime. These sermons were preached on the day of the execution. The condemned were present to hear the sermons, which drew large crowds. The sermon would not refer to the offender by name. They would be called the 'sinner' or the 'condemned'. The focus of the sermon was not the crime, for which, the person was being executed. The focus was on the smaller sins that led to the ultimate crime of murder. The downfall of the individual was a failure of the community. It was also a warning of the dangers of turning away from God.

The glamourous outsider and the attraction of villainy are part of the modern construct of the serial killer, but they have long roots. *The Life and Adventures of Bampfylde Moore Carew* was first published in 1745. This was a popular tale, most of it fiction, of the life and crimes of Bampfylde Moore Carew, the son of Reverend Theodore Carew. Carew's memoirs are a picaresque tale of his adventures outwitting the establishment and cocking a snook at authority. These are both long-standing traits in criminal biographies. *The Ordinary of Newgate's Account* contained biographies or autobiographies of all those who were hanged during each Old Bailey session. It was published from 1684 onwards (Linebaugh, 1977, 1991; Rawlings, 1992). These short historics faced two of the ongoing dilemmas in true crime: how can we judge the claims for authenticity and do these accounts glamourize perpetrators? Chibnall (1977) notes that crime news inevitably personalizes events in such a way that it produces both fame and infamy.

Despite the huge changes in production, distribution and consumption of news, crime has always been a popular subject matter. From the 1850s onwards, there was a huge expansion in cheap serialized fiction. This was the result of cheaper paper, steam-driven printers, the expansion of the railways and improved transport alongside rising rates of literacy. In the UK, advertisement duty (a tax on adverts) was removed in 1853, while stamp duty on newspapers was abolished in 1855. These developments led to the creation of the mass-market penny press (Springhall, 1994). In the 1860s, cheaper publishing meant that Fleet Street targeted this sensation fiction at the fast-growing youth market (Springhall, 1994). The market for popular, cheap, easily accessible fiction and non-fiction was filled by the 'penny dreadfuls'. In the UK, the Newsagents Publishing Company played a key role in this new market. Springhall (1994) notes that the term 'dreadful' was one that was used from 1870s onwards. The term is misleading. It reflects a middle-class moral panic about cheap serialized fiction being read by the newly emerging urban working class. The development of the term has become obscured. 'Penny dreadfuls' became dominated by gothic horror stories, tales of highwaymen and the underworld as well as domestic romances. These texts became a form of gothic escapism from the realities of the daily grind of working life.

The 1930s saw the development of the *True Detective* magazine (a popular tabloid magazine, published from 1924 until 1995) and hard-boiled detective fiction. These forms were incredibly popular. There were overlaps between the two (Murley, 2008). Leading writers of detective fiction such as Dashiel Hammett and Jim Thompson wrote for these magazines. These magazines were written in a style that has become hugely influential. There was a focus on the use of working-class speech and idioms. The focus was often on crimes that took place in working class communities or individuals struggling in the depression. These magazines followed a clear narrative structure of murder, hunt for the killer, capture, trial and execution. In this narrative, there was a strong pro law and order narrative. The sensationalist nature of these magazines was reflected in the covers. These were often of women, bound and gagged in ripped clothing (Murley, 2008). One can see here a theme that reappears in modern true crime, the marginalization of (female) victims alongside the fetishization of their suffering.

News stories were the basis for works of fiction. J.M. Cain's (1934) classic novel *The Postman Always Rings Twice* is inspired by the Ruth Synder case. Synder was executed, along with her lover, Judd Gray, in 1928 for the murder of her husband. Synder hoped to benefit from her husband's life insurance. At the trial, the couple turned on each other. The New York tabloids supported the execution of Synder. Ramey (2004) notes that this case became a cause celebre during the post-World War I period where the campaign for women's rights was gaining more momentum. The *Daily News* was able to obtain a photograph of the execution. The front page of 13 January 1928 was a full-page image of Synder in the electric chair. The headline was *DEAD*. The paper sold a half million more copies than usual that day (Ramey, 2004)

In Cold Blood

Truman Capote's 1966 'non-fiction novel' has been hugely influential on the development of the true crime genre. Capote's influence can be seen on many writers including Emelyn Williams' account of the Moors Murders case *Beyond Belief* (1967) and Gordon Burn's *Somebody's Husband, Somebody's Son* (1984). The influence lies as much in the style and approach as the subject matter. The full title is *In Cold Blood: A True Account of a Multiple Murder and Its Consequences* (Capote, 1966). This quasi-archaic usage of language creates echoes of earlier murder narratives. The title raises the fundamental ethical question raised by the 'non-fiction novel'. Capote did not, despite his claims, invent a new literary genre. For example, Hersey's *Hiroshima* (1946) used the techniques of non-fiction reportage and allied them with those of the novel. His work was a literary and public sensation.

Capote had enjoyed literary success before *In Cold Blood* (Capote, 1966) made him famous and wealthy (Clarke, 2006). Capote saw a short newspaper item that reported the murder of four members of the Clutter family in the small rural community of Holcomb, Kansas. The murders were carried out by Hickock and Smith who had recently been paroled from Kansas State Penitentiary. A former cellmate of Hickock's had worked on the farm. He wrongly informed Hickock that Clutter kept substantial amounts of cash in a safe in the family home. In the early hours of 15 November 1959, Hickock and Smith broke into the family home. They then bound and gagged the family and searched the house for the safe and valuables. When they were unable to find any, Smith slit Herb Clutter's throat and shot him in the head. They then shot his wife, Bonnie, and two youngest children, Nancy, 16, and Kenyon, 15. Hickock and Smith stole some property including a portable radio and $50 in cash. They were eventually arrested in Las Vegas and extradited back to Kansas. Hickock and Smith were both found guilty on four counts of first-degree murder and sentenced to death. They were hanged at Kansas State Prison in April 1965.

Capote travelled to Holcomb with his friend, Harper Lee. Capote worked on the book for six years. It was only published following the executions of Hickock and Smith. Capote interviewed members of the community and those involved in the investigation and prosecution and conviction of Hickock and Smith. This immersion in the story is a feature of modern true crime. Capote interviewed both men when they were on death row. *In Cold Blood* (Capote, 1966) portrays Smith as the more sensitive of the two – despite his role in the murders. The book was a huge literary and commercial success. To Capote's huge disappointment, it did not win a Pulitzer price. It was widely recognized as a ground-breaking work that brought Capote's undoubted literary gifts to bear on this story. Holcomb, a quiet rural community, was shattered by this senseless violent crime. Capote's portrayal of the killers probes the social and psychological factors that produced them.

Ever since its publication, *In Cold Blood* (Capote, 1966) has been the subject of debate. While its literary merit is rarely in doubt, critics have focused on its claim to veracity. Capote brings a skilled novelist's sensibilities to characterization. However, he also brought those skills to the plot. He invented dialogue and scenes to aid his construction of the narrative. Capote claimed that he did not need to use a tape recorder and was able to transcribe interviews from his notes. Tompkins (1966) identified inaccuracies in Capote's work. It has been alleged that Capote had funds to provide legal support to Hickock and Smith but did not use them as the executions would provide the ultimate ending to the book. Capote also invented a scene where the lead detective visited the graves of the Clutter family. Capote suggested that any criticisms of the book were the result of professional jealousy (Clarke, 2006). The influence of *In Cold Blood* (Capote, 1966) is beyond dispute. It is a key landmark in crime writing and wider 20th-century American literature. Capote himself became an iconic figure. He applied a New Journalism perspective, aesthetic and approach to crime writing. This is one that has been copied but seldom if ever better.

Serial killers

Modern true crime is an extremely broad genre that examines diverse types of crime and a range of experiences across the criminal justice system (CJS). However, the true crime landscape has been dominated by the serial killer. The term was not used until the 1980s. True crime has replaced the Western as the most popular film and TV genre. Within true crime, cases involving serial killers dominated the market.

Haggerty (2009) argues that serial killing is a phenomenon of modernity. Serial killing is set apart from other forms of murder – not just by societal fascination with the perpetrator. Wilson (2009) highlights that serial killing is planned rather than impulsive in the way that many other murders are. The planning, including the selection of potential victims, is part of the motivation for the crimes. For the killer, the victims are a means to an end – their own gratification. This sets serial killing apart from murders that are motivated by financial gain or take place in the context of abusive intimate relationships. Cummins et al (2019) argue that there is template for the reporting of serial killing. This template includes a nickname for the killers – the Moors Murders, the Yorkshire Ripper and Son of Sam being famous examples. These nicknames give the killers a status and media profile that their victims are denied. Artificial intelligence (AI) was recently used to generate a picture of Jack the Ripper (Landsel, 2024). The image was criticized for glamorizing a brutal murderer. The AI appeared to look like a raffish young British actor cast as Heathcliff in a modern remake of *Wuthering Heights*. These nicknames are often at odds with the banal reality of the killers. The Yorkshire Ripper was a lorry driver. This is explored in more depth in Chapter 8. The template also includes an exploration of the motivations of the killer. Inevitably, this focus on the killer(s) leads to the marginalization of victims and their families. True crime in all its formats – magazines, documentaries and podcasts – has adopted these elements in its symbiotic relationship with serial killing. They provide a narrative structure.

Serial killing has become a distinct modern form of murder. This is not to suggest that serial killers have not existed prior to the coining of the term in the 1980s. It is that the serial killer has become a modern archetype (Foucault, 1975). The serial killer is both a cultural phenomenon but also has become a psychological case with its own typology. The features of serial killing that make it a product of modernity include the random choice of the victims, the role of the mass media and the subsequent celebrity of the killers (Haggerty and Ellerbrok, 2011). The fact that serial killers identify and target victims is one of the elements that sets these crimes apart. This aspect of the crimes has become a key element in the popular representation of serial killers as planning their crimes but also evading arrest. There is an overlap between the true crime and psychological discourse as the murders are interpreted as leaving a distinct signature that allows experts to create a profile of the killer. In true crime, this allows for the audience to become 'citizen detectives'. Seltzer (2004, 2008) described true crime as a form of crime fiction. It is most apparent in this audience form of engagement with and relationship to the form. One of the ongoing attractions of detective fiction has always been the piecing together the clues and solving the puzzle. The difference here is that the cases are real.

The development of all forms of mass media has been a key feature of modernity. True crime has been a hugely successful and adaptive form. It has been able to maintain a prominent position in cultural life through the rise of mass media, including the recent explosion of social media. There is an almost insatiable public appetite for crime news. This is particularly for crime news that involves sexual violence and murder (Greer, 2010; Jewkes, 2019). True crime and high-profile cases provide the media and fiction writers with significant source material and huge audiences. Serial killing can thus be understood as a media event (Gibson, 2006). This is even more so in the era of 24-hour rolling news. True crime is often presents itself as a chance to 'move beyond the headlines' to consider a case in more depth. This has created a secondary market. For example, at the end of a case, when the jury returns a verdict, there will be a series of newspaper article followed by TV news specials. The TV news specials are usually fronted by a reporter who 'has followed the trial throughout'. It will include interviews with key police officers in the case. The officers outline the course of the investigation and how it was 'solved'. Short clips of key moments from the investigation such as the moment a suspect is arrested and a police interview are included. In the Lucy Letby case, Cheshire Police produced their own post-conviction video that explained how they had managed the investigation. These are discussed in more detail in the Lucy Letby case study chapter. These key scenes are then often recreated in a 'drama documentary' which is screened later. The focus in these post-conviction documentaries is usually the reporter – as a representative of the wider audience, who foregrounds their experience of the trial. The documentary format also usual includes interviews with psychologists or profilers who provide expert commentary.

Serial killers have become part of modern celebrity culture, which is such a prominent feature of the modern mass and social media landscape. This landscape includes politicians, film stars, prominent business figures and murderers. They can all carve out a little slice of fame and notoriety. Celebrity culture is flexible but also extremely volatile. One example of this would be the way that certain crimes and cases receive more attention than others. Leyton (1986) notes that 'no one ever became famous by beating his wife to death in an alley'. The symbiotic media/crime relationship means that certain crimes are almost guaranteed to attract audiences. Cummins et al (2019) show that in the UK, the Moors Murders case has been an almost constant feature of the media landscape for over 60 years. Egger's analysis (2002) of US serial killers concluded that they all enjoyed their celebrity status.

True crime on TV

Biressi (2004a) classified the rise of true crime documentaries as an 'emerging genre'. In the 20 years since, it has become a dominant one. The combination of powerful stories and new streaming formats resulted in the creation of a new TV phenomenon. Two prominent examples are *Making a Murderer* (Ricciardi and Demos, 2015–18) and *The Jinx: The Life and Death of Robert Durst* (Jarecki et al, 2015–24). Streaming allows for, in fact, encourages, binge watching. It has now become a stylized approach *not* to stream. The speed of modern media means that not streaming is a form of nostalgia. It plays on notions of the cliff hanger and earlier narrative structures. There is also an unstated claim that the work is of such quality that the wait for the audience will be worth. These claims for authenticity, artistry and value are made across all areas of consumption.

These new true crime documentaries with their large budgets and high production values are in a different category to the true crime and wider law and order features, such as *America's Most Wanted* (Linder and Chao, 1988–2021), that dominated the TV landscape. The high production values were combined with the writers being given much longer periods over which to tell the story. These factors combine and lead to the elevation of true crime. *Making of a Murderer* (Ricciardi and Demos, 2015–18) drew exceptionally large audiences. True crime documentaries follow a similar narrative structure to that of a trial. There is an attempt to construct a definitive version of events. *Making of a Murderer* (Ricciardi and Demos, 2015–18) was a departure in that it challenged conventions, for example, the traditional conception of legal authority. While it can be viewed as something of a departure, it used some of true crime's most consistent tropes – for example, footage of gruesome crime scenes and the way in which the identity of the victim was reduced to the manner of her death.

One of the paradoxes of the media representation of the serial killer is that following their arrest and conviction, they are portrayed as modern gothic monsters. However, prior to that they are average, unremarkable members of society. In the Lucy Letby case, the media and police officers who investigated the case constantly referred to her as 'beige'. She lived an outwardly normal life. Dennis Nilsen worked as a civil servant (Masters, 1985). Serial killers enjoy a form of social invisibility until they are arrested. Schmid (2006) notes the paradox of the serial killer – their alleged ordinariness allows them to hide in plain sight in society. When they are arrested, their whole life and crimes are subject to intense scrutiny and interest. This interest carries on long after the trial. In some instances, high-profile cases disappear from the public and media view. However, in cases such as the Moors Murders, the public fascination continues. There appears to be an almost endless appetite for the definitive history of crimes. In this process, banal events are endowed with a huge symbolic significance. Cummins et al (2019) illustrate this point using the example of Brady and Hindley going on a date to see the film *Verdict at Nuremberg*. This film was a mainstream Hollywood move, which starred among others Spencer Tracy and Montgomery Clift. However, this early date is often presented as a sign of foreboding – a sign that the relationship will lead to murder.

Mass media has always had an interest in crime, particularly violent crime involving attacks on women. Modern critics of true crime argue that these texts involve gratuitous violence to attract an audience. This may well be the case. However, this is not a new phenomenon. In 1888, the corpse of Annie Chapman, the second victim of Jack the Ripper (Jones, 2017) was on display for those prepared to pay a penny to see it. Modern-day Ripper tours are one of the biggest attractions in London. These tours can be regarded as an offshoot of true crime. Like true crime, such tours claim to provide an authentic experience or definitive account of the crime, attempting to create the experience of being in the East End of the 1880s, in the grip of the terror of these attacks. Sexual and other forms of violence against women are endemic within society. The National Police Chiefs Council (NPCC, 2024) reports the extent of violence against women and girls. The murder of a woman by man, often a former or current intimate partner, takes place every three days. Incidents of domestic abuse account for 18 per cent of all recorded crime in England and Wales. In the year ending March 2022, there were 194,683 sexual offences, of which 70,330 were rape. These tours continue the modern commodification of sexual violence and murder. The tours make claims to authenticity that do not stand up to any real analysis. The competition between the tour operators focuses on claims to authenticity. The modern East End is not the Whitechapel of the 1880s. However, the audience suspends disbelief and eagerly anticipates the denouement of the tour – the unmasking of the killer.

Caputi (1987) identified the Whitechapel murders as marking the beginning of 'the age of sex crime'. Since that point, Jack the Ripper has become a mythical figure. The fact that the case was never solved has created a space for all kinds of speculation and conspiracy theories. Alongside the Ripper tours, there have been innumerable dramatic treatments of the case, as well as volumes that claim to solve the mystery and name the killer. In these processes, the brutal murder of women and their lives have been marginalized. Rubenhold's (2019) *The Five* is an attempt to redress the balance and focus on the lives of Mary Ann 'Polly' Nichols, Annie Chapman, Elizabeth Stride, Catherine Eddowes and Mary Jane Kelly. When it was published, the author faced a barrage of criticism from so-called Ripperologists – self-appointed experts on the case. Most of this criticism was focused on the question of whether the victims were sex workers. In raising questions about this deeply embedded view, Rubenhold (2019) was highlighting the reality of working-class life for women in late Victorian London. She was also shining a lens on the engrained misogyny in the representation and analysis of the case.

Modern media use the term Ripper to refer to other killers. This places them in some grotesque tradition of the brutal violation of women. The most prominent example of this is Peter Sutcliffe being called in the press and by the police, the Yorkshire Ripper. There is no straightforward evidence as to when the term was first used. In a bizarre twist, the fake letter and tape that consumed so much of the police investigation quoted directly from letters sent to the press during the Jack the Ripper case. This was missed by the police. Caputi (1987) argued that these crimes should be viewed as a form of patriarchal terrorism. The influence of the Ripper case can be seen in many aspects of the modern media reporting of femicide. These include the romanticization of the perpetrator of violence, prurient reporting and the denigration and marginalization of victims. These features can be mapped onto much of true crime. In addition, there is an ongoing search for the 'truth' or the definitive account of the case and its aftermath. The cases that are key in the true crime canon, continue to produce films, documentaries and biographies.

One approach to the representation of serial killers is to view it as a form of the Gothic (Simpson, 2000). Serial killers and their crimes become modern-day monsters and myths (Halberstam, 1995). The attraction for the audience is that the Gothic is designed to create fear. However, this is done in a space where the audience is safe. True crime creates a similar environment as the audience know that the perpetrators have been caught. The external environment of Gothic fiction and drama helps to create the atmosphere of forboding. In addition, the physical appearance of individuals becomes a signifier of their underlying malevolence. In the case of true crime, there is a double shuffle that takes place. The seeming normality of the serial killer becomes, when they are convicted, a signifier of evil. This double shuffle is encapsulated in the mugshot. In her essay 'In Plato's Cave', Sontag (1977) describes photography as a means of creating and maintaining nostalgia. She notes that even when photographs appear or claim to reflect a social reality, there are, in fact, social constructs. The photograph is manipulated to produce a desired effect. Documentary or news photographs are presented as documenting a reality, but they do more than capture the reality of an event. The external thus represents evil. The modern media use mugshots or other photographs alongside reports of the crime. Even though the images themselves may be mundane, the audience project on to them their feelings of repulsion towards the killer and their crimes. The most famous example of this in the UK is the police photographs of Brady and Hindley taken just after their arrest in 1965. These photographs have appeared countless times in the British media in the past 60 years. Their appearance has become a key part of the representation of the case.

In the city

Not all true crime is concerned with events that have taken place in cities. However, the anonymity that the city provides has become a recurring theme in the true crime genre. The amoral serial killer can operate in this environment where it is alleged that the community ties of old have been destroyed. There is a strong element of nostalgia here. Nostalgia is always based on a partial, faulty or idealized vision of a past that certainly never existed. The emergence of the city and mass urbanization leads to new forms of social interactions and new forms of community. This can mean the creation of new identities and the chance to escape potentially stifling social structures. Such structures do, of course, exist in the modern urban environments.

In true crime, the serial killer becomes a metaphor for the extreme dark side of the city. In the true crime narrative arc, the serial killer can walk among us. They use the city to provide a cloak of invisibility. This allows the killer to identify potential victims. The city also attracts a wide range of people. In many areas, particularly poorer ones, there is a transient population. Burn (2011) and O'Hagan (1995) in their examination of the crimes of Fred and Rosemary West show the way that they targeted marginalized young women from fractured family backgrounds. This is not the case for all their victims. However, the Wests offered homeless young women a room in their house. Once they had moved in, the Wests sexually violated and murdered them. As O'Hagan (1995) observes, these very vulnerable children and young women were only really missing for a brief period. After a couple of weeks, in several cases nobody including the police were actively trying to find them. The Wests were clearly aware of this. They also had a ready-made, very plausible reply in the unlikely event of anyone tracing one of the victims to their home at 26 Cromwell St. They would be able to say that the victim had 'moved on and left no contact details'. Burn (2011) sees the city as offering an allure of freedom. This potential can be exploited 'The freedom conferred by masks. The freedom conferred by cities. In the city the forbidden – what is most feared and desired becomes possible' (Burn, 2011: 14).

The focus on the serial killer has led to the rise of the psychological autopsy. This explores the killer. Cummins and King (2014a) highlight the way that psychological profiling has become a key part of the serial killing industry. In true crime, forensic psychologists offer detailed explanations of the motivations of offenders who they have never and are unlikely ever to meet. In drama series, the psychological profiler has become a key character. The profiler is portrayed as a representative of rationality and science. They can offer greater insight than the old-fashioned detectives wedded to outdated policing approaches and over reliant on hunches. There are arguments about the effectiveness of profiling as an investigative tool (Trager and Brewster, 2001). However, the cultural status of the profiling and profilers remains high. As the novelist David Peace argues, it does not examine questions such as 'why that crime in that place at that time' (Interview with the authors, 2016). It can therefore only offer, at best, a limited and partial explanation. Wilson (2007) notes the victims of modern UK serial killers overwhelmingly come from marginalized groups: older people, gay men, prostitutes and working-class children. One of the reasons that these murders are often not adequately investigated or given a great deal of media coverage is the marginalized status of the victims (Wilson, 2007). Sitford (2000) shows that Harold Shipman was able to continue murdering patients, who were older and from working class backgrounds, even after serious concerns were raised.

Conclusion

True crime in all its formats, accounts of real crimes, podcasts, TV dramas and films, and reconstructions or investigations has become a cultural phenomenon. The genre has been able to adapt to new demands and opportunities offered by technological developments. This was the case in the mid-Victorian era when social and economic factors combined to create a wider market for the 'penny dreadful'. It was the case when the US tabloids and magazines such as *True Detective* produced lurid crime reports in the 1930s. The arrival of streaming and the podcast offered further new formats for the expansion of true crime. These processes are not linear. The podcast is not a modern version of the 'penny dreadful'. It is a new form with its own narrative arcs and conventions. It is possible to identify overlaps and similarity. The most important of these is the insatiable appetite for tales of sexual violence and murder.

3

Ethics and True Crime

Introduction

This chapter will discuss the ethical issues linked to true crime, first, highlighting clear-cut issues with the old-style murder narratives that have come to define the genre but also how this has become more complex as the genre has diversified in the wake of cultural and technological change. The growth of violent content in media culture has concerned media, academics and politicians for decades (Newson, 1994; Barker and Petley, 1997; Bryant and Thompson, 2002; Brown, 2003). Often, the debate centres on 'media effects' and the belief, underpinned by social learning theory, that engaging with violent content influences children and young people to commit violent acts themselves (Bandura et al, 1963). Indeed, the idea media violence causes actual violence is a tabloid news favourite that propels moral panics about certain content and genres with rhetoric often focusing on the detrimental impact of violent media on children and young people (Huesmann, 2007). For example, politicians and tabloid news often invoke media effects following fatal attacks such as school shootings in the US (Meindl, 2017; Petridis, 2017; Kaufman, 2019). However, critics of 'effects' studies argue this research field is in thrall to the 'hegemony of science' where experimental conditions wrongly define variables and attempt to isolate them to prove cause and effect, ignoring the complexity of media, social context and the futility of aggregating media violence from 'real life' in a 'mediatised society' (Brown, 2003).

That is not to say, however, that the sheer volume of graphic and disturbing content is not a cause for concern, with commentators worried about the harmful impact on the self and society (Cantor, 2003; Atkinson and Rodgers, 2016; Bridle, 2019). The era of mass media has intensified in the 21st century with social life now transformed by digital technology and culture; the number of violent media on offer has grown exponentially, becoming a 'hyper-real' spectacle across a range of formats and platforms. As Brown writes, 'the imagery of violence is rarely from the screen or newspaper, in an increasingly immediate, global and intertextual mode which makes fact-fiction divides daily less relevant' (Brown, 2003: 123). Thus, while there may not be a direct cause-and-effect relationship between violent media and actual behaviour, commentators identify how content normalizes violence and fosters demand for ever more graphic 'pornoviolence' (Ray, 2018). This occurs alongside a decline in empathy and compassion for the suffering of victims as violent content is taken for granted and it becomes more and more difficult to discern what is 'real' (Bauman, 1993; Giroux, 1995; Brown, 2003; Atkinson and Rodgers, 2016; Ray, 2018). Bauman (1993: 150) refers to how the 'carnival of cruelty' offered up by the media has eroded social life where often real suffering does not pass muster for viewers because 'the "reality" tends to be evaluated according to how closely it comes to the dramatic ingenuity and precision of a crime or disaster movie or to the productivity of an arcade game'.

Summing up the current state of violent content in digital popular culture, Atkinson (2019) identifies some troubling examples available to us in online spaces and straight to our devices: approximately 422,000 videos of staged beheadings or cut from video game footage; live streaming of rape and suicides; gaming controllers enabling the sharing of 'kills'. Reflecting on this, Atkinson notes how the shifts in the form violence takes and how we access it, is fostering harmful subjectivities as we are encouraged to enjoy ritual humiliation and victimization online.

The relationship between actual and simulated violence is complex. The previous discussion concentrates on graphic and disturbing content as harmful, rather than the issue of its veracity where the extent to which graphic violence 'looks real' is viewed as a big part of the problem. Thus, if staged beheadings and shootings in games look like they happened, they pose troubling questions for how we view and participate in simulated violence in contemporary mediascapes. In this vein, Brown (2006: 232) asks, 'how embodied does "real" victimisation have to be? How is the actant hurt?' Brown's key concern lies with the challenges virtual and online harms raise for law and justice (Brown, 2003, 2006), which have become ever more complex and difficult to resolve as technology innovates and transforms (Yardley, 2017). Moving on to discuss what this might mean in the case of fake images of child abuse, Brown considers the view that given the heinous nature of images, they demand legal recourse (Carr, 2002). However, she points out it would be impossible to apply this principle to all simulated violence but recognizes the links between real and simulated harms, nevertheless: '[i]t is clear that in the case in the case of paedophilia, child pornography, endlessly circulating, shifting, pixels affect real children's lives and the dignity of children; real humiliations and human pains are generated; and real relations of (patriarchal) power are reproduced and reinforced' (Brown, 2006: 233).

While we recognize that the problem of violent media crosses the boundaries between real events and fictive media, in recent years true crime has provoked particular concern because it takes real people's trauma and suffering and monetizes it for entertainment purposes (Yardley et al 2019; Hobbs and Hoffman, 2021; Menis, 2021). True crime has surged in popularity in the era of online streaming (Horeck, 2019; Pâquet, 2021). As Horeck (2019) observes, it is a genre especially well suited to the digital era with consumption shaped and enabled by current technologies: consumption via personal devices, binge-watching and listening, audience participation and multi-platform interactions. The rise of true crime podcasts also shifts some of the emphasis from the harms of visual violence to the cultural and (un)ethical work of violence and murder narratives which make up true crime podcast content.

Indeed, true crime poses numerous ethical questions. As stated, the obvious one is it draws on real suffering and tragedy for commercial and entertainment purposes (Greer, 2017), often dwelling on salacious detail and playing to voyeuristic drives (Browder, 2006; Murley, 2008; Seltzer, 2008). In addition, it has a reputation for elevating male killers and either disregarding or exploiting victims. On the face of it, newer formats and genres look to be more ethical as they claim a commitment to exposing violence and injustice; however, this often does not bear scrutiny and reveals a different set of ethical problems. In the discussions in this chapter and later on in this volume, we probe the ethics of true crime in more depth, exploring what the 'wrongs' of true crime look like across different genres and formats, and how online spaces create particular harms, before considering if true crime can ever be a progressive force for good.

The true crime murder narrative

Murley's (2008) audit of true crime, while acknowledging diverse formats and subgenres such as literary true crime and the different cultural work performed by various genres, picks out true crime's definitive features, such as the focus on a 'single murder event' and the centring of the killer's story and motivation, with the narrative often embellished with fictional elements. Murley also highlights how true crime simultaneously invites readers and audiences to identify with the killer, while also distancing themselves from him. A further convention is how true crime dwells on the details of violated and murdered bodies in visceral detail, within textual and visual imagery:

> In true crime ... graphic destruction of bodies is commonplace. True crime is obsessed with full-on visual body horror: autopsy footage, close-ups of ligature marks and gunshot wounds on bodies, bruises or lividity on flesh, and blood pools, stains and spatters in the physical

spaces where murder has occurred are all depicted in the genre, with varying visual intensity, causing some critics to refer to true crime as 'crime porn'. (Murley, 2008: 5)

What Murley describes here resonates with Seltzer (2007: 37), who argues that true crime strives to reconstruct the crime scene in all its gory detail or what he refers to as 'an aesthetics of the aftermath: a forensic realism'. The narrative and aesthetic of what we might refer to as traditional, or 'pulp' true crime, raises clearcut ethical questions relating to the foregrounding of the killer and the way true crime exploits victims as violated and murdered bodies whose humanity is disregarded. This type of narrative also exaggerates the competency of the police and the criminal justice system to solve and resolve crime, as well as encouraging retributive responses via the focus on rare and heinous crimes (Linnemann, 2015). Writing in *The New York Times*, Annie Nichol (2024), the sister of Polly Klaas, who was abducted from her bedroom and murdered in 1993, reflects on how media and politicians draw on true crime and use it to distort victims' stories for commercial and political interests, often driving a law-and-order agenda:

> It was difficult for me to feel a sense of justice in the years after Polly's death. Although her killer was caught and convicted, we grew up watching the brief beauty of my sister's life eclipsed by a political narrative that weaponised her innocence to propel an era of mass incarceration and true crime obsession. (Nichol, 2024)

We often associate true crime with infamous killers who have generated considerable cultural content with texts often lingering on the disturbing aspects of cases. As Biressi (2001) writes, high-profile cases involving serial killers in the US and the UK such as Ted Bundy, Jeffrey Dahmer, the Moors Murders, the Wests and the Yorkshire Ripper, have become embedded in collective memory and have come to define the true crime genre. Cummins et al (2019) point out that viewers and readers seek out these texts precisely because of the 'horrific details' therein. Echoing Murley, Browder (2006) identifies visual content in true crime books as a stock feature and key selling point for readers. As such, the framing of violent acts and violent subjects in this form of murder narrative is problematic because it exploits victims and turns violence into spectacle. Moreover, we also need to ask why people are attracted to 'real' suffering. As both Browder (2006) and Biressi (2001) point out, the actuality of true crime is one of its main draws, with readers often disparaging crime fiction in favour of 'real' killers and victims.

Indeed, true crime and the serial killer are co-dependent on one another. Murley (2008) observes how true crime gave us the figure of the socio/psychopathic killer with texts poring over the actions, life stories and motivations of male killers, to understand them in mostly psychological terms (Cantor, 2003). As McCabe (2022: 42) writes, 'true crime films and documentaries have inadvertently often glorified murderers by focusing on their actions as simultaneously horrifying and brilliant'. The way texts and serial killer 'fans' indulge in unsavoury identification with killers is widespread within serial killer culture across true crime and crossing over into fiction. For instance, cultural historian Phillip Jenkins (1994) identifies how the film *The Silence of the Lambs*, adapted from Thomas Harris' book, created the figure of the charismatic, intellectual and attractive serial killer, which then influenced how people perceived 'real' killers and fuelled assumptions about them as unique individuals. Concerning actual cases, we see how culture constructs the attractive serial killer via Ted Bundy's 'handsome genius' persona (McCabe, 2021). Moreover, the demand for serial killer murderabilia and serial killer tours represent particularly distasteful aspects of serial killer fandom.

Returning to Seltzer (1998, 2007) and the idea of a pathological public sphere or 'wound culture', Seltzer views violence (real and represented) as 'addictive' as it becomes increasingly spectacular. For Seltzer, the spectacle of violence and the need to understand it in pseudo-psychological and psychiatric terms has become embedded in public discourse and true crime is a central vehicle within this:

> This kind of crime and this kind of person have their places in a public culture in which addictive violence has become not merely a collective spectacle but also one of the crucial sites where private desire and public space cross. The convening of the public around scenes of mass-mediated violence has come to make up a wound culture: the public fascination with torn and open bodies and torn and opened psyches, a public gathering around shock trauma and the wound. (Seltzer, 2007: 48)

True crime beyond the murder narrative

We have a fixed idea of true crime as murder narrative, complete with macabre details of violence and sexually motivated murder, and a big focus on visual aftermath documented in poor quality documentaries and novels. However, once we move beyond the traditional murder narrative, the possibilities of what might count as true crime become evident. For instance, Horeck's (2019) analysis of true crime in the digital era includes a chapter on elevator assault videos captured by surveillance cameras. Horeck concedes these clips, which circulate rapidly across social media, are some distance from 'constructed "true crime" products and are presented as "authentic" moments of violence' (Horeck, 2019: 58). She argues that digital culture necessitates we expand how we define true crime to 'consider the relationship between new media interfaces and the capture of violent images' (Horeck, 2019: 58). In this case study, Horeck focuses on the criminalization of Black masculinity via surveillance technology and patterns of circulation in digital mediascapes.

The diversity of true crime predates social and technological innovation and is evident in literary titles from writers such as Norman Mailer, Gordon Burn and Truman Capote. As we explore in Chapter 8, Burn's form of literary true crime not only sought to understand the 'necessary conditions' for violence and murder but also the place of extreme crime in modern media culture. Moreover, Burn approaches his subject matter in the manner of a social scientist, adopting ethnographic methods to try and understand the subjectivity of violent subjects. More recently, Michelle McNamara's (2018) critically acclaimed book, *I'll Be Gone in the Dark: One Woman's Obsessive Search for the Golden State Killer*, offers a more enlightened take on the genre, exploring our relationship to violent events and their impact on victims, communities and place.

The focus on true crime solely as murder narrative and the rise of women-led podcasts has ignited a flurry of media and academic commentary seeking to explain why true crime is so popular with women (Browder, 2006; Vicary and Fraley, 2010; Hess, 2018; Pavelko and Gall Myrick, 2019). Explanations range from women gleaning survival tactics from true crime, seeking to understand the killer's motivation, to true crime offering a vicarious experience of risk and fear given how women are encouraged to be fearful and avoid risk in the context of patriarchal culture. However, when they explored men's and women's true crime preferences, Vicary and Fraley (2010) found that although they are often overlooked, male audiences exist, but they are more interested in stories about war and organized crime as opposed to serial killers.

In previous work, Wattis (2021, 2023) identifies the hardman story as a subgenre of true crime popular with male audiences which venerates men who excel at violence, who are often connected to some form of organized crime (Mayr, 2012). These stories may involve murder, but they are not murder narratives per se. Criminal protagonists often write texts themselves as biographies and memoirs, so they control the narrative and construct a particular version of themselves (Presser, 2008). In hardman stories, victims originate from the same criminal subcultures as offenders, such as rival gangs, and are often violent perpetrators themselves. In the British context, hardman stories explore histories of London gangland – most notably the Kray twins and their associates, but the genre also includes books written by lesser-known individuals who form part of local and place folklore. In addition, the hooligan memoir, written by men involved in organized football violence, represents a further subgenre of the hardman story. Certain 'characters' such as the Kray twins and Frankie Fraser transcend their criminal identity to become bona fide celebrities, surpassing the serial killer as a celebrity (Schmid, 2008). Penfold-Mounce (2010) refers to former gangland figures who actively pursue fame by drawing on their criminal pasts and affiliations as 'underworld exhibitionists'.

The hardman genre has generated countless books, documentaries and feature films, and, in the digital era, there are now large numbers of podcasts with a masculine bent either detailing the history of organized crime or featuring interviews with an assortment of violent male subjects who excel at violence. For example, criminal hardmen, those involved in combat sports or military violence such as former Special Air Service (SAS) operatives. These podcasts follow a different format from more familiar murder narratives and 'injustice narratives' (Larke-Walsh, 2020) that revisit previous cases and cast doubt on convictions. Rather, the digital hardman format involves subjects telling their own story, often reminiscing about formative years, criminal exploits and time spent in prison. As such, they often strike a celebratory tone that does not condemn criminal subjects but appeals to a hegemonic masculine ideal which venerates violence (Connell, 2005).

The rise of digital culture and its domination of social life have transformed true crime content while maintaining the cult of the serial killer. A glance at screen media streaming and podcast content indicates that the murder narrative and the serial killer are alive and well in the true crime universe. However, social change and shifts in technology and consumption have seen different true crime formats emerging, often claiming a higher purpose in exposing injustice and corruption (Bruzzi, 2016; Larke-Walsh, 2020). Documentaries such as *Making a Murderer*, *The Staircase* and the podcast *Serial* contrast with their lower-brow documentary predecessors in that they deal with the uncertainty of guilt as opposed to merely retracing murder events where the perpetrator has already been identified. Larke-Walsh (2020) refers to documentaries which question the guilt of those convicted and the actions of the police and the criminal justice system as 'injustice narratives' which she argues should be viewed as progressive texts which foster emotional engagement with harm and injustice beyond sensationalist entertainment.

Several commentators note how the #MeToo moment/movement has influenced media output and the media's approach to male violence against women (Hoffman and Hobbs, 2021; Banet-Weiser and Higgins, 2022; Gaston-Lorente and Gomez-Baceiredo, 2022; Horeck, 2024). Hoffman and Hobbs (2021: 143) view #MeToo as creating a 'prominent platform for a type of activism that reframes female victimhood by centring women's voices and experiences and calling attention to pervasive, systemic misogyny in the wider culture'. For instance, the woman-led true crime podcast has become a true crime subgenre. These podcasts demonstrate a feminist and feminine sensibility, combining murder narratives with comedy and self-help, and a greater acknowledgement of female victims and women's fear and experiences of male violence (Greer, 2017; Pâquet, 2021). Women make up the majority of listeners with the most popular podcasts such as *My Favorite Murder* generating parasocial relationships between audiences and hosts across social media platforms. Given stock true crime narratives often fetishize female victims and position themselves as cautionary tales which reinforce female vulnerability and fear, women-led podcasts such as *My Favorite Murder* have been praised as transgressive in encouraging women to subvert gender norms relating to feminine respectability and the feminine fear imperative (Hess, 2018).

More recently, documentaries examining sexual abuse cases, which foreground victim/survivors, have emerged as another new genre of true crime. These programmes have been praised for centring victims and addressing how formal justice often fails victims (Brown, 2019). As such, they have the potential to perform progressive ethical and cultural work challenging victim-blaming and rape myths by revealing the extent and harms of sexual abuse and its relationship to power and masculinity (Leung and Williams, 2019; Horeck and Negra, 2021; Mishra and Shewan, 2023). Horeck and Negra (2021) identify victim-centred documentaries concerned with sexual violence and abuse as a product of MeToo which they argue challenged the historical silencing of victims and created a space for their voices to be heard. They discuss how listening to survivors' accounts is an affective practice that elicits responses such as empathy and outrage from audiences and challenges dominant narratives about sexual violence.

Likewise, memoirs written by rape survivors allow victim/survivors to tell their stories on their terms away from the criminal justice space which often denies and distorts victims' experiences. Fernández-Morales (2023) notes the growth in academic, media and popular cultural outputs focusing on rape and sexual violence, of which she recognizes the rape memoir as a powerful medium for personal testimony and awareness raising about sexual violence. Echoing this sentiment, Leigh Gilmore (2017) refers to the survivor memoir as an 'alternative jurisdiction' for victim–survivors. Furthermore, in digital culture victims may communicate their story across multiple formats and platforms (Fernández-Morales, 2023).

True crime that appeals to men and focuses on 'hard masculinity' raises a different set of ethical concerns. On the face of it, this has less to do with voyeuristic violence and the objectification of victims. Victims are absent in hardman stories and if they do appear, they often originate from the same violent subcultures as perpetrators. However, issues arise in the way hardman narratives celebrate violent masculinity, which differs from responses to the serial killer, who is an object of both horror and fascination. In contrast, audiences admire the hardman, who is rarely subject to censure for his infamy and competence at violence. Wattis (2023, 2024) has previously written about the way notorious gangland figures who commit serious organized violence are embraced by the collective culture as domestic celebrities with their violence glossed over. They have become cult figures in lad culture, which endorses violence as a hegemonically masculine ideal, which also legitimates misogyny. Moreover, the gangster/hardman is a figure who cuts across fact and fiction. Writing about *Peaky Blinders*, a show that has revived the British gangster aesthetic, Larke Walsh (2020: 53) notes how 'the series, like so many examples of cultural and political discourse, stresses the normalcy of male violence and the celebration of those who are strong enough to fight their way to supremacy'.

Albeit with some exceptions (Ramos-Gay, 2016), in general, the hardman is a white working-class subject and along with other troubling aspects of masculinity, there may be links to right-wing ideologies. This link is clearest between right-wing extremism and organized football violence and the football hooligan. Back et al (2003) rightly argue that viewing racism in football purely through the lens of the 'racist/hooligan couplet' restricts the problem to violent extremism and obscures the wider issue of racism across football; nevertheless, one cannot ignore the historical links between organized football violence, racism and the far right across Europe (Crabbe, 2006; Ramos-Gay, 2016). Eric Dunning (2000: 151) outlines hooligan masculinity in the following way: '[t]he masculinity norms of the groups involved tend to stress ability to fight, "hardness" and ability to "hold one's ale" as marks of being a "man," and tests of masculinity are one of the things that football hooliganism is all about'.

Football hooliganism has inspired its own branch of the hardman genre in the form of memoirs, hooligan fiction, documentaries and feature films that celebrate violence and hard masculinity and offer a vicarious experience of the hooligan underground. Redhead (2010) disparages the hooligan memoir as 'hit and tell' (p 627), with most texts being of low quality, celebrating violence and following a 'hopelessly predictable format of "went by train/van, had a fight, wrecked their pub, took their end, came home"' (Dart, 2008, cited in Ramos-Gay, 2016). However, as with the gangster, popular culture presents the hooligan as a glamorous and 'cool' character who excels at hardman masculinity, with this appeal further reflected in the popularity of designer brands associated with hooligan culture.

One should be cautious when assuming connections between the enjoyment of hooligan culture and support for right-wing ideologies; nevertheless, the celebration of one can slip into support for the latter (Smith and Raymen, 2016, 2019), accelerated and amplified by connectivity and algorithmic choices in digital culture. In digital mediascapes, hardman podcasts exist alongside other violent masculine content which is likely to appeal to a specific 'community of interest' (Fish, 1980). This could include online fight pages (Wood, 2018), sites and social media accounts devoted to football violence/hooligan culture and combat sports. Analysing online fight pages, Wood (2018) cautions against assuming a uniform male audience and Bowman (2020) makes similar points about making simplistic links between mixed martial arts (MMA) and toxic masculinity, misogyny and violent right-wing ideologies. Bowman (2020) has illustrated alternative and diverse masculine practices within the MMA; but he also concedes that 'hard masculinity is often toxic' (p 406). The complex influence of violent images and texts across digital platforms, which have become social life and not just an adjunct to it, on subjectivities, worldviews and practices cannot be underestimated. As such, the celebration of violent masculinity and its presence in various forms on assorted online platforms has the potential to cross over and coalesce with toxic masculinity and extreme ideologies which may then enter the mainstream (Sugiura and Solea, 2023).

New true crime: a critical perspective

From the previous discussion, newer genres of true crime appear as less ethically problematic and, in some cases, perform progressive work in advocating for and recognizing victims who are often overlooked due to race and class (Horeck, 2019). The new breed of documentaries that expose injustice and question guilt have been lauded for their activism and the quality of journalism (Mumford, 2016; Larke-Walsh, 2019; Sawyer, 2014). For instance, the first series of *Making a Murderer* deals with the wrongful conviction of Steven Avery for sexual assault and attempted murder, with Avery freed 18 years into a 32-year prison sentence. However, in less than two years Avery, along with his nephew, was convicted of murdering Theresa Halbach. The whole premise of *Making a Murderer* is to draw attention to how the police and criminal justice system pursued Avery a second time, due to his outsider status in a close-knit small-town US community. The documentary is unashamedly one-sided in supporting Avery, and this sparked a whole movement demanding justice for him. However, Bruzzi (2016) takes issue with *Making a Murderer*'s biased narrative which, she argues, deploys aesthetic and narrative devices to shape viewers' opinions on the case by appealing to emotion. She also notes how the new breed of 'injustice narratives' (Larke-Walsh, 2019) impose a fake order on real life given the clear tensions between film-making agendas and the reality of crime, violence and justice. Bruzzi also points to how law and justice are often compromised within the documentary space, arguing that the 'documentary can clearly serve justice, just as the law can provide riveting entertainment; it is important to remember not to blur the two' (Bruzzi, 2016: 280). Relatedly, she identifies the afterlife of the documentary and how the pursuit of justice spills over beyond the documentary with harmful consequences.

Reviewing the second series of *Making a Murderer*, Nicholson (2019) comments on the impact of the first series on the family of the murder victims and how the show, despite its claims to a higher purpose, still defaults to gratuitous and disturbing forensic detail: 'One episode is given over to the practicalities of burning a body, another to how Halbach's blood ended up on the back door of her car. Both are as gruesome as they are revelatory. It is a sharp reminder that with crime there is always a victim.'

Writing about a recent Netflix documentary focusing on Ted Bundy, *Conversations with a Killer: The Ted Bundy Tapes*, McCabe (2022: 40) echoes this, arguing that even when programme makers set out to disrupt accepted true crime conventions and reject the serial killer as a compelling figure, audiences may miss the nuance and expect the usual true crime fare. In *Conversations with a Killer*, McCabe (2022: 40) notes how the show attempts to challenge the myth of the 'genius' killer who managed to evade the police, by highlighting the role of white male privilege and the 'objectification of, or the investment in, male dominance over women' that enabled Bundy to kidnap and murder women, sometimes in plain sight. McCabe (2022) makes the point, however, that audiences did not necessarily respond to the show in the way its creators intended. Moreover, despite the show's creator claiming he wanted to do something different with the serial killer documentary, it nevertheless deploys well-worn tropes such as horror rhetoric, homing in on the killer's appearance and dramatic music and production techniques. According to McCabe (2022), this results in audiences feeling dissatisfied at not getting what they came for in terms of a conventional murder narrative, when watching this more complex take on the serial killer which attempts to dismantle the mythos around Bundy. We further explore the true crime output devoted to Bundy and the perpetuation of the Bundy myth in Chapter 7.

The rise in feminist-inspired content that recognizes violence against women and its link to power and masculinity (Rodgers, 2022) demonstrates how true crime has evolved to incorporate victim advocacy which centres survivors' stories, as opposed to following stock narratives celebrating killers and dwelling on victims as wounded bodies. For instance, Pâquet (2021) praises podcasts that raise awareness about violence against women and revisit unsolved murders, as an alternative form of justice, albeit recognizing how some podcasts continue to objectify and sexualize victims. Likewise, Hoffman and Hobbs (2021) criticize *My Favorite Murder*, one of the most popular women-led true crime podcasts, which despite including victims in the conversation and offering female listeners a therapeutic space, nevertheless defaults to venerating the male killer and monetizing murder through live shows, excessive merchandizing and book deals.

Menis (2021) has concerns about how documentaries deal with sexual abuse and trauma, arguing that in the case of Jimmy Savile, victims became nothing but 'extras' serving the Savile narrative. She also questions if media discourse is the right space to tackle trauma and sexual abuse given its commercial motives. While Biressi (2004b) questions where the line sits between objectifying and empowering victims in documentaries. All of this is salient given that documentaries examining sexual abuse have become an established genre. Recent productions have been praised for centring victims and survivor testimony, raising awareness of the power dynamics and the harms of sexual violence and the frequent injustices meted out to victims who are frequently denied recourse to justice (Mangan, 2021; Latif, 2023). However, there are concerns that creating a new genre fosters expectations among audiences about format and content, specifically relating to the positioning and framing of survivor testimony (Horeck, 2024). This has led Horeck (2024) to question the weight placed on survivor stories and speaking out within anti-rape politics which risks commodifying accounts and places pressure and responsibility on victims to tell their story and to do so in a specific way (Serisier, 2018).

Conclusion

This chapter has explored the ethical problems raised by the true crime genre. First, we acknowledge the broader issue of the ready availability and accessibility of violent media content, particularly visual images, in the context of global late capitalism where existence has become increasingly mediatized and lived online, and truth, reality and simulation become ever more difficult to discern (Bauman, 1993; Brown, 2003, 2006; Yardley, 2017). This debate does not focus specifically on actual violence and suffering but rather on the fact that violent images have become more readily available, extreme and realistic, to the point they have superseded the real thing (Bauman, 1993). While eschewing simplistic effects type concerns about how watching and playing violent content leads to the commission of actual violence, commentators worry about the harms of mainstream leisure practices and what they are doing to us (Atkinson and Rodgers, 2016; Atkinson, 2019).

The deviant leisure perspective (Smith and Raymen, 2016, 2019) highlights how spectacular practices such as graffiti, hacking, protest and subcultures, viewed by cultural criminologists as transgressive (Ferrell et al, 2008), are not the issue from a social harm perspective. Rather, the deviant leisure lens identifies legal and acceptable pursuits such as tourism, gambling, fast fashion and online culture as inherently unethical activities that harm the environment, society and the self within a consumer capitalist order that actively encourages them. Raymen and Smith (2019) make the crucial point that applying ethics to 'deviant' leisure pursuits does not scan as they exist in a socio-economic context where a shared sense of ethical obligation simply does not exist:

> [t]o suggests that such activities 'deviate' from the moral norms and values of contemporary society is to make two fatal errors. First, it makes the false suggestion that there is a coherent and shared conception of ethics and morality which simply does not exist in a consumer capitalist society predicated upon the pluralistic values of sovereign liberal individualism ... the term 'deviant leisure,' as it is used in this book, follows the growing zemiological trend in criminology to consider the myriad harms that are embedded within some of the most popular and familiar forms of commodified leisure. (Raymen and Smith, 2019: 18–19)

So where does this leave true crime? With old-style murder narratives featured in magazines, books and documentaries, some of which are still alive and well on a variety of specialist television channels and online content, the ethical problems were obvious. Old-style true crime shamelessly invited voyeurism with its hyper-sexualized images of female murder victims accompanied by forensic detail and an unsavoury interest in male killers which reduced them to psychological pathology and ignored the links between violence, femicide and masculinity, and the acceptance of masculine violence in a patriarchal culture (Caputi, 1987; Downing, 2013; Wattis, 2018). Older forms of true crime remain intact; however, social change and digital culture have ushered in novel and diverse formats, genres and modes of consumption. As previously discussed, the true crime genre is well suited to a digital era of multiple platforms, connectivity and user-generated content (Horeck, 2019). However, this leaves us with a set of ethical dilemmas in the context of: '[a] complex leisure society and a culture firmly focused on high-definition screens and networked media. It is a land of voyeurism that Presdee (2000) had presciently anticipated as a culture enabled by technology to generate heightened forms of exhilaration but also new forms of victimisation' (Atkinson, 2019: 217).

So why might we consider true crime through the lens of deviant leisure? At the most basic, true crime is an engagement with real-life suffering as entertainment. This is nothing new, but consumer capitalism and digital mediascapes turn victims and violence into digital commodity objects which the convenience of connectivity, personal devices and binge culture accelerates (Hoffman and Hobbs, 2021). True crime in the digital age intervenes in law and justice (Bruzzi, 2016), continues to reinforce victim hierarchies along class and race lines (Slakoff and Duran, 2023), and legitimates murder and tragedy as cultural mainstays which true crime enthusiasts are invited to pick over with the wider public directed to who is worthy of outpourings of collective grief. At the most extreme, this may interfere with police investigations and exacerbate the suffering of victims' families (*The Economist*, 2023). With the arrival of new genres, new conventions and audience expectations emerge, which in the case of victim-centred documentaries risk commodifying and producing a stock experience of victimhood. In addition, other genres focusing on violent masculinity may promote toxic masculinities and bring extreme ideologies into the mainstream.

True crime has evolved and diversified. As we note, this comes with a new set of more complex ethical challenges. Still, we must recognize how this diversity encompasses a range of genres and experiences that perform quite different cultural and ethical work. There is a growing body of work exploring the value of analysing crime in popular culture for enhancing the criminological imagination (Rawlings, 1998; Rafter, 2007, Rafter and Brown, 2011; Wakeman, 2013; Wattis, 2018). As Rawlings (2007) highlights, popular criminology is a distinct and complementary discourse to academic theory and research that sheds light on different criminological knowledge and more emotional and philosophical takes on crime and justice. Brown (2011) echoes this when she writes about the fictive voice as equal but different to the ethnographic voice in refracting crime and culture. This might be envisaging a better way to deal with drug markets (Wakeman, 2013) or helping us grasp theory and how theory relates to everyday life (Rafter and Brown, 2011). This does not necessarily mean we approach texts as positive and progressive. This would be naïve given the availability of graphic media/digital violence, but even amid the harms of consumer capitalism and digital culture, journalism and creative work can, nevertheless, do something good. For instance, true crime can expose injustices and deploy emotion to foster empathy for victims, advocating for victims and empowering them to act agentively (Horeck, 2019; Touquet and Schulz, 2021). As such, true crime and popular criminology more broadly can offer alternative justice spaces (Pâquet, 2021) and alternative ways of feeling and thinking about crime, violence and victimhood.

4

True Crime and Punishment

Introduction

This chapter will explore the complex relationship between true crime narratives and wider *social* attitudes to crime and punishment. It begins with an overview of the development of penal policy and the politics of law and order over the past 50 years. As with any broad area of policy, there have been ebbs and flows. This analysis is influenced by Wacquant (2009a, 2009b, 2010, 2012). He uses Bourdieu's (1977) notion of the bureaucratic field as his main analytical tool for dissecting of the development of the 'neoliberal Leviathan'. Wacquant (2009a, 2009b, 2010, 2012) argues that the neoliberalism is more than the application of market mechanisms to wider areas of life. It is a political project that involves the dismantling of welfare provisions. Bourdieu's (1977) notion of the field is a way of exploring the competing discourses, political actors and organizational interests that exist in any area of policy. Having outlined developments in the policy areas, the chapter then examines how these issues are explored within the true crime genre. It concludes with a discussion the media and true crime responses to the case of the Central Park Five. This miscarriage of justice took place during a moral panic in the USA about violent crime. Following the exoneration of the five youths, the case has become representative of the racism that underpins the US carceral state

Since the mid-1970s, governments of all political persuasions have been committed to a tough law and order agenda. One of the most noteworthy results in England and Wales has been an increase in the prison population. Critical scholars in both criminology and media studies have consistently highlighted that there is a disconnect between representations of crime and the reality. Media coverage is dominated by crimes of violence. The figure of the serial killer looms large in the media landscape. The focus on the amoral killer, who has no contact with their victims before a murder, reflects but also enforces wider concerns about how we now reside in a society of anonymous strangers (Seltzer, 2013). Alongside this focus on the motivations of killers, popular representations of detectives have produced the model of the detective, such as Wallander – *obsessed with the job, broken by the job* (Cummins and King, 2017). In the fictional world, crimes of violence are solved by detectives with a flash of intuition or Holmesian brilliance. These portrayals obscure the reality of both the overall nature of crime and violent crime. The investigation of crime is far from removed from the fictional world of Sherlock Holmes or Miss Marple. Solving major crimes is much a process of the gathering and assessment of information. A major modern investigation will certainly require the analysis of thousands of hours of closed-circuit television (CCTV) and other footage from phones. Stranger attacks are rare. Interpersonal violence that is carried out in the context of a relationship between the perpetrator and victim is much more common. This chapter begins with a discussion of the development of a politics of law and order that Simon (2007) termed 'Governing through Crime'. It then explores true crime approaches to crime and punishment. There has been a shift in perspectives here. True crime has become increasingly critical of the failings of the criminal justice system (CJS). While still heavily influenced by long-standing tropes within cultural representations of law and order, the genre has also become the site of more critical voices.

The symbolism of punishment

On 5 January 1757, Robert-François Damiens attacked Louis XV, with a knife, at Versailles. The king was not seriously injured. Damiens was sentenced to death. Before he was torn to pieces by horses, he was subjected to four hours of brutal torture. After his death, Damiens' family had to either change their names or they were banished from France. His house was destroyed. The death warrant that outlines these punishments forms the opening to one of the most seminal works in the social sciences, *Discipline and Punish* (Foucault, 1975). Foucault (1975: 130–40) uses this example to illustrate that the punishment was not simply the result of the crime – attempted regicide. It reflected the cultural attitudes and power dynamics of the period. Durkheim (1972) emphasized that punishment has a deeply symbolic function. Punishment, in this model, does not deter or rehabilitate, its purpose is to strengthen societal bounds. The institutions and rituals of punishment play to an audience that understands the meanings of the symbolic elements. There are many examples of this: the wearing of wigs and robes by barristers and judges, the physical layout of a court including the dock and the pronouncement of sentences.

There is a wider symbolism that impacts on the politics of law and order. High-profile cases generate huge waves of public emotion that had an influence on the development of penal policy. Garland (2001) identified that the politicization of law and order means that the complexities of policy making can be replaced by more immediate, expressive actions or interventions. Such interventions mean that politicians can show that 'something is being done'. They also allow politicians to claim that the public's views are being considered. Hall (2006) argued that claims to represent 'public opinion' should be treated with caution. He suggested that populist politicians formed public opinion and then claimed to be responding to it.

Foucault (1975) used the creation of the modern prison as a case study in the dynamics and operation of power in modernity. For Foucault (1975), the technologies of disciplinary power that were and are used in the prison system are illustrative of how power functions. He contrasts Damiens' death warrant with Faucher's timetable that governed all prison activities. Foucault (1975) shows that there has been a shift from the spectacle of the gallows. Punishment had moved from the visible to the invisible. The end of public punishments including executions is often used to signify progress in penal policy. Foucault (1975) counters this and sees these developments as shifts in technologies of power. The new disciplinary processes produce 'docile bodies'. This is done by taken control of all aspects of prisoners' lives – including time and space. Foucault (1975) argued that similar techniques were adopted across the institutions of modernity – asylums, schools and factories.

Simon (2007) outlined a new form of governmentality, which he termed – 'Governing through Crime'. This analysis links penal policy with political debates and wider social changes that are driven by a fear of crime. This is not to suggest that all responses to crime are driven by irrational fears. It is to highlight that policies and individual responses can often be based on immediate emotional triggers than a more rational consideration. In these responses, the fear of being a victim of violent crime has had a key role. The development of gated communities, wider ownership of sports utility vehicles (SUVs), background and identity checks, and the explosion in the use of CCTV are all driven, in part, by a fear of violent crime.

Simon (2007) developed his analysis in the US context, where there are higher rates of violent crime. However, one can see that similar developments have occurred across other liberal democracies with lower crime rates, particularly of violent crime. In these cultural developments, the media has a significant role to play. True crime with its focus on serial killers, sexual assaults and random acts of violence is part of the wider cultural meme of 'fear of crime'.

Simon (2007) argued that 'Governing through Crime' is a result of the economic and political crisis of the late 1970s and early 1980s. In the post-World War II period, there was a general consensus among politicians, policymakers and academics around penal policy. This consensus was focused on the need for penal policy to play a wider role than punishment. Its institutions should have a rehabilitative function. For example, the probation service in England and Wales was committed to a focus on supporting offenders. Probation officers were qualified social workers based in the CJS (Cummins, 2021). Offenders were viewed as individuals who could be rehabilitated and go on to make a more positive contribution to society. There were always those in elites who did not share this view and argued for more punitive approaches. This perspective would argue for longer sentences and harsher conditions in prisons. This consensus among elites was often not one that was necessarily shared by the majority of citizens. Simon (2007) argues that the victim of crime, particularly violent crime, came to function as the dominant model of citizenship. In modern democratic politics, crime is a hugely significant issue (Garland,1996). It receives huge media coverage and is regularly identified as a key issue for voters. However, the range of responses to crime in liberal democracies has clear limitations. Punitive strategies are employed because they can be presented as evidence of the state's clear commitment to tackling the issues. Increasing rates of imprisonment and lengthening sentences can be quoted as evidence of being 'tough on crime'.

Law and order have become the site of some of the most intense party-political debates over the past 40 years. Being seen or allowing your opponents to portray you in any way as 'soft on crime' is now regarded as having a political death wish. 'Soft on crime' is one of those political phrases that can be used to mean anything, in the modern political environment. It is a shorthand for a set of positions that might include supporting due process and rights for those facing charges, arguing that long sentences do not have a deterrent effect and arguing that conditions in prisons should be seen as a question of human rights.

Penal policy is an area that can be heavily influenced by high profile cases and events, which come to be regarded as marking a shift in wider public attitudes (Cummins, 2021). In the US, the Attica Riot of 1971 and its brutal crushing is such an event (Thompson, 2017). Following the retaking of the prison, the official and dominant narrative blamed the prisoners. For example, it was claimed that hostages had had their throats cut. In fact, 10 hostages and 29 inmates were killed by law enforcement officials in the retaking of the prison. This armed retaking had been ordered by Governor Rockefeller. The official narrative was underpinned by deeply entrenched racist stereotypes, alongside a portrayal of the leaders of the riot as 'the worst of the worst', that is, violent criminals who were unreformable (Thompson, 2017). In fact, one of the leaders of the riot, Elliot James Barkley (21) was near the end of his sentence for a minor parole violation. He had originally been sentenced to four years for cheque fraud – an offence that was related to substance misuse issues (Thompson, 2017).

The Attica Riot and its aftermath became a symbolic turning point away from liberal penal policies and rehabilitative approaches. This shift culminated in Martinson's (1974) 'nothing works' thesis. Martinson's article was entitled 'What Works?' It was the report of a research project that reviewed 231 evaluations of rehabilitation programmes that took place in US prisons from 1945 to 1967. The evaluations included the assessment of a range of interventions, for example, psychotherapy and educational programmes. The outcome was a pessimistic one. It concluded that none of the programmes in the study could be said to be effective. The review was published as the dominance of the optimistic reformist approaches was beginning to wane. The paper soon became known as 'nothing works'.

The expansion in the use of imprisonment is most notable in the US where the prison population has been over 2 million since 2002. This represents a rate of imprisonment of 703 per 100,000. The rate of growth is astonishing. The prison population in 1990 was 1,148,702, a rate of 457 per 100,000. The US is something of an outlier, but a similar trend can be seen in England and Wales. In the period between June 1993 and June 2012, the prison population in England and Wales increased by 41,800 to over 86,000 (Ministry of Justice, 2014). The Ministry of Justice (MoJ) forecasts that the prison population will reach between 94,600 and 114,800 by March 2028 (MoJ, 2024). In the 2024 general election campaign, both the Conservative and Labour parties committed to increasing the number of police officers and increasing the capacity of prisons.

There are several factors that explain this shift towards more punitive approaches to law and order. Penal policy cannot be examined in isolation from economic, social and welfare policies as well as wider cultural attitudes (Lacey, 2008; Cummins, 2021). The shredding of the social state (Giroux, 2011) has been a key driver in the prison boom. Neoliberalism is often described as reducing or rolling back the state. The libertarian tradition that flows from Hayek (2014) and Friedman (2016) seeks to reduce the role of the state in regulating the market. There is, however, one area where the state has clearly expanded – in all areas of penal policy. In outlining the philosophical underpinnings of what came to be termed neoliberalism, Nozick (1974) laid out the role of the 'nightwatchman state'. The state had a clear duty to protect citizens and individual property rights. This was the one area where state intervention was considered not only legitimate but necessary. Welfare retrenchment has been accompanied by the expansion of the penal state. 'Workfare' and 'prison fare' are deeply interconnected (Lloyd and Whitehead, 2018)

Simon (2007) outlines the way that law and order became a political dividing line. In this analysis, parties of the Right shifted the debate to such an extent that nominally progressive parties felt that they had no option to move towards more punitive positions. Simon's (2007) work outlines the way that fear of crime, at a time of falling crime rates, became a huge factor in political debates. Political parties must appear to be strong on law and order.

Newburn and Jones (2005) show that this became something of a zero-sum game where the public is assumed to fear crime and resent criminals. The success of the Clinton Democrats presented a model that New Labour soon followed. After the 1997 election victory, Blair and Brown visited Washington to learn the lessons of the successful Clinton campaign. One of these lessons was that being tough on law and order as well as welfare policy was a key component (Cummins, 2021).

In modern politics, symbolism and presentation have become ever more powerful. This is particularly the case around penal policy. In this area, the key message is 'being tough'. Newburn and Jones (2005) highlight the success of the Bush campaign in the 1988 presidential election, in using the case of William Horton to portray his opponent, Dukakis, as weak on crime. Horton was serving a life sentence without parole when he was granted a weekend furlough. He did not return and was later convicted of offences including assault, robbery and rape (Newburn and Jones, 2005). The Bush adverts are an example of dog-whistle politics (Haney-Lopez, 2014). They played on a series of deeply embedded racist attitudes about Black masculinity and crime. The impact of the Horton adverts can be overestimated. However, they highlight the potential influence of media representations of crime and the responses to it (Hall et al, 1979). The campaign also demonstrates the way the rhetoric of a political debate can be as important as the substantial issues. Rhetoric can have real-world implications (Garland, 2001). Penal policy is replete with phrases – short, sharp shock; prison works tough on crime; tough on the causes of crime; the War on Drugs; the War on Terror – that have become, what Wacquant (2009a) terms, doxa. Doxa are, in effect, taken for granted phrases that restrict debate in policy areas.

In his analysis of penal populism, Garland (2021) notes that populism is usually regarded in academic criminological debates as inherently problematic. It is seen as a key factor in driving increasingly punitive penal policy (Cummins, 2021). Garland (2021) sees penal populism as part of wider form of political rhetoric. Populist politicians claim to be representing a long-suffering public – particularly the victims of crime – who have been let down by the liberal elites. There are two key assumptions here. One is that liberal elites are committed to less punitive penal policies. The other is that the public is in favour of more punitive policies. Garland (2021) sees penal populism as being characteristic of societies such as the USA where there are more elected officials such as judges and prosecutors.

Garland (2021) notes that 'the people' are imagined and their punitive views assumed. 'The people' is thus a political category rather than an actual group in the population (Laclau, 2006). Such calls assume that there is an agreement across society about penal policy. This is at odds with the reality. Hall (2006) went further, arguing that populist politicians create public opinion then claim to consult it. Garland (2021) argues that penal populism should be seen as a way of arguing for or representing a policy.

It is possible to place penal populism in the wider spectrum of populist discourse. It shares many features, in particular the notion that populists represent a revolt against a liberal elite. Garland (2021) presents a challenge to academic criminology that is ignored or derided by populist discourse. At the same time, he notes that there are a clear examples where liberal progressive politics have led to significant changes in penal policy. The abolition of the death penalty in the UK, for example, was the result of debates within elites (Flanagan, 2012). In his annual report, His Majesty's Chief Inspector of Prisons for England and Wales highlighted the crisis in the prison system in the UK. The 2023/24 report (Taylor, 2024) emphasized a series of ongoing issues: staff, shortages and a lack of experienced staff, overcrowding, lack of constructive activities and education, violence and bullying, drug misuse and a lack of mental health support. Despite these failings, in the 2024 general election both the Conservative and Labour parties committed to building more prison places. There is comparatively little debate about the effectiveness of the expansion of the prison estate.

Punitive attitudes are deeply embedded in the political landscape. These attitudes reflect wider social attitudes and the othering of marginalized social groups (Garland, 2001; Cummins, 2021). One result is a continued call for 'tougher' punishments, longer sentences and harsher conditions in prisons. The decline of the 'rehabilitative ideal' (Garland, 2001) is one of the most important shifts in penal policy of the past 50 years. A more dominant idea is Becker's (1968) model of rational choice theory where offenders are making a rational choice to commit crime. Punishment or other sanctions are part of a cost–benefit analysis that offenders make; thus, harsher punishment will change the nature of these decisions.

True crime and punishment

Crime remains one of the mainstays of the news media. The true crime boom has demonstrated that there is an almost insatiable appetite in popular culture for works that examine crime and responses to it. Crime and punishment, despite a general political consensus, remain key areas of public debate. Recent high-profile crimes such as the abduction, rape and murder of Sarah Everard by a serving police officer crystallize questions about the nature of modern society. In September 2021, Wayne Couzens was sentenced to a whole-life term for murdering Ms Everard. The case led to an outpouring of anger from women about the levels of sexual harassment and danger that they face in their daily lives. The excessive use of force in the policing of a vigil for Ms Everard led to further public outrage. A review led by Baroness Casey was established to examine the culture and standards of London's police service. This reported concluded that public confidence in the police was completely broken (Casey, 2023).

Despite wide coverage, the workings of the CJS are hidden to most members of the public. The majority have little direct contact with, or knowledge of, the working of the institutions of the CJS. The representation of the role of the police on TV in both documentaries and drama is at odds with the day-to-day reality of the work. Reality TV and fly-on-the-wall documentaries that follow officers on the beat are a particular popular subgenre (Rackstraw, 2023). This subgenre was developed in the US, in the late 1980s and early in 1990s. Technological developments meant that filming was made much easier. The narrative arc of the format reflects the populist law and order politics of the time. This was the period that saw rising crime alongside the escalation of the 'war on drugs' in an era of law-and-order rhetoric, rising crime and the ramp-up of the war on drugs in the late 1980s and early 1990s. Rackstraw (2023) notes that hundreds of US police departments have 'co-operated' with such shows over the past 40 years. These programmes are both popular and ubiquitous. Rackstraw (2023) found that over 90 per cent of Americans had seen at least one of these shows and that the audience views these programmes as an accurate portrayal of policing.

Reality TV's overwhelming positive view of policing has been classified as 'copaganda'. Rackstraw (2023) notes that it is difficult to untangle cause and effect here. Viewers may choose to watch these programmes because they assume that the content will be supportive of the police. This genre presents a very inaccurate portrait of police work. In particular, the shows present the police as constantly solving crime and making arrests. In her analysis, Rackstraw (2023) shows that in the most popular US policing reality TV show, *Cops*, officers have made arrests in 89 per cent of the cases shown. This is at odds with data that shows that most crimes are more likely to be unsolved than not and that most police officers infrequently make arrests. The overall impact of the genre is to distort the role and impact of policing. Rackstraw (2023) found that the genre has an impact on policing. Officers engage in more proactive policing while being filmed. They make more stops and arrests for 'quality of life' crimes.

The genre has developed in the UK to include programmes such as *24 Hours in Police Custody*. The title is a reference to the length of detention that is allowed under the Police and Criminal Evidence Act (Home Office, 1985). It also presents the police facing a race against time to collect evidence, interview and make decisions about the case. Doyle (2003) argues that reality TV true crime shows such as *Cops* are grounded in what are assumed to be common sense notions of law and order. The virtual ridealong gives officers the opportunity to outline their motivations for joining the force – which are an idealized version of serving the community. The police are presented as the thin blue line protecting society from chaos. Cases are solved usually by the arrest of a suspect.

The influence of the media on attitudes to crime and punishment have been long been a key feature of debates in this field (Reiner, 2010). These predate the true crime boom. For Conservatives, media representations are seen as part of the wider progressive undermining of traditional institutions. Critical perspectives see the media as restricting debates about crime in two ways. Media coverage, with its focus on violent crime, plays a key role in the fear of crime. It thus exaggerates legitimate concerns about crime. There is also a tendency to represent the police as being shackled in the fight against crime by a focus on the rights of individuals. and emphasizes the bureaucratic and other restrictions under which the police operate. This is seen as undermining due process and legitimatizing what can be termed a 'maverick' approach to policing.

Life on Mars and *Ashes to Ashes* were two hugely popular TV drama series that satirized the attitudes of policing in the 1970s and 1980s in the UK. The character of Gene Hunt – a racist, homophobic, misogynistic detective who routinely assaulted suspects, was written as a satire. However, he became a cult hero – particularly to those on the right who felt that he represented old-school policing that had played a key role in the fight against crime. These views are summed up by Peter Hitchens – a columnist for the *Daily Mail*: 'Our first line of defence used to be people more or less like Gene Hunt in "Life on Mars" and "Ashes to Ashes". Yes, they did rough up criminals (or "suspects" if you must). They got away with it because they always roughed up the right one' (Hitchens, 2010).

The Central Park Five

In this section, the arrest, trial, conviction and subsequent exoneration of the Central Park Five will be used as a case study to examine the impact and representation of high-profile crimes. There are certain crimes that define an era. This is one that can be seen to straddle two. The initial crime was seen to represent the late 1980s/early 1990s era of urban high crime. More recent examinations of the case have seen it as an example of racial injustice and symbolic driver of mass incarceration. In the 1980s, New York was a city that faced huge economic and social problems. It had become a symbol of industrial decline. Crime, particularly violent crime, rose significantly. Alongside increased unemployment and poverty, crack cocaine use reached epidemic proportions. The crack epidemic was one of the key drivers in the homicide and other violent crime. Users committed offences to feed their habits. Drug dealers fought turf wars to control the lucrative drug market (Bourgois, 1995). These developments combined to impact on the direct victims of crime but also the wider population. The police and other agencies struggled with the surge in violent crime. This helped to create a sense of urban crisis. This forms the backdrop to the Central Park Five case.

In 1989, a white female jogger was brutally assaulted, raped and left for dead in Central Park, New York. The jogger, Trisha Meili (Meili, 2003), was an investment banker, who regularly ran in the park. Five Black and Latino teenagers – Kevin Richardson, Raymond Santana, Antron McCray, Yusef Salaam and Korey Wise – were arrested by the police and confessed to the crime. McCray, Richardson, Salaam, Santana and Wise faced charges, including assault, attempted murder, sexual abuse, rape and sodomy of the jogger. They were also charged with other attacks on people in the park that night (Burns, 2011). The boys were tried in two groups. They were convicted in 1990 and sentenced to between 5 and 15 years. Four of the five adolescent boys were sent to juvenile detention. Korey Wise was tried and convicted as an adult. He was imprisoned in a maximum-security prison. The convictions were only overturned in 2002. Matías Reyes, who was serving a life sentence for rape, assault and murder, confessed to the Central Park attack. In 2014, the five men were awarded a settlement of $41 million by New York City (Burns, 2011).

The case took place in a period where there were concerns about violent crime, particularly in the urban areas. The debates about the case focused on long-standing issues in the American penal system: race, class, gender and the influence of media representation. The media coverage portrayed the five teenagers as out of control animals. It used the term 'wilding' to refer to gangs of young Black men, who allegedly went on crime sprees and indiscriminate attacks on citizens. The focus on the gender, class and race of the victim and the defendants played on deeply entrenched racist stereotypes and constructions of alleged Black criminality (Alexander, 2010). The *New York Daily News* front page of 21 April 1989 was a picture of a police officer at the scene of the crime. The headline was 'Wolf Pack's Prey: Female Jogger Near Death after Attack by Roving Gang'. The paper then went on to outline a version of events that followed the racist tropes of the headline. It stated that a group of 30 youths were in the park. The paper called the group a 'wolf pack'. The article claimed that the group had been involved in a series of assaults of people in the park. The *News* then reported a group of at least a dozen youths grabbed the jogger and dragged her to an area of heavy undergrowth and trees before subjecting her to violent sexual assaults. Mayor Ed Koch called the attack 'the crime of the century'. Donald Trump, then a New York real estate magnate, took out newspaper adverts calling for the execution of the five teenagers – before they had been convicted.

In 1991, Joan Didion wrote an essay, published in The *New York Review of Books*, which is a critical analysis of the case and the way that it was reported

(Didion, 1991). Didion (1991) explores how the media discourse amplified deep schisms within New York and wider American society. The ongoing moral panic about violent crime was intensified by the coverage of the case. Didion (1991) questions whether the coverage meant that the accused were denied a fair trial. Didion (1991) highlights the flaws in the confessions. She presents a powerful critique of the ongoing impact of race and class in the US penal system.

Duru (2003) in his analysis of the case shows how the myth of uncontrollable Black sexuality has been a factor in previous miscarriages of justice including the Scottsboro Boys. The Scottsboro Boys were nine African American teenagers, accused of raping two white women on a freight train in Alabama in 1931. The teenagers were convicted by an all-white jury. Eight of the group were sentenced to death. Protests led to the case being taken to the Supreme Court, which ordered a retrial. The boys were again convicted. They collectively served over 100 years in prison. The case led to significant changes including the makeup of juries and the right to counsel (Gildersleeve, 2009). In 2013, the state of Alabama posthumously pardoned the Scottsboro Boys.

Simon (2007, 2014) highlights that fear of crime has been a major driver of mass incarceration. The original trial of the Central Park Five took place as the rise of the imprisonment was reaching a peak (Cummins, 2020). The USA saw the development of a huge prison industrial complex with over 2 million people in US jails. An oft quoted statistic is that the USA has 5 per cent of the world's population and has over 25 per cent of the world's prisoners (Cummins, 2020). The USA's history of slavery, racial segregation and discrimination is a key factor in the overrepresentation of young Black men in the modern penal system (Wacquant, 2001 and 2002). Black men represent 13 per cent of the US male population but 35 per cent of all men serving state or federal sentences of more than a year. One in three Black men born in 2001 can expect be incarcerated at some point in their lifetime (Hinton et al, 2018).

The challenge to mass incarceration has become an issue of civil rights. This movement includes organizations – *Black Lives Matter* – think tanks such as Vera Institute, the Stop Mass Incarceration Network as well as local community groups and academics. The case of the Central Park Five has been used by campaigners to illustrate the injustices of the US penal system. In 2002, a convicted serial rapist and murderer already serving time confessed to the Meili attack. Matias Reyes was a positive DNA match to evidence found at the crime scene. On 19 December 2002, a New York Supreme Court justice vacated the convictions of the five previously accused men. In 2003, the Central Park Five sued New York City. The city fought the case for over a decade before settling the case and paying $41 million dollars in damages. In 2012, the award-winning filmmaker Ken Burns released a documentary about the case. During his election campaign in 2016, the future US President Donald Trump also issued a statement stating his belief that the Central Park Five were guilty. He also stated that New York city authorities should not have settled the court case (Rios, 2020). This statement was part of Trump's populist dog whistle about race and crime.

In 2016, Netflix streamed *13th*, a documentary film by Ava Du Vernay. The film was an analysis of the historical construction of the racist stereotype of the Black male offender and the US prison boom. The title of the film comes from the Thirteenth Amendment, which abolished slavery and involuntary servitude. However, involuntary servitude was not abolished as a punishment for crime. Du Vernay then produced, in 2019, a miniseries for Netflix, *When They See Us?* This series begins with the events of 20 April 1989. We follow the trial and subsequent incarceration. The series shows the men trying to adapt to life after they have been released. It shows the difficulties that they face in obtaining employment. They are required to register as sex offenders. Alexander (2010) outlined the barriers to integration that ex-offenders face. These impact disproportionately on Black men and women. Trump who had, by then, become the US president, is shown in an interview at the time of the case again calling for the death penalty. Part four of the series concentrates solely on the experiences of Korey Wise, who was tried, convicted and incarcerated as an adult. Wise's story is used to demonstrate the brutality of the prison system (Riso, 2020). The audience see his mental health deteriorate. He experiences hallucinations. Wise is brutalized by fellow inmates and has to move into solitary confinement for his own protection. Even though the events are historical, the case is used as representative of the current brutality of the US penal system.

When They See Us? contributed to the movement that seeks to end mass incarceration and racial injustice. In 2019, Elizabeth Lederer, the chief prosecutor in the case, resigned from her position as a law professor at Columbia University. In March 2020, Linda Fairstein, who had been head of the sex crimes division of the Manhattan District Attorney's office and led the investigation, sued the makers of the film. She claimed that she was portrayed in the film as a racist determined to jail innocent children of colour.

The case of the Central Park Five was an immense miscarriage of justice. It demonstrates how race, class and a politics of fear drive punitive penal policies. The influence of the media at the time of the original attack helped to create a highly charged emotional atmosphere, in which, the wrongful convictions took place (Didion,1991). There are those including the 45th president, who continue to view Antron McCray, Kevin Richardson, Yusef Salaam, Raymond Santana and Korey Wise as guilty. Later true crime and dramatizations of the case have focused on it as a symbol of the failings of the US justice system.

Conclusion

True crime engages its audiences with a series of compelling narratives that examine the darkest areas of human behaviour. There appears to be an insatiable cultural appetite for material that explores criminal offending – particular the most violent crimes. The true crime boom has coincided with a punitive turn in penal policy. Media portrayals of crime can help to shape perceptions. This is particularly the case where individuals may have limited real-world experiences with crime itself (Simon, 2007). True crime, as with its cousin detective fiction, provides comforting resolutions to complex social problems. It also creates a clear moral universe. This contrasts the amorality of 'evil' of criminals with the wider values of society.

It is not surprising that true crime concentrates on the most sensational and unusual of cases. The focus of true crime can help to skew public perceptions about the nature and extent of crime. The most obvious example is the focus on serial killers and other high-profile cases that represent only a small fraction of overall offending. The concern is that this focus on certain forms of violence may increase fear and anxiety about crime. This public fear can be a driver of calls for even more punitive policies. True crime focuses on individual rather than structural explanations of criminal behaviour. There is a clear link here between the execution sermons of Puritan New England and modern true crime.

True crime as a genre can also be a site for critical perspectives on the agencies of the CJS. There is an increased focus on miscarriages of justice and wrongful convictions. In addition, true crime podcasts, in particular, provide a space for the voices of marginalized individuals, families and communities to be heard. This space can also be one where alternatives to retribution and punishment can be discussed in more detail that is allowed for in the wider media and public discourse. True crime is a form of entertainment that represents the commodification and monetization of crime. This means that its focus will be on the most extreme forms of crime and punishment such as violent offences and incarceration in maximum security settings. True crime's influence on the debates about justice, punishment and the treatment of both criminals and victims appears unlikely to wane in the near future.

PART II

Case Studies

5

Norman Mailer's *The Executioner's Song*

Introduction

Norman Mailer's *The Executioner's Song* (2012) has become a classic of the true crime genre. Mailer's work is divided into two books – Book 1 *Western Voices* explores nine months in the life of Gary Gilmore. This period ends when Gilmore commits two senseless murders in the course of two robberies: one at a gas station and one at a motel. The second book, *Eastern Voices*, is concerned with the period of the trial, Gilmore's conviction and his subsequent execution. When the Court sentenced him to death, Gilmore requested execution by firing squad. In so doing, he waived his right to appeal. However, the case was taken up by opponents of the death penalty, including the American Civil Liberties Union (ACLU). *Eastern Voices* examines the way that Gilmore became a media celebrity. It also explores the case as an example of the hyper commodification of crime and punishment (Hamerton and Hobbs, 2022). This case was a forerunner of what was to come in the age of social media and an expansion of 24-hour rolling news.

In this vast sprawling work, Mailer uses a range of genres and literary techniques. The use of a wide range of voices – there are over 100 characters – means that every imaginable explanation of Gilmore's conduct is explored at some point. Despite this, Mailer does not provide the reader with anything that can be read as an authorial explanation or judgement. *The Executioner's Song* (Mailer, 2012) has become widely recognized as a classic of the true crime genre. Mailer's 'true crime novel' – it won the Pulitzer Prize for fiction in 1980, has been hugely influential on true crime writers such as Gordon Burn. The macho brutal killer Gilmore can be viewed as the ultimate subject for Mailer. However, the book confounds expectations both in style and its portrait of Gilmore. The case and Mailer's work played a significant role in debates about the reinstatement of death penalty in the USA. The work raises a series of ethical questions about the relationship between the media and the criminal justice system (CJS).

Norman Mailer

Norman Mailer became one of the most prominent and controversial writers in post-war USA. He was born in 1923 and grew up in Brooklyn. He graduated from Harvard in 1943 with a degree in engineering. He was drafted in 1944 and served in the Pacific (Lennon, 2013). His wartime experiences were the basis for his first novel *The Naked and the Dead* (Mailer, 2018a), which was originally published in 1948. Mailer's novel received huge critical claim. It is widely recognized as a classic of the literature of war and one of the finest American novels of World War II. The themes of the novel, particularly its construction of masculinity, reoccurred throughout Mailer's career. The success of the novel made Mailer a major figure in American letters, a position he maintained until his death.

Mailer explored the conformity of post-war Eisenhower America. His 1957 essay 'The White Negro' (Mailer, 2017) argued that the twin horrors of the atomic bomb and the concentration camps had created a form of 'psychic havoc' that produced conformism while expanding the power and influence of state institutions. Mailer's work was influenced by the Beats, particularly Kerouac and Ginsberg (Shoemaker, 1991). Mailer argues that the existentialist hipster is a model for the individualism that is required to reject the conformity of consumerist America. Mailer's work was criticized by James Baldwin for its crude stereotyping and racialized sexual politics (Baldwin, 1988). It repeated deeply entrenched racist notions of the hypersexualized Black male, notions that remain and are tied to constructions of alleged Black criminality.

From the publication of 'The White Negro' in 1957 (Mailer, 2017) onwards, Mailer was a controversial public intellectual. The feminist classic *Sexual Politics* (Millett, 1970) contains a withering critique of his work. Millett (1970) argued that Mailer's work was based on and reinforced patriarchal values. He responded with 'The Prisoner of Sex', an article published in *Harper's Magazine* (Mailer, 1985). In this article, Mailer argued that biological differences meant that equality between the sexes was impossible. Mailer relished his role as a 'male chauvinist pig', particularly in his 1971 Town Hall debate with Germaine Greer (Mead, 2017).

The Armies of the Night: History as a Novel/ Novel as History (Mailer, 2018b) is an account of the 1967 antiwar Vietnam War march on the Pentagon. It was originally published as a long essay in *Harper's Magazine*. Mailer (2018), in the style of New Journalism, places himself at the centre of the events over the course of the march. These include his being arrested. The book was widely acclaimed. It won a Pulitzer Prize for nonfiction, a National

Book Award and a George Polk award for magazine reporting. It was a key document of the political and social convulsions that the USA experienced in the late 1960s. In *The Executioner's Song* (Mailer, 2012), Mailer appeared to have discovered an ideal subject – the outsider, who in refusing to appeal his death sentence, exposed the hypocrisy of the liberal establishment. The final work is more complex and nuanced.

Gary Gilmore

Gary Gilmore was born in Texas in December 1940. His father, Frank, was a petty criminal. Gilmore was originally registered as Faye Robert Coffman. His father's brushes with the law meant that the family were using an alias at the time. Gilmore never used the name Coffman. The theme of family secrets and identity is one that reoccurs. In 1948, the family settled in Portland, Oregon. Gary's brother Mikal Gilmore became a journalist and wrote for *Rolling Stone*. In his memoir, *Shot in the Heart* (Gilmore, 1994) he describes their father, Frank Snr, as an abusive and violent man, who beat Gary and his elder brother Frank Jnr. The sons also witnessed domestic violence in the family home.

Gary Gilmore was 36 years old when he was executed on 4 January 1977. He had spent a sizeable proportion of his life in institutions. He was convicted of stealing a car at the age of 14 and sent to a reform school for a year. He committed petty offences as an adult and served a sentence in Oregon State Correctional Institution for larceny. Released a year later, he resumed his criminal activities. Between 1960 and 1961, he was incarcerated at the Oregon State Correctional Institution on a larceny charge. In 1962, in Vancouver, Washington, he was arrested for driving offences and received another custodial sentence.

In 1964, Gilmore received a sentence of 15 years imprisonment for assault and armed. He was released from Oregon State Penitentiary in 1972. He committed an armed robbery and was recalled. Gilmore was in constant trouble with prison authorities. At one point, he was treated with anti-psychotic medication. He was finally transferred to a maximum-security prison. In *The Executioner's Song* (Mailer, 2012), it is revealed that Gilmore's favourite film was *One Flew Over the Cuckoo's Nest*. There were certainly similarities between Gilmore and McMurphy. *One Flew Over the Cuckoo's Nest* (Kesey, 2005) is one of the most influential American novels of the 20th century. The 1975 film adaptation by Milos Forman with Jack Nicholson in the role of McMurphy was an outstanding critical and commercial success. The film won all five of the major awards: Best Picture, Best Screenplay, Best Director, Best Actor and Best Actress. The original novel was based on Kesey's experiences as a nursing assistant on a ward in a large psychiatric hospital. Kesey had famously been a volunteer in US forces experiments with LSD, which had taken place at the same hospital (Cummins, 2018). McMurphy is transferred to a state mental hospital – it was filmed in Oregon – from prison where he was serving a sentence for statutory rape. McMurphy has engineered the move through his disruptive behaviour in prison. He thinks that the regime will be easier. The struggle between McMurphy and Nurse Ratched, who controls the ward, is at the heart of the drama. McMurphy challenges her authority at every opportunity. The film and the novel present McMurphy as a rebellious antihero (Anderson, 2003; Cummins, 2018).

Gilmore was paroled on 9 April 1976. He moved to Provo, a small town in Utah, to live with his cousin, Brenda Nicol. She found him a job in her father's shoe-repair shop. Gilmore began a relationship with 19-year-old Nicole Baker Barrett. In this period, Gilmore continued to be involved in petty criminality. He also drank heavily. Gilmore was violent towards Barrett, and she ended the relationship. Shortly after the end of the relationship with Barrett, Gilmore committed two armed robberies during which he murdered two people. On 19 July 1976, he robbed a gas station. He shot and killed the attendant, Max Jensen. By Gilmore's own account, Jensen complied with all his demands. Despite this, he made Jensen lie on the floor, and he then shot him in the head. The proceeds of the robbery were around $100. The next day, Gilmore's pickup truck was being repaired in Provo. While waiting for this work to be completed, Gilmore robbed a nearby motel. He shot the manager, Ben Bushnell. As in the previous murder, Gilmore's victim had complied with all his demands.

Gilmore was tried only for Bushnell's murder. The trial lasted just three days. Gilmore was convicted on 7 October and sentenced to death. In July 1976, the US Supreme Court had reinstated the death penalty. Gilmore chose not to appeal and insisted that the punishment be conducted. He chose death by firing squad. Civil liberties groups including the ACLU sought to appeal on his behalf. The result was that for the final three months of his life, Gilmore became a media celebrity. The case crystallized a series of arguments around crime and punishment including the death penalty. The media circus that followed Gilmore's conviction and sentence is examined in *Eastern Voices*, Book 2 of *The Executioner's Song* (Mailer, 2012). Gilmore clearly revelled in his newfound fame. The bizarre scenario of a death row prisoner demanding the Courts conduct the sentence while his would-be defenders argued that the penalty was unconstitutional was a tabloid media dream. Gilmore twice went on hunger strike. He also attempted to end his own life in a pact with Nicole.

After a Supreme Court ruling, Gilmore was executed by firing squad in January 1977. His last words, 'Let's do it', were widely quoted in the media. Some have suggested that they inspired Nike's slogan 'just do it'. Gilmore's corneas were transplanted. In 1977, the English punk band, the Adverts released a hit single – *Lookin through Gary Gilmore's eyes*. The song's lyrics describe the patient's realization that the successful operation was only possible because of a donation by an executed double murderer. *The Executioner's Song* (Mailer, 2012) is the most detailed discussion of the case in popular culture. Along with Mikal Gilmore's memoir, it presents an unsentimental bleak view of Gilmore's life encapsulated in the brutality and senselessness of the murders of two defenceless working people. Mailer adapted the novel into a TV film. Tommy Lee Jones won an Emmy for his performance as Gilmore. Roseanna Arquette played Nicole. Mikal Gilmore's memoir was also made into a TV film with Sam Shepard playing the brothers' abusive father Frank Snr.

The death penalty

The Gary Gilmore case is inextricably linked with debates about the death penalty. His execution ended a de facto ten-year moratorium on the use of the death penalty in the USA (Culver, 1985). The death penalty has been abolished in most democratic countries. However, this is not the case in the USA where there is strong opposition to its abolition (Finley, 2024). The fact that Gilmore did not appeal and was eventually executed by firing squad meant that the case, which may have only received limited coverage, became a huge news story.

In an era of rolling news and social media, viewers can feel overwhelmed by the number of stories and the players within them. Many news stories, including violent crimes, are part of the news cycle for a brief period before the caravan moves on. The media saturation has other important implications for the relationship between consumers of and actors in the news cycle. Social media allows individuals to play both roles. Bolter and Grusin (1999) argue that with so many competing interests for our attention as media consumers, even violent crimes can become just another story. Gilmore's crimes did not receive huge media coverage. The case became 'news' when he chose not to appeal and insisted that the Court enact the death sentence.

The Supreme Court decision *Furman v. Georgia* (Thorne, 2022) placed an effective moratorium on the death penalty. The case held that the death penalty was an unconstitutional breach of the Eighth Amendment. The Eighth Amendment prohibits 'cruel and unusual punishments'. The Supreme Court held that the application of the death penalty was 'arbitrary and capricious'. The decision did not ban the death penalty, but its use was suspended until states could bring forward legislation that would create a sound legal framework for its application. The decision at the time was seen as a landmark in the move towards the abolition of the death penalty. Boudreau (2006) notes that the legal processes of the death penalty – the initial trial and the appeals – allow states to create the impression that this is distinct from thirsty revenge.

Mailer presents Gilmore's refusal to appeal as a challenge to the CJS and the liberal elite's hypocrisy and double standards. Gilmore was sentenced at the beginning of the Carter presidency. However, the emergence of the New Right and Reaganism was on the horizon. Law and order policy was marked by a shift towards more punitive policies (Shelden and Vasilie, 2017; Simon, 2014). It is possible to see the beginnings of the era of mass incarceration (Wacquant, 2001; Clear, 2009). It is symbolic of wider attitudes towards punishment. The death penalty was and remains a totemic policy. Derrida (2013) argues that the origins of the notion of the legal subject can be found in the development of commercial law. Hence phrases such as paying a debt to society. Gilmore presents no explanation and shows no remorse for his crimes. *The Executioner's Song* (Mailer, 2012) shows that Gilmore commits his crimes because of debt as he is behind on payments on his '66 Mustang truck. The car is hugely symbolic in modern US culture. The truck is named after a breed of horse most associated with the rugged individualism and freedom of the mythic West (Kelton, 1991).

Mormons are no longer the majority population of modern Utah. However, Mormonism has clearly had a huge cultural, social and political influence on the development of the state. The Mormon doctrine of *blood atonement* held that, for capital crimes, the blood of the perpetrator must be spilled as part of the act of retribution. The doctrine is no longer widely held. It was behind the policy of administering capital punishment by firing squad or decapitation (Bartkowski et al, 2023). The fact that Gilmore chose death by firing squad added to the media and wider popular interest in the outcome of the appeals. Gilmore's death ended the moratorium on the use of the death penalty. Since 1976, there have been 1594 executions in the USA. Texas has used the death penalty significantly more than any other state. It has executed 589 of its citizens. The next highest state is Oklahoma which has executed 125 citizens in this period. There have been eight executions in Utah since 1976 including Gilmore's (Death Penalty Information Center, 2024). As discussed in Chapter 4, racial injustice has casted a long shadow over the US penal system. The imposition of the death penalty is an area where these racial disparities are readily apparent (Steiker and Steiker, 2016).

Gilmore sold the rights to his life story to journalist and filmmaker Larry Schiller. This process is discussed at the beginning of Book 2 *Eastern Voices*. Schiller was something of a media/crime fixer. He was the last man to interview Jack Ruby. He had also produced a book *The Killing of Sharon Tate* (Schiller, 1970) with Susan Atkins. Atkins was a member of the Manson family and had been convicted for her part in the murder of Sharon Tate, alongside other offences. Atkins testified for the prosecution at the grand jury in return for the state not seeking the death penalty. Schiller later published a book *I Want to Tell You – My Response to Your Letters, Your Messages, Your Questions* (Simpson, 1995) in which O.J. Simpson's thoughts in jail are juxtaposed with some of the over quarter of a million letters he received. He knew the value of a story. His efforts to get the principals signed up and as much information as possible from Gilmore form a key part of the overall discussion of the case. Mailer uses this to expose the double standards that the wider society applies. Gilmore's story becomes a commodity. *Western Voices* is concerned with a world away from this media circus. A world that is rarely covered in mainstream media – the world of the working class struggling to survive. Mailer took Gilmore's story from Schiller and produced a modern classic.

Western Voices covers the period following Gilmore's release from prison. It is not difficult to see how Gilmore would be an intriguing character for a writer with Mailer's history and personal background. Here was a subject that allowed him to explore many of the key themes in his work including the construction of modern masculinity and the power of the state. It also allowed him to explore the motivations and actions of part of the liberal Eastern Coast elite. Despite being a Harvard graduate and an award-winning novelist, essayist and leading public intellectual, Mailer was never at ease in the literary milieu. His public persona was of a pugilist railing against developments in contemporary culture – particularly the influence of the second wave of feminism. Gilmore's choice to die rather than rot in jail is seen by Mailer as both morally valid but also heroic.

Gilmore was released from prison in April 1976. The period until his arrest is told in the mid-Western voices of those around him. There are three key women in Gilmore's life: his cousin Brenda, his partner, Nicole, and his mother, Betsey. Mailer uses their insights to paint a bleak portrait of working-class life. *Western Voices* is written in a style that has similarities to the emerging approach that came to be known as 'dirty realism'. The term was coined by Bill Buford in *Granta Magazine* in 1983. It was associated with writers such as Raymond Carver (1938–88) who wrote in a flat minimalist style. Carver's short stories in collections such as *What We Talk About When We Talk About Love* (Carver, 2009) were concerned with characters struggling to make ends meet. The women in *Western Voices* have experienced dislocating and often traumatic lives. Nicole is 19 and has been married twice. Following their initial meeting, Nicole appears to have had a positive impact on Gilmore's behaviour. However, this is a short-lived period. Mailer shows Gilmore, who was 35 when they met, is obsessively possessive and brutally violent towards Nicole. She ends the relationship. Gilmore commits the murders shortly afterwards.

Mailer's sparse evocative prose allows him to avoid cliched stereotypes. He admires Gilmore for the decision he has made, which will lead to his execution. This does not mean that he does not include details that show a much darker side. These include Gilmore demanding sex with Nicole on the first date (Mailer, 2012: 41). Mailer includes Gilmore's stories from prison, which show him to be both violent and racist (Mailer, 2012: 44 and 65).

The characters around Gilmore, particularly Nicole and Bess, are portrayed in a much more sympathetic fashion. Despite the number of characters, who are deployed to build a portrait of Gilmore, Mailer as the author remains absent so the reader is left to make up their own mind or construct their own explanation for Gilmore's crimes. From its title onwards, *Western Voices* is concerned with the foundational myths of the West and the USA. The action takes place in Provo, Utah, which Mailer (2012: 28) describes as a city with 'the desert at the end of every street'. The Western myth includes criminal antiheroes such as Billy the Kid. Mailer stops short of portraying Gilmore as anti-hero. He does show the impact of his chaotic family life and periods in institutions. Gilmore, as his mother and cousin both note, simply does not know how or have the skills to survive on the outside. One of the challenges that Mailer faces in *The Executioner's Song* is that his readers know the outcome – there is no dramatic tension. The first readership of the novel would be familiar with the detail that shocks the contemporary reader. In *Western Voices*, Gilmore's return to crime has an inevitability about it. The reader is still shocked that the crimes themselves are so brutal.

Mailer does not appear to have fallen for Gilmore's superficial charm. Gilmore remains at a distance. After the publication and success of *The Executioner's Song*. Mailer, along with other intellectuals, participated in the campaign for the release of Jack Henry Abbott. Abbott was serving a prisoner sentence for murder, bank robbery, forgery and prison escape. Abbot was released on parole. Abbott had contacted Mailer when he was working on the Gilmore case. He claimed that he would be able to provide Mailer with a more realistic portrait of prison life (Loving, 2016). Like Gilmore, Abbot had spent all his adult life in prison. Abbott wrote to Mailer, who was stunned by the quality of the writing. He compared the letters to the writings of Eldridge Cleaver's *Soul on Ice* (1968). Mailer arranged for a book advance and the letters were published as *In the Belly of the Beast* (Abbott, 1981). Abbott's book received critical claim. He was released on parole. For a brief period, he was a literary celebrity – he was even interviewed on *Good Morning America*. In July 1981, after six weeks as a free man, Abbot stabbed a waiter to death following an argument in a New York café (Loving, 2016). Abbot took his own life in prison.

Eastern Voices

In her review of *The Executioner's Song*, Didion (1979b) saw the first half of the book as a Western. The Western was one of the most popular genres in TV drama, film and popular fiction. The classic Westerns and stars such as John Wayne were seen as the embodiment of the American pioneering spirit and rugged individualism. In *John Wayne: A Love Song*, Didion (1968) explored these themes. She became famous for her urbane essays that mapped the dislocation of US politics in the aftermath of the explosion of 1960s counterculture. Despite this, she writes of the power of the myth of the Old West as embodied in the character played by Wayne throughout his movie career.

Gilmore is clearly not a hero who would appear in a John Ford movie or be played by Gary Cooper. *Western Voices* presents a wide range of explanations for Gilmore's commission of these brutal crimes. Despite the voices of those closest to him and Gilmore himself, the reader is left with a confusing sense of doubt (Ricks, 2008). One of the key features of true crime as a genre is that it seeks to offer explanations and answer the why questions. Mailer (2012) does not offer a definitive authorial answer to Gilmore's motivations. In contrast to the trial, there is no verdict. Gilmore, particularly in the period when he is fighting for the verdict of the Court to be conducted, becomes a more complex character. Mailer (2012) sees a series of endless contradictions.

Western Voices is part of the revisionism of the Old West. Reflecting the wider cultural context, films such as *Soldier Blue* (1970) sought to use the Western genre to question foundational myths (Langford, 2003). *Soldier Blue* (1970) was inspired by the 1864 Sand Creek massacre of Native Americans. The film is shocking in subject matter but also in its depiction of violence. The film was widely interpreted as an allegory of US involvement in Vietnam. It appeared shortly after the 1968 My Lai massacre. Lt William Calley Jnr who commanded a platoon responsible for the massacre was convicted of 22 counts of murder. He was sentenced to life but served three and half years under house arrest. He sentenced was then commuted by President Nixon (Smith, 2020).

In *Western Voices*, the female characters are pivotal. The portrait of Gilmore and his actions prior to the murders, is based on the perspectives provided by his mother, his cousin and his girlfriend. In contrast, *Eastern Voices* is dominated by the professionals in the legal system, who are all male, and Gilmore himself. There are two key elements to *Western Voices*. The first is the legal and ethical questions that the case raises. The second is the way that Gilmore becomes a media celebrity and how this celebrity is exploited. The writing of the novel is, of course, part of this process. Mailer is following a tradition in crime writing that focuses on the perpetrators. He avoids glamourizing Gilmore.

If *Western Voices* is read as society against Gilmore, *Eastern Voices* can be read as *Gilmore vs the Legal system*. True crime accounts of miscarriages of justice and wrongful convictions have played an especially key role in campaigns against the death penalty. *Dead Man Walking* (Prejean, 1993) is a memoir by Sister Helen Prejean, a Roman Catholic nun. It explores her work as a spiritual advisor to two convicted murderers on death row. They were held at Louisiana State Penitentiary – known as Angola. The prison is based on a former plantation. Louisiana has one of the highest rates of incarceration among the individual states The prison has a history of racism, brutality and violence that is endemic within the US prison system (Pelot-Hobbs, 2023). The book, which was made into an Oscar-winning film, explores the impact of the process of conducting an execution has, on the members of the legal profession involved and the families of the perpetrators and victims. Prejean wrote a further volume, *The Death of Innocents: An Eyewitness Account of Wrongful Executions* (Prejean, 2006). Mailer's work can be placed into a slightly different category. It also exposes the brutal reality of the death penalty, but it is not an overtly abolitionist novel.

In the section that examines the trial, Mailer (2012) focuses on the way the legal process can be viewed as a complex game with its own rules but also a code of behaviour that governs the conduct of the players. This is a counterpoint to the liberal construction of the court room as a space where the truth about events and people can be revealed. For example, the lawyers on both sides know that Gilmore's confession to the murder of Bennie Bushnell had not been obtained legally. Despite this, the defence team decide not to run a defence that the gun went off accidentally (Mailer, 2012: 375).

The drama in *Eastern Voices* takes place in the claustrophobic courtrooms where the decisions about whether Gilmore lives or dies are taken place. In this section, Gilmore is presented as regaining or re-establishing his humanity. The usual processes are reversed here. Gilmore is, in effect, arguing that he should be executed. Mailer (2012) sees this determination to force the Court to follow through with the sentence as Gilmore reaffirming his identity and autonomy. It echoes one of the themes of Mailer's earlier work – the individual/common man reasserting himself in the face of the state power. The structure of the traditional courtroom drama is turned on its head. There is no search for the true facts of the case or attempts to establish the guilt of the accused. Gilmore does not dispute the verdict. It is the refusal to enact the death sentence that is the focus of legal arguments. Mailer (2012) portrays Gilmore as a martyr – a very unusual one – to the US legal system. In doing so, the author's famous hostility to the progressive metropolitan elite is clear.

Larry Schiller is a key character in *Eastern Voices*. He had worked with Mailer on a biography of Marilyn Monroe. Mailer was hired to write an introduction to a book of photographs of the American icon. This expanded to an essay. After *The Executioner's Song*, Schiller and Mailer were reunited on the project that became *Oswald's Tale: An American Mystery* (2007). *Oswald's Tale* has echoes on the style and method that Mailer used on his work on Gilmore. It includes a detailed account of Lee Harvey Oswald's life and movements in the USSR and USA prior to the Kennedy assassination. It focuses on the period he spent in Minsk and the months in Dallas before 22 November 1963. The work was not met with the sort of acclaim that *The Executioner's Song* had received.

Eastern Voices was critical of the distorting effect of media coverage. Mailer paints a less than flattering portrait of the journalists covering the case. Schiller thinks that the press pack is lazy and lacks initiative. The press does not go further to explore the story (Mailer, 2012: 791). A key theme of this section is the way that reporters, by their presence, shape the news and inevitably become or place themselves at the centre of the story. The trends that Mailer identifies here have intensified since. Mailer despite his partnership with Schiller recognizes that this is a commercial enterprise. Schiller has made an investment in Gilmore and his story. That investment needs to be protected. Gilmore via his lawyers gives written answers to questions from a journalist from *Playboy Magazine*. The questions have been sent to Gilmore's lawyers, who then ask them on prison visits and transcribe the answers. This is then written up as an interview. Schiller then develops this into the project that produces *The Executioners Song*.

The symbiotic relationship between crime and the media is explored in *Western Voices*. Gilmore becomes the focus of intense media interest. He signs a deal with Schiller, he gets fan mail and signs autographs. The concluding chapters of the work switch from this and focus on the period shortly before and after the execution is conducted. Mailer (2012) switches the perspective between the witnesses. In this period, Mailer portrays Gilmore as courageously acceptance of his fate. Earlier, Gilmore has told interviewers that he deserves to die. Mailer (2012) shows the brutality reality of the execution. This is a powerful ending creating tension even though the reader knows the outcome. The endless commodification of Gilmore does not end with his death. It continued with the publication of the book and the successful film.

Conclusion

The Executioner's Song (Mailer, 2012) is a complex and often ambiguous work. It is often linked to *In Cold Blood* (Capote, 1966). However, despite similarities, there are major differences. The similarities are in the ethical questions that are raised but also the doubts about the authenticity of sections. Capote consistently claimed that none of the material was fictional. Mailer (2012) in his Afterword outlines areas where he had altered text. Gilmore's decision to seek that the death penalty was conducted meant that the media coverage of his crimes expanded and intensified. There was, of course, the important public policy issue that the sentenced if conducted would end the effective moratorium on the death penalty. Since 1977, American penal policy has become more punitive (Simon, 2007). Within the politics of the punitive shift, the death penalty has a hugely significant symbolic value. In the 1992 presidential election campaign, Governor Clinton flew back to Arkansas to ensure that the execution of Ricky Ray Rector took place (Newburn and Jones, 2005). The other element of the case that ensured it received such media coverage was the fact that Gilmore chose not to appeal. In fact, he was insisted that the Courts carry it out. The appeal was from organizations such as the ACLU, opposed to the death penalty and aware of the implications of Gilmore's decision. Mailer's achievement is to bring all the themes together. He paints a picture of an individual who has been brutalized by his upbringing and the state institutions where he had spent most of his adult life. The chaos and violence of the last months of freedom lead to an almost inevitable brutal outcome. Mailer (2012) is not a sentimentalist; he does not excuse Gilmore or suggest he should be viewed as a hero. He is asking profound questions about the causes of violence and how society should prevent it and respond to victims. Mailer's (2012) work remains a key text in the history and development of the true crime genre.

6

British Serial Killers on Screen

Introduction

This chapter is a case study of three dramas about British serial killers and contrasts the humdrum nature of such texts with their US counterparts. Representations of British serial killers on screen draw on a long tradition of British filmmaking, dating back to the documentary film movement of the 1930s, and on the tropes and techniques of this body of work, the British New Wave of the 1950s/1960s, British soap operas, police procedurals and the work of renowned British filmmakers and playwrights who focus on the 'ordinary' aspects of British life.

Serial killers on screen

The serial killing industry (Haggerty, 2009) is discussed in the opening chapter of this monograph along with Greer's (2004) concept of mediatized murder and its links to modernity (Bauman, 1989). This discussion provides the theoretical framework for this chapter, which focuses on serial killing on screen with specific reference to the representation of the British serial killer, which will be examined through three examples. Jarvis (2007) argues that true crime is a spectacle to be consumed with the 'serial killer as the gothic double of the serial consumer' (Jarvis, 2007: 326). At the time of writing, he identified over 1,000 films on the Internet Movie Database (IMDb) which feature serial killing. There has been an explosion in the UK in recent years of films and TV documentaries on serial killing (Cummins et al, 2014; Fanning and O'Callaghan, 2023), increased home-grown products, US imports and the rising popularity of Nordic Noir (Creeber, 2015) have all added to this body of work. Fanning and O'Callaghan (2023: 16) cite Jack the Ripper as the first serial killer to whet the public's appetite 'for titillating real life murder stories' and go on to argue that the rise of crime thrillers in Hollywood, particularly film noir (Duncan and Müller, 2024), added to this. Following this, expanded news media and the rise of TV in the home in the 1960 and 1970s made household names of serial killers such as Brady and Hindley, The Zodiac Killer, Son of Sam (David Berkowitz), Ted Bundy and John Wayne Gacy (Fanning and O'Callaghan, 2023). All have featured in more than one dramatic production documenting their exploits ever since. Bonn (2014: xviii) argues that 'serial killers are transformed into larger-than-life celebrity monsters though the combined efforts of law enforcement authorities, the news and entertainment media and the public' and goes on to examine the way in which representations of the cases are a significant part of this phenomenon.

Celebrity and notoriety

Rojek's (2001) work on celebrity culture is also instructive here, in that he sees notoriety as one route into celebrity status. Celebrity (he argues) is a cultural fabrication with mass media representation (Hall, 1997) as the key principle in the formation of celebrity culture. In addition, public preoccupation with celebrity is based on the democratization of everyday life. Their 'ordinary' and 'the everyday' nature is a key theme of discussion of serial killers; interviews with friends or neighbours of serial killers, once their crimes are discovered, often focus on the fact that the killer seemed so 'ordinary' or 'normal' often accompanied by a sense of disbelief and the serial killers discussed later in this chapter all fit this pattern.

Rojek (2001: 15) argues that notoriety is a route into modern-day celebrity: 'The figure of notoriety possesses colour, instant cachet and may even in some circumstances be inverted with heroism for daring to release the emotions of bloodied aggression and sexuality that civilised society seeks to repress.'

Penfold-Mounce (2010: 4) adds 'the joy of transgressive criminality leads to the celebrification of those who dare to cross boundaries'. Ferrell (1998: 38) states 'adrenaline and excitement, terror and pleasure seem to flow not just through experience of criminality …. but through the many capillaries connecting crime, crime victimisation and criminal justice', while Katz (1988) suggests that crime is seductive. Thus, serial killers, particularly those who feature as the subject of film and TV drama, achieve a celebrity based on 'transgression, deviance and immortality' (Rojek, 2001: 31) and, interestingly, public reaction to them may differ as a consequence of such representations. Serial killers such as Brady and Hindley and the Wests achieve long-term celebrity status based on public revulsion while other notorious criminals, such as the Krays, despite being gangland killers who tortured many of their victims, still seem to be regarded with a kind of public benevolence; they have been celebrated in two feature films, the most recent of which, *Legend* (Helgeland, 2011), focuses on the style and glamour aspect of their 1960s working class hero status.

Haggerty (2009) sees mass media and the use of celebrity culture as one of the cultural and institutional factors that shapes serial killing. Drawing on Bauman's (1989) work on the Holocaust, he identified other factors as a society of strangers, a means/end rationality that is derived from value considerations, cultural frameworks of designation and opportunity for action.

Fritz Lang's *M* (1931) is a film which perfectly illustrates the ideas advanced by Haggerty (2009) and is accepted as being the first cinematic portrayal of a serial killer (Ebert, 1997). The rise of the impersonal society as a diseased society, opportunity, the focus on means and end and the celebrity status afforded to the killer by newspaper coverage are all key features of *M* (Lang, 1931). Based on a real life case, the film stars Pete Lorre, later to star in many Hollywood crime classics of the 1940s, as Hans Beckert, a serial killer who targets children. It is an example of an early procedural drama and highly influential on the modern true crime drama (Ebert, 1997). It is credited with forming two genres, the police procedural and the serial killer movie, and the style of the film, shot in black and white, was to be highly influential on US film noir in the 1940s, partly facilitated by the fact that Lang and many other Jewish actors and directors located to the USA as the Nazis took power in 1930s Germany. The blurring of lines between the criminal underworld and the force of law is another feature of the films that have influenced crime drama; Channel 4's *Red Riding* trilogy (Jarrold et al, 2009), based on David Peace's quartet of *Red Riding* novels (Peace, 2008a, 2008b, 2008c, 2008d), provides a contemporary example (Cummins et al, 2019).

Beckert's/Lorre's outburst late in the film: 'I can't help myself. I haven't any control over this evil thing that's inside me' is also significant in that discussion of the concept of evil and the serial killer forms an important part of both populist and academic discussion (see Chapter 11 on the Lucy Letby case).

A very British affair: three case studies

Here we will examine one British film and two TV dramas, made between 1977 and 2020, to illustrate the way in which representations of British serial killers tend to focus on the ordinary, the mundane and the low-fi nature of British policing in contrast to the big budget, high-tech production of their American counterparts. First, British film and dramas tend to be made on low budgets. For example, *10 Rillington Place* (Fleischer, 1971) a British film about the serial killer John Christie who was active in the 1940s and 1950s, was made on a budget of £1 million in 1971 (£12 million in today's currency). Contrast that with the US film *Zodiac* (Fincher, 2007), which documents the manhunt for the Zodiac Killer, who operated in the San Francisco Bay area in the late 1960s and early 1970s, one of the USA's most infamous unsolved crimes. The film is a high production values Hollywood blockbuster and had a £65 million budget (£96 million today).

Popular US TV drama *Criminal Minds* made between 2005 and 2022 (Davis, 2005) features a group of profilers working for the Federal Bureau of Investigation (FBI) as members of the Behavioural Analysis Unit, who are called in to help local police departments, usually to track down serial killers. *Bones* (Hanson, 2005) is a police procedural comedy drama made between 2005 and 2017 with a focus on the way forensic anthropology and forensic archaeology are used to solve FBI cases where human remains are found. Again, serial killing is to the fore. Both of these dramas are big-budget productions running over a number of years. They feature multi-disciplinary teams set up to solve crimes where budget is no issue. The *Criminal Minds* team fly everywhere by private jet. *Bones* feature high-tech technology (some of which does not exist in reality!) to assist in their work and again features a multi-disciplinary team. It will be seen in the discussion of the case studies that this contrasts sharply with the portrayal of British policing. While US dramas such as *Criminal Minds* (Davis, 2005) and *Bones* (Hanson, 2005) focus on an extraordinary approach to solving crime, in British film and TV drama the focus is very much on the ordinary, the everyday. The police are portrayed as having limited resources; quite often it is the commitment and tenacity of one detective that is at the heart of the drama, late nights in the office with a glass of whisky a recurrent theme. They are also often portrayed as incompetent (Cummins et al, 2014).

UK real-life true crime cases do show some evidence of this. Despite the huge manhunt and resources devoted to tracking down the Yorkshire Ripper, Peter Sutcliffe, in the 1970s and 1980s, he was eventually apprehended by two police officers on the beat who pulled him over for a faulty taillight (Burn, 1984). The focus on the ordinary and the everyday in these films and dramas is very much part of the British tradition of filmmaking, dating back to the 1930s.

The documentary movement, Ealing and the British New Wave

Hanley (2011) argues that the British documentary film movement of the 1930s was the beginning of a particular tradition of British filmmaking. The movement began at the film unit of the Empire Marketing Board in 1930, headed by John Grierson, who saw documentary film as a way in which to elevate and understand society using innovative methods in filmmaking. The depiction and aestheticization of everyday life were highly influential on later British film directors (Ruffert, 2019), and many of its productions are now highly regarded. *Housing Problems* (Elton, 1938) and *Listen to Britain* (Jennings and McAllister, 1942) are but two examples. Hanley (2011) sees the Ealing Cinema productions, made between the 1930s and the 1950s, as another important stepping stone, featuring as they do location shoots, regional and working-class accents and a focus on glimpses of working-class life, of ordinary people doing ordinary things.

The traditions of the documentary film movement and Ealing Studios are also key features of the British New Wave movement of the 1950s, highly influenced by the documentary filmmaking style with the aim of valuing 'the creation of a sense of place not advancing the plot' (Hanley, 2011: 23) with protagonists defined and limited by their environment. The focus is on working class, youth and authenticity, a kind of filmic equivalent of punk rock, which was also referred to as new wave.

The British New Wave is commonly perceived as comprising nine films released between 1959 and 1963 (Zarhy-Levo, 2010): *Room at the Top* (Clayton, 1959), *Look Back in Anger* (Richardson, 1959), *The Entertainer* (1960), *Saturday Night and Sunday Morning* (Reisz, 1961), *A Taste of Honey* (Richardson, 1961), *A Kind of Loving* (Schlesinger, 1962), *The Loneliness of the Long Distance Runner* (Richardson, 1962), *This Sporting Life* (Anderson, 1963) and *Billy Liar* (Schlesinger, 1963). Pre-dating this is the free cinema movement of the mid 1950s, which featured Lindsay Anderson, Tony Richardson and Karel Reisz, who all went on to direct New Wave films, which was established to provide an antithesis to mainstream British cinema at the time which its founders regarded as unadventurous, class bound and uninteresting. British cinema was seen by them as a reflection of 'a nation chronically dominated by the hegemonic high cultural protestations of its capital city' (Hanley, 2011: 25).

It is no surprise, then, that the majority of the New Wave films were set in the North of England, feature films yet influenced by the documentary style, seen by many as a progression from the free cinema movement, which only produced documentaries. The other important link is to the developments in other cultural products of the time. Tony Richardson, a key figure in the New Wave stated in 1959: 'It is absolutely vital to get into British films the same set of impact and sense of life that, what you can loosely call the Angry Young Man cult, has had in theatre and the literary worlds' (Zarhy-Levo, 2010: 234). John Osborne's *Look Back in Anger* (Osborne, 1956) is the most well-known example, and Richardson went on to direct the film version. All of the New Wave films were based on novels and stage plays, already labelled by critics as 'kitchen-sink dramas' or part of a social protest movement and the description of the New Wave films as 'kitchen-sink dramas' has stuck. A review of *Saturday Night and Sunday Morning* (Reisz, 1961) in *The Times* described it as 'one of those films, the product of a new generation of British writers and directors, which are dedicated to the work of bringing the cinema into closer touch with the lives of the mass of people' (Zarhy-Levo, 2010: 241). Press notices for the film *A Taste of Honey* (Richardson, 1961) foregrounded the director's desire to create a film that would seem real, achieved by placing actors in realistic location settings that was not achievable in the stage version and also by the casting of regional actors. Other reviews referenced the stylistic similarities to the French Nouvelle Vague cinema movement (Zarhy-Levo, 2010: 243).

The three examples of British serial killers on screen discussed here, very much reflect the legacy of the British New Wave, with their kitchen-sink approach to the ordinary realities of everyday life: tales of ordinary people, with humdrum lives, doing extraordinary things in mundane locations. Place, illustrated via location shooting, is central to all, whether in the North or South of England and regional accents and casting are all key features.

The Black Panther

The Black Panther (Merrick, 1977) is a British crime film, made in 1977, featuring the real-life crimes of serial killer Donald Neilson, a former soldier, who killed three men during a series of robberies of sub-post offices and kidnapped Lesley Whittle, an heiress, in 1970, with the intention of blackmailing her family, but she died while he was holding her captive. Neilson was sentenced to life imprisonment in 1978, convicted of four counts of murder. He died in prison in 2011.

Patterson (2012) reviewed the film on its re-release following a British Film Institute (BFI) restoration in 2012 and describes it as 'a gripping and responsible true crime movie' and compares it to 'the gothic occult novels of David Peace and the *Red Riding* Trilogy' (Patterson, 2012: 1). The initial release in 1977 was highly controversial, given that it came the year after Neilson's conviction. Neilson's arrest in 1975 followed closely on the heels of the arrest of Peter Cook, the Cambridge Rapist, and coincided with the period in which Peter Sutcliffe, the Yorkshire Ripper, began his killing spree. Patterson (2012) sees the backlash against the film as being based on the fact that the film outlines the way in which the media are portrayed in the film, particularly around their intervention in the kidnap of Lesley Whittle. He sees the film as 'a victim of the media's dishonesty and malevolence' because of the portrayal of journalists in the film. 'The Faux Outrage' (Patterson, 2012: 1) from the media and its accusations of poor taste and bad timing is neatly encapsulated by the fact that Sue Lawley on the *Tonight* programme described it as a 'sick film' despite the fact that she had not actually seen it. The press backlash and resultant council banning of films in local cinemas meant that it disappeared without a trace for 35 years.

It is certainly a dark film, made on a low budget and is an excellent example of the way in which British true crime films vary from their US counterparts. It is focused very much on the character of Neilson, with an attempt, as with many other true crime texts, to try and understand 'why' he did what he did, given his ordinariness. All of the examples in this chapter feature ordinary men doing extraordinary things leading people to question why. David Peace, author of the *Red Riding Quartet* (Peace, 2008a, 2008b, 2008c, 2008d) which were made into TV films for Channel 4 and which Patterson (2012) refers to in his review, has talked eloquently about the eternal question posed by much true crime writing; 'why in that place at that time?'. He concludes that this is the wrong question. Scholars of true crime should ask the supplementary question 'why do people think that there has to be some sort of logical answer to that question?'

The Black Panther (Merrick, 1977) begins, as many true crime films do, with the statement 'This Is a True Story' and date headlines appear on the screen at regular intervals to emphasize the authenticity of the events represented. It begins with Neilson, played convincingly by Donald Sumpter, unknown at the time although more recently he has appeared in *Game of Thrones* (Benioff and Weiss, 2011–12), *Les Misérables* (Hooper, 2012) and *Chernobyl* (Renck, 2019). The film opens in a bleak Northern industrial landscape, setting the tone for the film, and we see Neilson in military camouflage, camping out in the woods, meticulously preparing for his next crime. In the next scene the camera pans round a post office, an ordinary shop in an ordinary town. Neilson botches a robbery and leaves his balaclava behind, then we are back to him running through the Northern landscape, skinning a rabbit and eating outdoors, then to a terraced house where his wife and daughter are introduced. Upstairs, he is a family man, something of a Victorian dad akin to James Mason's character in *Spring and Port Wine* (Hammond, 1970). He explains his absences from home as 'working away', which his wife seems to take at face value; downstairs in his cellar, he is surrounded by military regalia, guns, camping gear and maps.

The secret life of the family man is a recurring theme in many serial killer cases, Peter Sutcliffe, the Yorkshire Ripper, being a prime example. Neilson also keeps scrapbooks to record his exploits, another common theme and often the downfall of serial killers. Neilson undertakes two post office robberies both of which end in murder, and we see him pasting reports of the shootings into his scrapbook. By this point the media have given him the nickname 'The Black Panther' and an open newspaper in is house reads 'Hooded killer is public enemy no. 1'. Other newspaper clippings refer to 'heiress' Lesley Whittle, although she is heiress to her father's wealth created through a coach company, again part of the 'ordinary' fabric of the film. The film cuts to the Midlands with Neilson checking out a drainage hole by a railway line and then to the home of Lesley Whittle for the first time.

The rest of the film documents the kidnapping of Lesley Whittle and the police hunt to find her. We see Neilson entering her home with a sawn-off shotgun and tools, from where he takes her to the drainage shaft that he has previously identified. The interactions between Whittle and Neilson are nicely portrayed by Sumpter as Neilson and Debbie Farrington as Whittle. Her portrayal of 'scared' is powerful in its simplicity, and there is a tenderness in the dialogue with Neilson in which he tries to reassure her that all will be well and that his intention is to collect a ransom as soon as possible. 'I don't want to harm you' he tells her, 'you are a good girl' while she responds with 'I'll be a good girl, I won't be any trouble, please don't hurt me.' He offers her hot soup then proceeds to tie her feet and put a metal noose around her neck, the horror of the situation contrasting with the tender dialogue. She records a ransom message on tape, and as he leaves to deliver it, she pleads for him to come back, and he reassures her that he will. Patterson (2012: 1) argues that Sumpter's portrayal of Neilson characterized him as inadequate (we have seen his bungled post office robberies despite meticulous preparation and his macho displays at home), trapped by his decisions resulting in rage. He states 'he remains, if not sympathetic, then human' (Patterson, 2012: 1).

The extraordinary setting of the drainage tunnel is contrasted in the next scene where Neilson is back in the family home with his wife cooking breakfast. We then see Whittle's brother in the family home listening to the ransom message. Despite being told not to by Neilson, the brother contacts the police. As previously discussed, whereas the police in contemporary US dramas appear to have limitless resources and highly advanced technological support in tracking down suspects, the very 'Britishness' of the police force and their seeming lack of resources is a key feature of the UK true crime film, whether set in the modern era or, as with *The Black Panther* (Merrick, 1977), 50 years ago. The police are portrayed as having no real sense of urgency, no plan and are seen in the settings of local police stations despite there being a national awareness of the crimes being investigated. The failings of the West Yorkshire police force in relation to the hunt for the Yorkshire Ripper have been well documented (Wattis, 2020) and are foregrounded in the recent ITV drama about the case, *The Long Shadow* (Arnold, 2023). The bumbling policing approach of the 1970s is definitely on show in *The Black Panther* (Merrick, 1977).

Neilson's bungled attempt to call the brother at a pre-arranged telephone box to arrange delivery of cash leads to the press getting wind of the case, and it is soon plastered all over local and national news broadcasts. Panic and rage engulf Neilson as he sees a *Daily Express* newspaper headline. He returns to Whittle, still captive down the drainage shaft, tells her there has been a delay and gets her to record a new message. The tension rises as Neilson's panic is palpable in the darkness. There is another final attempt to rendezvous with the brother by which time the police are closing in and, as a police helicopter hovers overhead, Neilson stands in a field screaming 'it's all going wrong'. He returns to Whittle, no longer wearing his mask. She is still tethered round her neck by a wire noose. Neilson is angry 'they are trying to trap me' he shouts. There is the sound of the wire clanking, and we know that Whittle is dead (at his trial Neilson would claim that this was an accident).

The film ends with Neilson on the run. A police patrol car spots him lurking outside a shop. As the police officers try to arrest him, he pulls out a shotgun and forces them to drive him away at gunpoint, but they overpower him, and he falls out of the car in front of that most British and ordinary institution, a chip shop. Customers rush out to help the police officers and Neilson breaks down in tears as he is chained to a drainpipe. The shabby ordinariness of the ending is reflective of the tone of the whole film and his capture, by chance, is also typical of the ending of many British true crime stories.

See No Evil

See No Evil (Menual, 2005) is a two-part drama made for Granada TV to coincide with the 40th anniversary of the trial of Ian Brady and Myra Hindley, known as the Moors Murderers. It was made with the co-operation of the victims' relatives and won best drama at the 2007 British Academy of Film and Television Arts (BAFTA) awards.

In 1966, Ian Brady and Myra Hindley were convicted of the abduction, sexual assault and murder of Lesley Ann Downey (aged 10), John Kilbride (aged 12) and Edward Evans (aged 17). Many years later, they also admitted to killing Keith Bennett (aged 12) and Pauline Reade (aged 16). Three of the bodies were buried on the Saddleworth Moors located just outside Manchester, and it is also suspected that Keith Bennett was also buried there, but his body has never been found. The Moors Murders represent the dark side of Manchester's history with Brady and Hindley providing a Northern counter point to the celebrity culture of 1960s swinging London. Brady and Hindley are prime examples of celebrity based on notoriety.

See No Evil (Menual, 2005) tells the story of the Moors Murders using the techniques and tropes of the British kitchen-sink dramas previously discussed. The influence of the British New Wave style serves to contextualize the Moors Murders in time, space and place, and in doing so produces a chilling portrait of the killers and their crimes. It is steeped, then, in a particular version of the North with a focus on working class solidarity and community; the influence of kitchen-sink drama is apparent, the focus on the ordinary and the everyday. Brady is presented as an aloof outsider, but Hindley is deeply rooted in the community, within her family, and the drama shows Hindley in the family context, exploring, in particular, her relationship with her sister, Maureen.

The opening shots of *See No Evil* (Menual, 2005) is of the Moors and their bleak beauty and amplifies the image of isolation through the sound of howling wind. This shot establishes the drama's narrative and also emphasizes the importance of place. Brady and Hindley, in time honoured serial killing tradition, were given a nickname, the Moors Murderers, although not all of their crimes actually took place on the Moors but as the drama unfolds, the viewer becomes aware that this is where the bodies are buried. Place, then, is central to their story and the opening shots of the Moors establish this fact. The use of inside/outside (King, 2013) is a key feature of 1960s kitchen-sink dramas with the enclosed indoor spaces, often emphasized via the hand-held camera technique borrowed from the French New Wave (Zarhy-Levo, 2010), representing entrapment with the outside representing escape and freedom from the mundane (King, 2013). In *Saturday Night and Sunday Morning* (Reisz, 1961), Albert Finney escapes from the confines of his factory job to the countryside outside Nottingham where he goes fishing with a mate. In *The Loneliness of the Long-Distance Runner* (Richardson, 1962), Borstal Boy Tom Courtenay uses running through the countryside as an escape from the confines of the Borstal and its monotonous routines. In *A Kind of Loving* (Schlesinger, 1962), Alan Bates and June Ritchie escape to the open spaces of a huge Northern park from the confines of the semi-detached house Bates and Ritchie share with her mother. Escape from a humdrum existence is a key feature of many of these films. In *Billy Liar* (Schlesinger, 1963), the main protagonist plans to escape his Northern shackles as an undertaker's clerk by going to London to be a scriptwriter. The Moors are a place where Brady and Hindley escape, taking picnics and alcohol on days out, taking photographs of each other in locations which we later learn have a dark secret to hide.

The authenticity of the drama is once again established by the opening captions. 'This is a true story. Some scenes have been created for the purposes of dramatization but what follows is based on extensive research.' The 'Northernness' of the drama is part of its essential fabric. *See No Evil* (Menual, 2005) is a Granada TV production, made in Manchester, and the cast are also chosen for their Northern credentials. Sean Harrison, as Brady, Maxine Peake as Hindley, Joanne Froggett as Hindley's sister, Maureen, and Matthew McNulty as her husband David, had all previously appeared in Northern-based TV or film dramas.

Following the opening shots of the Moors, the action moves to the cobbled streets of Gorton, Manchester. Brady and Hindley are introduced as workplace colleagues. They have mundane jobs. They are ordinary people. The establishing of the relationships between the four main protagonists forms a major part of the first part of the drama. The bond between Brady and Hindley is established in the indoor spaces of evenings at home, often spent with Maureen and David (the Smiths) and Brady's strange obsession with the works of the Marquis de Sade and Adolf Hitler are revealed, as is his sense of superiority, his self-image as an intellectual among lessor beings. 'Does a dog have a soul' he asks the bemused David Smith at one point, but we see the way that Smith falls under his spell as Brady tries to persuade him to take part in a bank robbery. The scenes set on the Moors begin to hint at the significance of the place but also evokes the iconography of Emily Bronte's *Wuthering Heights* (1847), the Moors and the lovers, inextricably linked in the public imagination. Indeed, during his appearance at a Mental Health Tribunal in 2013, Ian Brady alluded to the public fascination with the dark gothic nature of the Moors and referenced Bronte's work (King et al, 2016).

This is interspersed with a more traditional police procedural plotline. As in *The Black Panther* (Merrick, 1977), the police are disorganized and under pressure. The detective at the centre of the case, DC Joe Mounsey of Lancashire Police, has to fight bureaucracy to investigate the case, a staple of the police procedural (Cummins et al, 2014). Mounsey begins to link missing children cases across Greater Manchester (each area has its own police force and co-operation is non-existent), beginning with Pauline Reade, Lesley Ann Downey and Keith Bennett. Mounsey is played by George Costigan, another actor with strong Northern credentials.

As the action skips between cobbled streets, sparsely furnished working class family homes and bleak and ill-equipped 1960s police stations, the text exudes a British ordinary-ness which makes the extraordinary action of Brady and Hindley even more shocking.

The drama shies away from explicit portrayals of the child murders, with everything being left to the imagination, but the ending of the first part of the drama, where Brady kills 17-year-old Edward Evans with an axe, is a more shocking scene and a crescendo to the opening episode. Set on the Hattersley estate outside of Manchester, in the house Brady and Hindley shared with Hindley's gran, near to the flat where the Smiths live, the scene is key to the discovery of their crimes in that they involve David Smith in clearing up the post-murder mess, and he goes to the police the following day.

Brady is arrested at the end of the first episode and the second part of the drama follows a more traditional police procedural format, with Mounsey at the centre, leading a search for bodies on the Moors. These scenes are recreated from real-life news footage and pictures from the 1960s with police officers and volunteers poking the ground with long sticks looking for human remains, iconic 1960s images, again adding to the authenticity of the drama. There is initial doubt about Hindley's involvement in the crimes, but the shocking discovery of a suitcase Brady has placed in a left-luggage locker at Manchester Central Station containing pictures and an audio tape of the torture and murder of Lesley Ann Downey proves her guilt and thus establishes her status as 'the most evil woman in Britain' (Cummins et al, 2019).

The final part of the drama deals with the impact on the lives of the Smiths, given a hard time by locals who believed that David Smith was also involved in the murders, the public spectacle of the trial and Brady and Hindley's emergent celebrity status, an early example of mediatized murder (Greer, 2004).

In drawing on the style and techniques of the British New Wave, *See No Evil* (Menual, 2005) sets out to avoid the salacious titillation that can be found in other dramatizations of serial killing. It emphasizes Brady and Hindley's ordinariness which meant that they were able to commit these crimes without coming under suspicion. The focus on characterization and the relationships between key players also sets it apart from many other serial killer dramas and relates to a very British tradition, not only kitchen-sink drama but also the plays of Dennis Potter and the films of Ken Loach. It attempts to privilege truth over spectacle and, in this sense, goes some way to addressing the moral and ethical issues involved in producing such an adaptation. Unlike *The Black Panther* (Merrick, 1977) the drama was well received; the co-operation of victims' families goes a long way to explaining this and, obviously, a great deal of time had elapsed between the crimes and the dramatization. Its BAFTA award for Best Drama Serial at the 2007 ceremony, is testament to this. However, the case remains embedded in the British psyche and remains an ongoing reference point in terms of the modern serial killer narrative and a benchmark in terms of discussion on crime and evil. The drama makes no attempt to answer the 'why?' question and is all the more powerful for it.

Des

Des (Arnold, 2020) is a three-part ITV drama made in 2020, which begins with the arrest of Dennis Nilsen (Des to his friends). Nilsen, a serial killer and necrophile, is known to have murdered at least 12 men between 1978 and 1983. He was convicted of six counts of murder and two attempted murders, and sentenced to life imprisonment in 1983. He was given a whole life tariff in 1994. Nilsen is played by David Tennant, a performance which is a million miles from his zany manic *Dr Who* (Newman, 1963) persona. He bears a striking resemblance to Nilsen. In a *Guardian* review, Lucy Mangan (2020: 1) describes Tennant's 'brilliantly controlled, understated yet commanding performance as the perfectly ordinary, union-leading, valued-by-colleagues monstrous narcissist'. The context of the drama is provided by the 1980s homelessness crisis and Mangan (2020: 1) goes on to add: 'There is an almost visible miasma enveloping every scene of evil, of sadness, of bleak loss.'

It begins with the statement 'This is a true story' and the discovery of body parts in a drain at Nilsen's home and his subsequent arrest. The drama focuses on Nilsen's interviews with the police. Nilsen's narcissism is clear as he seeks to establish control in these scenes. Alongside this theme, the drama contains many of the elements of a police procedural, particularly British procedurals (Cummins and King, 2014b). DCI Peter Jay (Daniel Mays), the detective leading the enquiry, has much in common with fictional detectives like Wallender. He is jaded and world weary. Jay battles bureaucracy but is also under pressure from superiors and the public to get a result. The portrayal of Jay, in his sheepskin coat, smoking and drinking heavily, has echoes of 1970s classics, most notably *The Sweeney* (Childs, 1975). Those nods to previous British crime dramas give *Des* (Arnold, 2020) a particularly British feel. Mays' previous credits include *Ashes to Ashes* (Graham and Pharoah, 2008) whose main protagonist, Gene Hunt, also owes a debt to *The Sweeney* (Childs, 1975). The third strand features the writer Brian Masters (played by Jason Watkins). His Nilsen biography *Killing for Company* (Masters, 1985) is the basis for the drama, and we see interviews between Masters and Nilsen in which Masters is keen to answer the 'why did he do it?' question.

The drama's opening titles play out over real footage of London in the 1980s with a particular emphasis on homelessness, the context in which Nilsen picked up his victims. We see Nilsen at work in a job centre in Kentish Town, travelling home on the bus to Surbiton, London. Again, an ordinary man who did extraordinary things. Following his arrest, colleagues expressed shock that their friend could have done such atrocious things, another common feature of both true crime drama and real-life cases (see Chapter 11 on Lucy Letby). Later, we see his spartan living arrangements, a sparsely furnished flat with a one-bar electric fire, very much redolent of the British kitchen-sink drama. As the police prepare to arrest Nilsen after the discovery of human remains, an officer points out that they have found partial remains and asks him where the rest of the body is. 'In the cupboard' Nilsen responds nonchalantly and his 'matter of fact' responses to police questioning is a key feature of the drama. 'Are we talking one body or two?' he is asked. '15 or 16' he replies and points them to a previous address where more bodies are discovered. He is articulate and clinical, similar to Ian Brady's in his approach to his crimes, and as the drama unfolds, we learn about his modus operandi. Picking up homeless men, offering them food, drink and a bed for the night, sleeping with them, killing them and then chopping up the bodies. 'It's a relief to get this off my chest' he tells the detective inspector (DI) in his first interview. We also learn that he kept some of the bodies for a period of time before cutting them up, to keep him company. These are horrific revelations to those listening. When his solicitor asks him the 'why did you do it?' question Neilson responds 'I do not really know … I was hoping that you could tell me that.'

The relationship between the media and serial killing is foregrounded in the drama. Beginning with an interview with the drainage worker who was called out to Nilsen's house and discovered the first remains, the media latch on to the story causing a headache for the police investigation, another common theme in British police drama. 'Media blackout from now on' a senior officer tells the investigation team and Mays' broken by the job DI constantly fights against the bureaucracy, another common theme, particularly towards the end of the case when Nilsen has produced a number of names of victims, and they have been identified. Senior detectives want to call a halt at six, enough to prosecute, Mays' DI wants to fight for justice for the families of the rest of the victims. He goes rogue, another key theme, often regarded as first established by Clint Eastwood's DI Harry Callaghan in *Dirty Harry* (Siegal, 1971) and continued through British 1970s dramas like *The Sweeney* (Childs, 1975). He asks for more manpower but is turned down on the grounds of cost. As the drama progresses, he becomes frustrated and alienated.

The scenes where Mays' DI interviews Nilsen and those between Nilsen and Brian Masters, an author who decides he wants to tell Nilsen's story, are very much two-handers, a technique often used for dramatic events in British soap operas, where a full episode features the interactions of two characters, giving the text a theatrical quality (Adams, 2024).

In both of these scenarios the emphasis is on Nilsen's controlling and narcissistic nature. He holds back, revealing only what he wants to reveal, piece by piece. It is his show. He complains about the food in prison, claims he should be rewarded for helping the police, asks Mays' DI to bring cigarettes, is reluctant to remember/release names of victims. He is playing the police investigators. Tennant puts in a masterful performance as Nilsen, capturing his strange, detached personality. He goes on a long rant about the public and the media's obsession with the macabre and ponders on why people are so interested, neatly encapsulating how the serial killing industry was in full swing during the 1980s. Mays' DI presses him for more details, the police need evidence, confessions are not enough. Nilsen pretends not to understand. Their scenes together are powerful in that they illustrate much of what we know about the self-obsessed nature of serial killers and their need to let the world know what they have done (Cummins et al, 2019).

The scenes between Masters and Nilsen are similar in character. At their first meeting Neilson gives Masters book containing sketches of his victims and reveals that having power over a beautiful body was a great motivation for him. He tells him he watched TV with the dead bodies for company. He asks the questions. 'I'm not entirely sure of your intentions … why would you want to write about a monster like me?' again getting to the heart of the public's obsession with true crime. He also reveals, again, his views on the public's appetite for the macabre, describing self-righteous public condemnation while consuming the grizzly details of serial killing and indulging in it at arm's length. 'I have responsibility for my story, and it is to be told correctly' Nilsen tells Masters and raises the issue of others making profit at his expense. Masters is drawn closer to Nilsen in each visit (he continued to visit Nilsen in prison for many years) following the completion of the book. Masters states that 'I'm here to comprehend because the law cannot comprehend beyond guilty and innocent.' He tells Nilsen he wants to know about his upbringing, 'the whole picture'. It is apparent from the outset that he is trying to answer the eternal 'why?' question. 'You keep looking for simple answers' Nilsen tells him.

Masters and Nilsen continue to meet, their relationship grows closer and it becomes apparent that Masters is fascinated by him. As the trial approaches, Nilsen thanks Masters for his company and asks him if he can borrow his tie. Masters is in court for the duration of the trial. To the surprise of the investigating team, Nilson pleads not guilty to all charges in court, despite having confessed to a number of murders and given details of the victims. His next two-hander with Masters sees Nilsen moving towards a 'mad not bad' defence. 'Am I mad?' Nilsen asks and argues that he did not plan the killings and that he should be seen as having diminished responsibility.

Nilsen is eventually convicted and given life sentences. The final scene belongs to Nilsen and Masters, following the publication of Masters' book. 'I read your book' Nilsen tells him, 'absolutely terrifying'. 'Good?' asks Masters. Nilsen hands him a pile of notes and questions why the book is not just called 'Nilsen'. His narcissism is on show again, but his critical thinking processes about serial killing and the media also re-appears. 'It's disrespectful not to name victims' he tells Masters, 'I robbed them of their life please don't rob them of their identities.' This is a criticism which has been levelled by academics and commentators about many accounts of serial killers and more recent publications such as Hallie Rubenhold's (2019) book *The Five: The Untold Lives of the Women killed by Jack the Ripper* and Louise Wattis' (2020) *Revisiting the Yorkshire Ripper Murders* have sought to redress the balance.

It is a strange thing to write, but there is a tenderness in this final scene in its kitchen sink-like setting of the prison visiting room. Many big budget serial killer films on TV dramas end with back-slapping and celebration. There is a weird kind of sadness in Nilsen's final question 'when will it be my turn?' meaning for the celebrity status given to previous serial killers. He did not live to see it happen courtesy of ITV, but the popularity and reception of *Des* (Arnold, 2020) illustrates that mediatized murder (Greer, 2004) is still big business and a popular part of the entertainment industry.

Conclusion

The three examples discussed here, despite being made in different time periods, all, it has been argued, draw on a rich British history of film and TV drama and use the techniques of those texts to contrast the ordinary, the mundane and the humdrum with the extraordinary actions of the perpetrators. *The Black Panther* (Merrick, 1977) draws its authenticity from the fact that it was made immediately following the crimes portrayed and its low budget adds to the 'kitchen sink' atmosphere created. *See No Evil* (Menual, 2005) is a Northern production in many of its aspects and therefore nods heavily to the British New Wave, particularly in its use of place and space. *Des* (Arnold, 2020) is set in the context of a social crisis (homelessness) and draws on the techniques of British police procedurals and soap operas with a focus on character relationships. Overall, the representation of British serial killers remains a very British affair.

7

Darkness Doubled: The Bundy Myth

Introduction

There is a close relationship between the various genres that go to make up true crime. This chapter will explore the media's relationship with the serial killer, Ted Bundy. True crime has focused on producing 'psycho' biographies which combine lurid details of crimes with a pop psychology explanation of their behaviour (Haggerty, 2009; Cummins et al, 2019). Serial killing has become the focus of intense academic interest. The serial killer has become what Foucault (1975: 42–3) termed 'a new specification of individuals'. In this case, the new specification could be termed the serial killer/celebrity. Serial killers are set apart from other killers. There is usually no prior relationship between the perpetrator and the victim. Such crimes are planned by the perpetrator. The selection and targeting of potential victims are part of the motivation of the killer (Wilson, 2009). These features form part of the myth of the serial killer genius or criminal mastermind that is such a stock feature of true crime in this area. The other distinguishing feature is the fame and notoricty that is attached to serial killers. In a world where serial killers become 'celebrities', one of the biggest 'celebrities' is Ted Bundy.

Serial killing is defined as a series of murders that occur over a period of time with a so-called 'cooling-off' period between each crime (Dietz, 1986). Before discussing the case of one of the most famous/infamous serial killers, Ted Bundy, this chapter will briefly explore the criminological literature that seeks to explore the motivations of serial killers. The academic literature has produced a typology of serial killers. These classifications have been used to assist in criminal investigations and the new discipline of psychological profiling.

Ressler et al (1986) played a key role in the development of psychological profiling. They categorized serial killers as 'organized' and 'disorganized'. This classification was based on psychological profiles and other factors such as clues from the crime scene. Bundy was the archetypal organized serial killer. Ressler et al (1986) saw these individuals as intelligent and methodical. Such killers exercised a sense of control over their victims. In this typology, the killer is seen as planning the murders in advance, often establishing some form of trust with the victim before killing them. Disorganized serial killers, in contrast, act impulsively without the level of planning that organized killers use to commit their crimes. It is suggested that this lack of planning is evidenced in the chaotic crime scenes. Ressler et al (1986) suggest that this group of killers is more likely to be socially isolated. Another typology was developed by Holmes and Holmes (2009). This approach examines the motivations of the killers. They identified subsets of serial killers including visionary, missionary, hedonistic and power-control. Visionary killers are seen as being driven by psychotic or delusional ideas. Victims are grounded in the killer's delusional worldview. Missionary serial killers are focused on groups that they deem to be undesirable. They have a belief that their actions are morally justified. Holmes and Holmes (2009) identified a separate group of killers – hedonistic killers. These killers are driven by seeking sexual gratification. It is suggested that the act of murder often follows the torture of victims, which, increases the sexual pleasure. Jeffrey Dahmer would be an example of a hedonistic killer. The final group in this typology is power-control killers who seek to assert dominance and control.

Leyton (1986) argues that the psychological typology approach cannot answer questions that relate to the cultural and historical nature of serial killing. It can provide insights into the motivations of individuals. It provides few insights into the targeting of victims. It does not seek to address broader sociological questions such as the status of victims. Modern UK serial killers' victims tend to come from groups that are marginalized in some way, for example, older people, gay men and sex workers, (Wilson, 2009). This marginalized status can be a factor in the failings in initial investigations and relative lack of media coverage of such cases (Egger, 2002; Wilson, 2009).

The crimes of Ted Bundy

Bundy committed a series of horrendous and shocking crimes (Williams, 2020). The media during his trial and in the vast number of books, films and dramas about the case, portray him as charming and intelligent (Drekle, 2011), a wholesome all-American boy, who happened to also be a rapist, serial killer and necrophiliac (Michaud and Aynesworth, 2000). Bundy has been a constant media presence since his arrest and trial. He was executed in 1989, the 30th anniversary in 2019 saw two Netflix series exploring the case.

Bundy admitted to the murder of 30 women in the 1970s. It is widely believed that he may have killed more women (Sullivan, 2019). There are some suggestions that he may be responsible for the deaths of over 100 women (Rule, 2000). Bundy was born in 1946, in Burlington, Vermont. He grew up believing that his mother was his older sister. His grandparents were deeply religious. This deception was a way of covering up the shame that was attached to illegitimacy at that time. Bundy was born at a home for unwed mothers (Rule,2000). His father is unknown. His mother moved with her son to Tacoma, Washington. In 1951, she married Johnnie Bundy.

Bundy attended the University of Washington, graduating with a degree in psychology in 1972. He was accepted to and attended law school in Utah, though he never earned his degree (Sullivan, 2020). Bundy was politically active. He worked on the re-election campaign of Daniel Evans, Governor of Washington. Bundy followed Evans' Democratic opponent, recording his speeches (*NY Times*, 1973). This later added to the myth of Bundy as a charming man leading a double life.

Bundy lured his victims into his car by pretending that he was injured and needed help. He then raped and killed them. Such features of his crimes would place Bundy in the organized serial killer category (Ressler et al, 1986). It is not clear when Bundy started his killing spree. In 1974, women went missing and there were rumours that they were last seen in the company of a young man called Ted (Sullivan, 2019, 2020). DeLisi (2023) suggested that Bundy had killed in his adolescence. DeLisi (2023) bases this hypothesis on the nature of the crimes that Bundy committed in the period 1974–78. This failure to account for all of his potential victims has added to the Bundy myth that continues to drive popular cultural interest in the case. It also reflects the way that violence against women and girls is marginalized (Strid et al, 2013; Walby, 2023). The full extent of Bundy's crimes may well never be known (DeLisi, 2023).

In 1974, Bundy was attending law school in Utah. There was a further spate of women disappearing. In 1975, Bundy was stopped by the police. A search of his vehicle found a crowbar, a face mask, rope and handcuffs. Bundy was arrested. The police linked him to more serious crimes. He was arrested for the kidnapping of Carol DaRonch. Bundy had approached DaRonch when she was shopping one night in November 1974. He claimed to be a police officer investigating a break-in of her vehicle. He flashed a badge to reassure her. He lured her to his Volkswagen. DaRonch appeared in the Netflix documentary (Berlinger, 2019a). She told how she had managed to fight off Bundy. She later was able to confront him in court. He was convicted and received a 1- to 15-year jail sentence.

Alongside the charm of the all-American boy, another key element of the myth of Ted Bundy is his ability to escape from prison. He escaped on two occasions. The first time, he was defending himself on a murder charge. During a trip to the courthouse library, he jumped out a window and made his first escape. He was captured eight days later. In December 1977, Bundy escaped again. He then travelled to Florida. On the night of 14 January 1978, Bundy broke into the Chi Omega sorority house at Florida State University. He attacked four of the young female residents. He killed two of the students: Margaret Bowman and Lisa Levy. On 9 February, Bundy kidnapped and murdered a 12-year-old girl named Kimberly Leach (Dekle, 2011).

Bundy became a celebrity during his trial. He was convicted of the murders of Margaret Bowman and Lisa Levy, and sentenced to death. In 1980, he was convicted of the murder of Kimberly Leach and received the death penalty. Bundy spent nine years on death row appealing his sentence. He was executed by electric chair in 1989. Huge crowds gathered outside the prison at the time of the execution (Saltzman, 1995). Bundy's body was cremated. No public ceremony was held. Before Bundy was executed, he requested his ashes be scattered in the Cascade Mountains of Washington state, where he murdered at least four of his victims.

The Stranger Beside Me

Ann Rule's memoir of working with Bundy has become one of the bestselling and most influential true crime products. Following its success, Rule went on to become one of the most successful true crime writers. She is also a key figure in the development of true crime. Her memoir is one of the key texts in the genre. Before this success, she had worked in law enforcement. She had also written for *True Detective* magazine. She was, therefore, well versed in the conventions of true crime and had a knowledge of the criminal justice system (CJS). The nature and extent of Bundy's crimes, combined with his charm and the escapes from prison, have meant that the case continues to be a rich source for writers and filmmakers. *The Stranger Beside Me* (Rule, 2000; first published in 1980) is one of the earliest examples. Ann Rule met Ted Bundy while they were both volunteers at Suicide Crisis Clinic in Seattle in 1971. Bundy was a student studying psychology at the University of Washington. They developed a close friendship.

The Stranger Beside Me is a biography of Ted Bundy. However, it is also a semi-autobiographical piece of work. The exploration of the relationship between the writer and the subject matter has become an integral part of the true crime genre. The book can be termed a 'memoir biography' as the author simultaneously provides accounts of her own life experiences that entwined with that of the subject's life. Jena (2023) argues that in The Stranger Beside Me Rule's voice and conscience fluctuates. There are periods when she describes having a close personal friendship with Bundy. She then has doubts and feels that he may be connected to the disappearances. Rule, perhaps not surprisingly as no one would want to believe that a friend had committed such crimes, outlines how she maintained some hope that Bundy was not a rapist and killer. Eventually, Rule comes to realize that Bundy has manipulated and exploited her.

The Stranger Beside Me was influential in the construction of the image of Bundy as a charming charlatan, who was able to move in polite society while committing his crimes. The author and the reader know the reality. However, Rule does appear sympathetic to Bundy at some points. Rule became a hugely successful true crime writer. In an interview in 1994, Rule was clear on how she went about choosing which news stories to develop into one of her bestsellers. 'I'm looking for a protagonist, a subject who is as many of these as possible: attractive, rich, brilliant, successful, charismatic, has love in his life – basically all the things that we think we would be happy if we had, but they always want more' (Katz, 2017). In the same interview, Rule went on to state that the public want to explore the stories of those, like Bundy, who in her words 'don't look like they have committed a murder'.

Beale (2015) was extremely critical of Rule's most famous work, particularly the relationship that Rule had with Bundy when he was in prison. Rule was criticized for her ambivalent attitude to Bundy. There are clear echoes of the criticism that Capote faced following the publication of *In Cold Blood* (1966). This criticism did not have any impact of the sales of The Stranger Beside Me or her later works. The audience members are in a similar ambivalent position as the author – attracted and repulsed but still drawn to the case.

Conversations with a Killer: The Ted Bundy Tapes

Since Rule's (1980) memoir, books, articles, films and documentaries about the Bundy case have appeared at regular intervals. The commodification of serial murder and sexual violence against women and girls has meant that cases like the crimes of Bundy are revisited and exploited time and time again. Indeed, we must acknowledge that this chapter, and similar academic commentaries, are also culpable in reproducing the cult of sex crime and femicide.

Part of modern true crime relationship with murder and serial killing is the endless search for the 'definitive account' of the case or the solving in the long-standing mystery. There is little mystery in the whodunnit sense about many of the cases such as the Moors Murders (Cummins et al, 2019), John Wayne Gacy (Linedecker, 1993; Amirante and Broderick, 2011) or the Yorkshire Ripper (Bilton, 2003) that receive the most attention. The memoirs of police officers involved in such cases appear at the end of their careers. Topping's account of his role in the Moors Murder case was published in 1989. The main interest for readers was the fact that Topping was in charge of the police operation that saw Brady and Hindley, separately, in 1987, return to the Moors in an attempt to locate the bodies of Pauline Reade and Keith Bennett (Topping, 1989). Brady and Hindley finally confessed to the murder of both children. This is an unusual example. In many other cases, the attempt to provide a definitive account or a new perspective is more exploitative.

The Stranger Beside Me was made into a TV miniseries. The nature of Bundy's crimes means that there have been a series of films. These include *Bundy: An American Icon* (2009). This is a slasher/horror film that went direct-to-video, an indication of its overall quality. *Bundy: The Deliberate Stranger* (2019) is a true crime account of the case. Larsen was a reporter for the *Seattle Times*. Larsen was a political reporter. Larsen had interviewed Bundy during the 1972 election campaign for Governor. Bundy was working on the team of Daniel J. Evans who was seeking re-election. Larsen moved from political reporting to crime. He subsequently covered the homicides in the Seattle area and followed the case up the execution of Bundy in 1989. The book was adapted into a two-part TV movie.

The series does not include all of Bundy's crimes – it omits the first five murders and the kidnap and murder of 12-year-old Kimberly Leach. Larsen's (2019) book demonstrates his journalistic skills as he outlines his relationship with Bundy. He also explores the impact of the crimes on victims' families and the officers involved in the investigation. Bundy remains very much the focus and the centre of the narrative. Larsen (2019) presents Bundy's all-American boy persona as one of the key factors in the failure of authorities to catch him earlier. It also a key component in ongoing public fascination with the case. In this and similar discussions of the case, there is no critical analysis or deconstruction of the 'all-American boy' persona or what it might tell us about white American masculinity.

Extremely Wicked, Shockingly Evil and Vile (2019b) stars Zac Efron as Bundy. Efron became famous for his leading role as Troy Bolton in the *High School Musical trilogy* (2006–08). He also starred in the musical film *Hairspray* (2007). Efron is playing against type as a serial killer. However, his casting emphasizes the 'Bundy charmer' trope that is a consistent feature of many of these treatments of the case. This film includes the standard Bundy charming serial killer/celebrity tropes. *Extremely Wicked* tells the story of Bundy's crimes from the perspective of his girlfriend, Elizabeth Kloepfer. The film begins with a death row visit. It then moves back in time to the night they met in a bar in Seattle in 1969. These scenes contrast the bleakest of settings death row with the vibrancy and normality of the bar. The viewer knows that Bundy uses the setting of the bar and his social confidence to deceive Kloepfer. Confidence and charm that we know he will use to trick the women he murders. She becomes a victim of Bundy. This romantic relationship continues to develop while Bundy, unbeknownst to Kloepfer, was committing murders. The film shows Bundy's arrests, escapes and trials. This is paralleled with Kloepfer's mental breakdown as she recognizes the enormity and depravity of Bundy's crimes. However, the romance is presented in the film as a conventional love story. The film does not include the abusive behaviour that Bundy inflicted on Kloepfer. Bundy's sexual abuse of Kloepfer's younger daughter is not included (McCann, 2021)

The same is true of *Ted Bundy: American Boogeyman* (2021), which stars Chad Michael Murray as Bundy. Murray first rose to prominence for his role on the US teen drama *One Tree Hill*. The title of *Extremely Wicked, Shockingly Evil and Vile* is a reference to the judge remarks on Bundy's murders while sentencing him to death. The film is based on the memoir written by Bundy's former girlfriend *The Phantom Prince: My Life with Ted Bundy* (Kendall, 2020).

The nature and extent of Bundy's crimes meant that he was a suspect in other unsolved crimes. This is a shocking indicator of the deeply engrained nature of sexual violence and femicide within American society (Messing et al, 2023). *The Riverman* (2004) is based on *The Riverman: Ted Bundy and I Hunt for the Green River Killer* (Keppel and Birnes, 2010). *The Riverman* tells the true story of how Bundy was interviewed by detectives who were searching for a serial killer known as the *Green River Killer*. Keppel was a criminology professor at the University of Washington. He was approached by local law enforcement agents to help profile a serial killer who targeted sex workers. Keppel interviewed Bundy several times. However, Keppel was seeking to gain information about Bundy's crimes. Bundy confesses to several unsolved murders in the hope that Keppel will delay his execution. The interviews generated little of use in the investigation.

There are uncanny echoes of *The Silence of the Lambs* (Harris, 1988), where a serial killer, Hannibal Lecter, is interviewed by the FBI to provide insights into the psychological profile of a serial killer. Demme's 1991 film adaptation received critical acclaim and was a huge box office success. It is one of only three to win all five of the 'Big Five' Academy Awards. Most viewers of *The Riverman* would make connections between the film and *The Silence of the Lambs*. Lecter fascinates the audience for two reasons. The first is that he is an intelligent and cultured character. At the same time, he is an almost gothic figure akin to a vampire, symbolic of evil (Oleson 2005, 2006; Garcia, 2020). The same could be said of Bundy.

Bundy features in many documentaries that look at serial killers. For example, the 1984 documentary *Murder: No Apparent Motive* explores the cases of Ed Kemper and Ted Bundy. Kemper killed eight people in 1972 and 1973. Kemper murdered female students he had picked up hitchhiking in Santa Cruz, California. He took them to isolated areas to kill them before mutilating their bodies (Matera, 2021). Kemper was convicted and requested the death penalty. The moratorium placed on capital punishment by the Supreme Court of California meant that he was sentenced to life imprisonment. He remains incarcerated. The title of this documentary is not an ironic use of language but reflects a wider cultural failure to face the reality of male sexual violence. Kemper and Bundy had clear motives – the dominance and degradation of women for their own pleasure.

Bundy and his crimes have been a feature of the true crime and popular cultural landscape since his first arrest and escape 50 years ago. The images related to Bundy and his crimes have become iconic. These include Bundy waving to reporters in Court as he conducts his own defence, wanted posters, mugshots and the Volkswagen Beetles that he used to kidnap his victims. Even the pictures of Bundy in Court are part of the myth of Bundy (McCabe, 2022). They play a key role in the narrative that society was somehow deceived by this handsome, white, middle class, educated, embodiment of suave modern masculinity.

Conversations with a Killer

McCann (2021) notes that the title of the memoirs *The Stranger Beside Me* (2000; first published in 1980) and *The Phantom Prince* (2020; first published in 1981) emphasize the notion that Bundy operated in plain sight. There is a psychological defence mechanism at work. The reality of the murders that Bundy committed might be too devastating to contemplate. *Conversations with a Killer* (Berlinger, 2019a) contains a series of interviews with journalists, lawyers and law enforcement officials. These are all white men. The result contrasts Bundy's masculinity with these men who embody a traditional masculinity. This strand of masculinity does not include the sexual violence that Bundy inflicted. McCann (2021) notes that Rule (1980) highlights the way that law enforcement showed for contempt for Bundy.

Berlinger's documentary is based on interviews with Bundy and law enforcement officials. Bundy, like other high-profile killers and offenders, was surely aware of and keen to protect his public image (Cummins et al, 2019). Netflix promoted the series as though it was a horror movie – 'maybe don't watch this one alone'. The tapes were recorded when he was appealing against the death sentence. In these taped conversations, Bundy is the most unreliable of unreliable narrators (McCabe, 2022). The image of a happy, secure and carefree childhood he presents is totally contradicted by the interview with Sandi Holt. She was the sister of a childhood friend of Bundy. Holt suggests that Bundy was bullied at school partly because he had a speech impediment. She also suggests the portrait of Bundy as an all-American success – an academic achiever, a social success and a high school sportsman – is also a myth. McCabe (2022) suggests that in these taped interviews, Bundy's arrogance is clear. This arrogance is confirmed by the law enforcement officials, who make it clear that his confidence was linked to his socio-economic status. This was, in turn, one of the key factors in his ability to avoid detection. It was also a reason that Bundy was able to escape twice. Berlinger's film demonstrates the failings of law enforcement agencies. This is an area of the Bundy case that is often underplayed.

Burn Bundy burn

The final episode of Berlinger's *Conversations* focused on the execution of Bundy in Florida in 1989. Bundy's execution drew crowds and there was something that might be called a carnival atmosphere. The death penalty as well as being the ultimate punishment performs a highly symbolic role. It is a form of theatre (Conquergood, 2002) as well as a state function (Garland, 2010). Public executions drew significant crowds. The introduction of private executions was intended to prevent mob violence and social disorder (McGowen, 1994; Linders, 2002). It also meant that the actual execution was witnessed by members of the elite and state officials. There were, of course, reports of executions that took place behind prison walls. Bundy's execution had echoes of the public executions of the 19th century (Saltzman, 1995). Before his death, Bundy spoke with a radio host, James Dobson (Caputi, 1989). In this final confession, Bundy blamed pornography and alcohol. Bundy ended the interview by stating his belief in Jesus Christ. The interview reflects key elements of the Bundy myth. Bundy uses the third person throughout displacing responsibility (Caputi,1989). The fact that the interview took place is further evidence of the role of Bundy's status in the construction of the Bundy myth. This final interview is a modern form of traditional gallows literature (Saltzman, 1995). Saltzman (1995) concludes that the wider media comments on the execution highlighted that the carnival style event were thoughtless, an affront to the solemnity of death. This populist response was a challenge to the state's control of the narrative.

The Netflix documentary *Conversations with a Killer: The Ted Bundy Tapes* does include some more challenging perspectives that confront issues of masculinity and patriarchal violence (McCabe, 2022). This is a critical perspective that is absent from much of the true crime treatments of Bundy. Berlinger's films about Bundy were followed up by *Conversations with a Killer: The John Wayne Gacy Tapes* and *Conversation with a Killer: The Jeffery Dahmer Tapes*. The three series use a similar mixture of archival footage and recordings made while the killers were incarcerated to explore the cases.

Documentary can be an immensely powerful and emotionally engaging form. The potential power of the documentary is not necessarily diminished in the age of streaming. Social media forums allow for a collective response (Larke-Walsh, 2020). Larke-Walsh (2020) analyses the feature length documentary *Southwest of Salem: the Story of the San Antonio Four* (Esquinazi, 2016). The film tells the story of the wrongful conviction of four young gay women for the sexual assault and rape of two children – nieces of one of the accused. The film shows the young women were targeted in a society where homophobia was deeply entrenched. The convictions took place during a moral panic about satanic abuse. The film had a significant role in the overturning of the wrongful convictions.

The viewer engages with a documentary about Bundy in a different fashion to a film that stars Zac Efron. This is not to say that a work of art cannot provide valuable insights. Documentaries use a range of techniques to engage the viewer and challenge perceptions. These include the use of audio-visuals, for example, music being played under photographs of victims. In this case the photographs are mostly of young women taken from college year books. These pictures usually show optimistic young women full of energy about to set out on their adult lives. The poignancy of these photos is apparent for the viewer as they know their lives were cut short in the most brutal way imaginable. This shifts the focus to the impact of the crime without stepping into more salacious areas. This approach avoids the presentation of the mutilated female corpse as entertainment (Penfold-Mounce, 2016, 2020).

Berlinger's series highlights how deeply engrained the Bundy myth has become (McCabe, 2022). This is despite the nature of his crimes. The basic facts of the case, including the levels of degradation, humiliation and violence that Bundy inflicted on his victims are widely known. Despite this, the Bundy myth remains deeply entrenched within popular culture. The Bundy case is an outlier in the application of Christie's (1986) notion of the 'perfect victim'. In the context of 1970s USA, it is hard to think of more perfect victims than white, attractive middle-class female college students. In other cases, the social status of the victims has played a vital role in the media coverage (Wattis 2020). Here, the status of the victims is trumped by Bundy's. Law enforcement and other officials repeat the idea that one of the reasons that Bundy was able to commit his crimes undetected for so long was his social status.

A Google search for imagines of photographs of Bundy produces a series of pictures that reflect a particular version of US American middle-class masculinity (McCann, 2021). It is, of course, a matter of judgement as to whether Bundy was charismatic. He seemed able to charm some individuals even in the most unlikely circumstances. The amazing comments by the judge who sentenced him to death illustrates this. Dade County Circuit Court Judge Edward Cowart told Bundy, 'You're a bright young man. You'd have made a good lawyer, and I would have loved to have you practice in front of me, but you went another way, partner.' He added, 'I don't feel any animosity toward you. I want you to know that. Take care of yourself.' The tragedy is not the degradations that Bundy has inflicted on the young woman, he has murdered and the pain their families and friends endure, it is Bundy's failure to realize his potential and enjoy the advantages of being a white middle-class professional (McCann, 2021).

Mangan (2019) questioned the value of the Berlinger productions asking what if anything they contributed to the understanding of Bundy and his crimes. Within true crime, there are high profile cases such as the Moors Murders, the Yorkshire Ripper and Bundy where there appears to be an insatiable appetite for information about or stories related to the case (Cummins et al, 2019). McCann (2021) contrasts the widely viewed photographs of Bundy with the picture that appears at the end of *The Stranger Beside Me* (1980). The photograph shows a moment when Bundy lost his temper while on trial for the murder of Kimberly Leach. It is an image of the cool self-contained Bundy that dominates. In this picture, Bundy's face is contorted with rage and aggression. Rule suggests that this might be the final image that Bundy's victims saw. Rule suggests that this is the real Bundy behind the mask. There is no real basis to this speculation from Rule. It reinforces the notion of the diabolical hiding beneath the suave exterior.

Conclusion

Fascination with violent crime and the individuals who commit such acts is not new. However, the creation of the serial killer as a figure in popular culture can be seen as symbolic of modern societies obsession with violence, particularly sexual violence, and murder (Benham, 2015). Serial killing is rare but serial killers are everywhere – in all forms of media: news, true crime, films, documentaries, novels and podcasts. In modern celebrity culture, the serial killer is an important trading commodity. Murderabilia is big business. Serial killers are aware of their media status and value. Bentham (2015) illustrates this by using the example of Richard Ramirez – the Night Stalker. Ramirez was convicted of 12 murders and 11 counts of rape. He terrorized the Greater Los Angeles and San Francisco Bay areas in the 1980s. He was sentenced to death. He died on death row awaiting execution. Ramirez signed his artworks 'Richard Ramirez Night Stalker'. The demand for such pieces was so high that he had his own art dealer (Bentham, 2015).

Schmid (2006) argued that the serial killer has a mythic status akin to that of the cowboy as an outlaw figure in American culture. The reality of their actual existence has been lost in the mythical status that they have achieved in popular culture. This is true for both cowboys and serial killers. The comparison should end there as the serial killer is inflicting degradation on victims (Bentham, 2015). However, like the cowboy, the serial killer has become a figure that is feted for their ability to outwit authorities. This is, of course, one of the key elements of the myth. The 'success' of serial killers is more often due to institutional failings rather than anything else. The attraction of the serial killer becomes difficult to understand. The myth of the serial killer means that the true nature of their crimes (Caputi, 1987) becomes secondary.

This chapter has explored the enduring fascination of the Bundy myth. Bundy is one of the most famous *celebrities/serial killers*. Bentham (2015) notes that his public image has more in common with a character such as Highsmith's Tom Ripley. The facts of the case, including his two escapes, helped to create this image. The media representations since have cemented it. This image obscures the abject reality of his horrific crimes.

There have been some more recent attempts – for example, McCabe (2022) and McCann (2021) – to deconstruct this myth. This is a difficult task in the face of the deeply engrained cultural representations of the suave, charming and sophisticated Bundy, who used his intelligence to outwit law enforcement and trick his victims into his Volkswagen Beetle. Bundy is a modern version of the villain in Gothic fiction. The attraction of the Gothic is not only that it creates fear but also that the monster is also attractive (Ingebretsen, 1998). In fiction, fear alongside the dual nature of the anti-hero is a main factor in the audience enjoyment. The Bundy myth is a perfect example of this. In the battle between the truth and fiction, the myths have overwhelmed a more sober analysis. Bundy's social status seems to have obscured the nature of his crimes, the misogyny that drove them and the failings of institutions that allowed him to commit them.

8

Fear of Masks: The Crimes of Peter Sutcliffe

Introduction

This chapter will trace the ways in which true crime texts and true crime-based dramas have represented the crimes, investigation and aftermath of the murders and assaults carried out by Peter Sutcliffe – the so-called Yorkshire Ripper. The chapter uses bricolage as a research method to produce a case study analysis of cultural representations of the case, drawing on a range of source materials including true crime accounts, podcasts, news documentaries, TV dramas and works of fiction. This method explores the impact of the crimes but also allows for a deeper examination of how the case has become embedded within the collective memory. The chapter includes an in-depth examination of *Somebody's Husband, Somebody's Son* (Burn, 1984), a true crime account which differs from much of the content produced about these murders. Influenced by Capote and Mailer's fact-based narratives, Burn's work also falls into what might considered to be literary true crime. In contrast to other popular true crime treatments, Burn sought to produce a psycho geographical analysis of the case, exploring the socio-cultural and historical context in which the attacks and murders occurred, and how this shaped police, media and public responses. Burn's 'deeper dive', which involved extensive 'fieldwork' spending time in Sutcliffe's hometown thus acts as a counterpoint to the general psychological autopsy approach that dominates how we understand the figure of the serial killer (Davis, 1993; Webber, 2010) – a frequent focus in true crime serial murder narratives (Murley, 2008).

The crimes of Peter Sutcliffe

In October 1975, Wilma McCann, a 28-year-old mother of four young children was murdered by Peter Sutcliffe in the Chapeltown area of Leeds.

Wilma McCann was hit over the head with a hammer and stabbed over a dozen times. Her mutilated body was found on playing fields close to where she lived. The murder was to be the first committed by lorry driver from Bingley, Peter Sutcliffe. Prior to murdering Wilma, three women survived attacks by Sutcliffe in the summer of 1975: 14-year-old Tracey Browne was attacked on the outskirts of Halifax; Anna Rokuljski was attacked in Keighley; and Olive Smelt was also attacked in Halifax. Sutcliffe went on to murder 12 more women: Emily Jackson (42), Irene Richardson (28), Patricia Atkinson (32), Jayne McDonald (16), Jean Jordan (20), Yvonne Pearson (21), Helen Rytka (20), Vera Millward (40), Josephine Whittaker (19), Barbara Leach (20), Marguerite Walls (47) and Jacqueline Hill (20). A further five women survived attacks by Sutcliffe between 1975 and 1980: Marcella Claxton, Maureen Long, Marilyn Moore, Uphanda Bandaya and Teresa Sykes. Sutcliffe was arrested in Sheffield by uniformed officers carrying out a routine number plate check in January 1981.

Up until the conviction of GP Harold Shipman – there is speculation that Shipman may have murdered over 200 of his patients – Sutcliffe was the most prolific serial killer in British criminal history. This case is often understood as a series of murders targeting sex workers and while it is true that early murder victims were linked to sex work, this was not always as clear-cut as police and media made it out to be (Kinnell, 2008). Indeed, police began to draw parallels with the Whitechapel Murders of 1888 following the murder of Irene Richardson in February 1977, increasingly referring to 'Jack the Ripper type murders' in news coverage and on public information posters (Yallop, 1988). The unknown killer of five women in 1888 spawned the ripper mythos in the figure of Jack the Ripper who also targeted women connected to prostitution. The crimes have become deeply embedded in British popular culture. There is a whole Ripper cultural industry – including walking tours of London (Jones, 2017), numerous cultural artefacts and the pseudo-science 'ripperology'. The 1888 murders have also been constructed as a gothic mystery in the mould of Stevenson's Dr Jekyll and Mr Hyde and have become as much a part of the fabric of the mythic history of London as the Blitz, black cabs or the fog. Until recently, with the publication of *The Five* (Rubenhold, 2019) the lives of the Ripper's victims have received much less attention than theories, offered by the aforementioned ripperologists – the more outlandish the better for sales – as to who the killer might have been. Rubenhold set about to tell the stories of five women, whose lives were defined by poverty and hardship. Before this, news and culture had treated the Whitechapel victims as props in the story of the unknown killer's story, condemning them as prostitutes who deserved their fate, while also picking over the details of their mutilated bodies.

Feminist writers identify how Whitechapel set the cultural template for sexually motivated murder as a crime of misogyny where the male killer is elevated and the female victim is othered and hated (Downing, 2013). Caputi (1987) argues that the modern sex crime originated from the Whitechapel narrative, referring also to 'ripper repetitions' to understand how culture has applied the 'ripper' formula to subsequent cases involving male murderers and female victims. As such, the myth serves to legitimatize masculine violence, specifically violence against women in the context of patriarchal culture (Downing, 2013). Returning to the Sutcliffe murders, it is not clear when or by whom, but at some point, early on in the case, police and media began to refer to the murderer as the Yorkshire Ripper.

Most of Sutcliffe's attacks took place in the red-light areas of Leeds and Bradford; however, Sutcliffe also attacked women in Manchester and smaller towns across West Yorkshire. This strengthened the police's belief that they were searching for a man obsessed with killing sex workers. Indeed, the focus on prostitution remains an immensely powerful narrative in both true crime and academic discussions of the case. As Kinnell (2008) argues, media and academic commentaries remain wedded to the idea that Sutcliffe was a 'prototypical prostitute killer' even though only four victims were selling sex at the time of their murders. Sutcliffe's legal team invoked the 'prostitute killer' trope to plead a defence of diminished responsibility, claiming that Sutcliffe was suffering from schizophrenia and was motivated by messages from God telling him to kill 'prostitutes'. Even after 50 years, the broadcast of the TV docudrama *The Long Shadow* in 2023 prompted further debates about the status of the victims and their involvement or otherwise in sex work.

The police's fixation with a killer driven by a hatred of prostitutes led to assumptions that 'respectable' women were somehow not at risk. When 16-year-old Jayne McDonald was murdered in Chapeltown while walking home from a night out, police claimed the killer had mistaken her for a 'prostitute'. However, as police surveillance increased in the red-light districts of Leeds and Bradford, Sutcliffe began attacking women outside of these areas and from 1978 onwards, all subsequent attacks were perpetrated on women with no links to prostitution.

The case is notorious for the misogyny and indifference police directed at victims linked to prostitution who were denigrated and blamed because they were women who were perceived to have taken risks and who did not live up to proscribed standards of feminine respectability (Jouve, 1986; Smith, 2013; Wattis, 2018). In Christie's (1986) outline of the media and cultural construct of victims, sex workers would be far removed from the notion of ideal victimhood. This leads to victim blaming but also shapes the extent and nature of media attention and how police respond and investigate murder cases, which is often determined by the perceived status of victims (Jiwani and Young, 2006). Moreover, Smith (2013) documents how police prejudice extended to any of the victims they perceived as demonstrating 'low morals' (Yallop, 1988) by going out at night unaccompanied, suffering with their mental health or having more than one boyfriend.

A further noteworthy feature of the case is the climate of fear it created. Once it became apparent that the killer was targeting women with no links to prostitution and that all women were potentially at risk, the 'Ripper' threat pervaded everyday life for women across West Yorkshire and beyond. Safety advice from police, media and other institutions such as the Universities of Leeds and Bradford urged women to restrict their lives and not to go out alone at night. This sparked a backlash from feminists who took issue with women being held responsible for the threat posed by a male killer and responded with Reclaim the Night marches in Leeds and Bradford (Mackay, 2015).

The five-year police 'hunt' for the Yorkshire Ripper was the biggest manhunt in British police history and is renowned for a catalogue of investigative failings which allowed the killer to attack women with impunity before Sutcliffe was eventually caught in 1981 (Byford, 1981; Yallop, 1988). Errors include the fact that police interviewed Sutcliffe nine times and failed to look into his previous convictions. In addition, their belief that they were looking for a 'prostitute killer' meant that statements from surviving victims who did not fit this victim profile, including, most crucially, accurate descriptions of their attacker, were ignored and omitted from the investigation. The gravest error the police made, however, was the blind acceptance that the hoax tape and letters sent to the police in 1979 by a man claiming to be the killer, taunting the police and discussing his next attack, were genuine. The man heading up the Ripper investigation at the time of the tape and letters, Assistant Chief Constable George Oldfield, was convinced the man calling himself 'Jack' was the killer and as Joan Smith (2013) writes, this fixation with a 'ripper figure' resembling the Whitechapel murderer was pivotal in steering the investigation in the wrong direction.

As Caputi (1987) writes, the tape and letters reinforced the Ripper myth and formed the basis of a large-scale publicity campaign including leaflets distributed across West Yorkshire with samples of what was thought to be the killer's handwriting. Posters of the letters appeared on billboards across the country. The tape was also played on the radio, in schools, youth clubs pubs and nightclubs in case anybody recognized the voice of the killer. It was also possible to ring a police hotline to 'hear the voice of the Ripper'. Wattis (2020) notes that the responses overwhelmed the police and as one officer commented produced '100 per cent rubbish' (Yallop, 1988). In the wake of Sutcliffe's conviction in 1981, the Byford inquiry and subsequent report), which was only made public in 2006, set out to understand the failings in the case. The report identified the weight given to the hoax tape and letters as one of the investigation's most serious errors. Byford (1981) highlights how evidence at the time did not support George Oldfield's view that the perpetrator had sent the letters and tape, and belief in their authenticity led to a huge diversion of resources and misdirected the investigation. This meant that suspects including Sutcliffe were eliminated based on handwriting samples and voice identification because the voice on the tape had a Northeast accent.

Sutcliffe's eventual arrest occurred by chance in Sheffield's red-light district, during a check on his car prompted by a faulty brake light and false licence plates. Uniformed officers noticed the car and made the arrest. As such, the breakthrough was not down to the five-year resource-intensive murder investigation. Sutcliffe was found guilty of the murder of 13 women, following his trial in 1981. His plea of diminished responsibility was dismissed, and he was sentenced to life imprisonment. Sutcliffe was transferred to Broadmoor Special Hospital in March 1984 after being diagnosed with paranoid schizophrenia. Under new legal provisions, he was sentenced to a whole life term in 2009. His appeal against this was dismissed in 2011. Sutcliffe was transferred back to prison in 2016. He died of COVID in Durham in 2020.

True crime and the Sutcliffe case

The symbiotic relationship between media culture and the serial killer is now a given, reflected in the growth of media output devoted to serial murder and the elevation of killers to modern celebrities (Jenkins, 1994; Seltzer, 2008; Murley, 2008; Schmid, 2008; Haggerty, 2009). Given the nature of Sutcliffe's crimes, it is hardly surprising that considerable cultural output has revisited the case in books and documentaries. For instance, a brief unrefined Google search, yields over 500,000 results. More recently, Sutcliffe's death in 2020 prompted renewed interest in the case with the popularity of the true crime podcasts expanding popular criminological commentary on the case. Indeed, it is a requisite that alongside other 'infamous' cases, podcasts should include an episode that covers the so-called Ripper case – examples include *I Could Murder a Podcast* (Season 2 Episode 1), *These Walls are Thin*, *The Last Podcast on the Left* and *Casefile*.

There is a collection of true crime texts that represent definitive accounts of the case. *Wicked Beyond Belief: The Hunt for the Yorkshire Ripper* (Bilton, 2003) is a classic of the investigation-focused true crime genre. In the preface, Bilton (2003) stipulates that he is not interested in Sutcliffe or any psychological analysis (Morrison, 2003). The result is a lengthy and devastating outline of the investigation into the murders, highlighting how later murders might have been prevented had it not been for earlier investigative errors. Of course, Bilton possesses the benefit of hindsight; nevertheless, he presents the flaws of investigation in forensic detail.

Both Bilton (2003) and *The Byford Report* (1981) identify how during the Ripper investigation, the major incident room became overwhelmed due to the sheer volume of information that was being collected. This led to huge backlogs in processing information and a serious fault in the central card index system, which meant that information about Sutcliffe was never collated in one place or cross-referenced.

However, as Bilton (2003) points out, many errors appear to stem from failure to follow basic investigatory procedures. For example, when Sutcliffe murdered Jean Jordan in Manchester, he posed as a punter and paid her £5. Jean's body was not found for nine days; however, in her handbag was the £5 note given to her by Sutcliffe. In the intervening nine-day period, Sutcliffe returned to the body to remove what could be a vital clue but failed to do so and in the process left further evidence. Indeed, the note was a brand-new issue traced to 34 firms in the local area. This meant that it must have been in the wage packet of an employee, one of whom was Peter Sutcliffe. On the back of this, Sutcliffe was interviewed, but the police did not search his car or house.

Indeed, as we now know, Sutcliffe was interviewed nine times; however, police failed to link clues that would have pointed to Sutcliffe as the perpetrator. As discussed earlier, at one point, he was ruled out because he did not speak with a Geordie accent like the voice on the infamous hoax tape. The cover of the first edition of *Wicked Beyond Belief* includes a montage of photofits based on descriptions of the killer provided by victims who survived attacks. At the centre is the mugshot of Sutcliffe following his arrest. What the cover captures is the fact that the photofits proved to be remarkably accurate but were ignored by police because the women either did not fit the police's assumed victim profile or they were deemed unreliable witnesses.

In common with many true crime narratives, Bilton's promises the 'full' or 'true' story of the case. In doing so, he strays from reflecting on the investigation to discussing prurient details. For instance, Bilton reveals that Sutcliffe wore a 'killing suit' when he murdered his victims. This garment was made from a V-neck jumper, which protected his knees, and exposed his genitals. This allowed Sutcliffe to kneel, stab his victims and masturbate over their bodies. The discussion of sexual details of this nature reinforces the idea of the sexually motivated male killer and echoes the sexualization of the Ripper narrative, which acts to objectify victims, and is a common feature of true crime and popular culture more widely (Caputi, 1987; Bilton, 2003; Downing, 2013). Notwithstanding, Bilton deploys the 'killing suit' as evidence that Sutcliffe was a 'sick and perverted murderer' rather than mentally ill. In a bizarre twist in 2003, the *Bradford Argus* reported that a former Detective Constable Alan Foster who had worked on the Ripper case, had handed in the item of clothing that Bilton had described as the killing suit. The so-called suit was among Sutcliffe's belongings which he had been ordered to burn when the case ended, but he had kept it (*Telegraph and Argus*, 2003).

It is common in cases involving serial killers, or a series of murders, for claims to be made about additional victims whom the police do not link to the case in question. In classic true crime style, Bilton identifies a dozen additional cases which bear similarities to the attacks and murders perpetrated by Sutcliffe. Two of these involved male victims who were attacked from behind with a hammer. Bilton also notes that Sutcliffe was arrested carrying a hammer in a red-light district as early as 1969.

In contrast to Burn's *Somebody's Husband, Somebody's Son*, Bilton offers little in the way of critical cultural, social or historical analysis of the crimes or the failed organization. Morrison (2003) argues that Bilton's lack of interest in Sutcliffe means that there is a crucial element missing from the narrative. At the same time, however, ignoring the killer, avoids mythologizing him by placing him at the centre of the narrative.

Yallop (1988) began writing *Deliver Us from Evil* during the Ripper investigation and before Sutcliffe's arrest (Wattis, 2018). The text combines an exposé of police failings, chronology and details of the murders with socio-historical commentary, victims' stories and Yallop's own investigative take on the case. Much true crime resembles detective fiction in terms of narrative structure and a progression towards answers. Moreover, detective fiction often involves the detective as a maverick outsider, who outperforms the police and solves the case, typified in the figure of Sherlock Holmes (Brown, 2003). Yallop positions himself in that space. As Wattis (2020) notes, the narrative in *Deliver Us from Evil* centres on a mission to reveal the 'truth' of the murders and other crimes that occurred during this period.

One of Yallop's concerns in the book is the murder of Joan Harrison in Preston in 1975. Due to the victim's lifestyle, police initially linked it to the Ripper case. This was reinforced by the hoax tape which referred to 'Preston '75'. When Sutcliffe was caught, however, it transpired he was not responsible for the murder and in 2006, DNA evidence identified Joan Harrison's killer as convicted sex offender Christopher Smith. *Deliver Us From Evil* was published in 1988 and within the book Yallop considers the possibility that two serial killers were at large during the period when Sutcliffe was murdering women. Thus, in common with Bilton (2003), he contends that Sutcliffe may have been responsible for further unsolved murders in the North of England. This resonates with Hilary Kinnell's (2008) view that when sex workers are murdered, this is ignored by the media, unless there is a possibility that the murder can be linked to a newsworthy serial killer. Writing about the murder and disappearance of five sex workers in Teesside in the late 1990s and early 2000s, Wattis (2020) makes a similar point, observing how at the time, local and national media attempted to link the cases to Christopher Helliwell and Steve Wright. Again, this relates to the 'ripper' template and the assumption that when sex workers are murdered the perpetrator is a 'prostitute-hating' lust murderer (Downing, 2013).

Wattis (2020) highlights the ambiguous nature of Yallop's (1988) work which includes both progressive and gratuitous content. On the one hand, Yallop offers social commentary on gender politics, feminist history and the social marginalization and legal repression of sex workers. Indeed, Yallop's in-depth description of place and people humanizes sex workers and positions them within the community, as opposed to outside it. He also writes about victims' lives in detail, taking them beyond the hyper visibility as mutilated and violated bodies (Jouve, 1986). On the other hand, the book does also objectify victims, inviting a voyeuristic gaze via its frequent graphic descriptions of sexually motivated murder. Moreover, the use of free indirect speech to invoke the 'voice' of Sutcliffe centres the killer, reinforces the text as 'his' story and further embeds the serial killer in the realm of myth and horror.

There has also been a series of true crime dramas based on the case. For example, the docudrama *This Is Personal: The Hunt for the Yorkshire Ripper* was broadcast in 2000. This was written by Neil McKay and produced by Jeff Pope. The team also produced two subsequent dramas *See No Evil: The Moors Murders* (Menual, 2005) and the award-winning *Appropriate Adult* (2011), which was based on the experiences of Janet Leach who acted as an appropriate adult when Fred West was interviewed by the police. Under the Police and Criminal Evidence Act (Home Office, 1985), adults with mental health problems or learning disabilities are afforded additional protections in police custody and interviews. These include the role of the appropriate adult, often a social worker, who is present at interviews.

Pope and Mackay's earlier docudrama, *This Is Personal*, examined the Sutcliffe murders from the point of view of the police investigation, specifically the personal and professional impact on Assistant Chief Constable George Oldfield, who led the Ripper investigation from 1977 to 1979. The show documents the considerable psychological strain placed on Oldfield and other officers involved in the investigation. Following the fiasco of the hoax tape and letters, Oldfield was moved sideways; he subsequently retired on health grounds and died of heart failure at age 61. The show does not dwell on the details of the murders, and it does not objectify victims in the ways common to much true crime content. Nor does it shy away from the failings of the investigation and the deeply problematic leadership and macho culture of 1970s policing which was instrumental in why the investigation floundered. Writing in *The Guardian*, Sweeting (2000) views the drama as a realistic portrayal of personal obsession, police incompetence and 'the state of 1970s policing'.

The Long Shadow is the most recent drama based on the case and was broadcast to widespread critical acclaim in late 2023. It is based on Michael Bilton's (2003) *Wicked Beyond Belief* but purposely focuses on the victims, moving away from the killer and the trope of heroic police which often defines this type of drama. Instead, *The Long Shadow* examines the misogynist and macho police culture so closely associated with the case (Wattis, 2017) and concentrates on the backstories of victims and their families. For example, the drama paints a moving portrait of the way that Emily Jackson, driven by grief at the death of her son and financial hardship, decides to sell sex with the audience aware that this will have devastating consequences. The drama also shows the personal impact on Marcella Claxton, who suffers a miscarriage after surviving a hammer attack, as well as the police's dismissal of Marcella's accurate description of Sutcliffe, rooted in deeply entrenched misogyny and racism.

There is a danger that modern viewer assumes such attitudes are 'of their time' and not present in modern policing. But the broadcast of the series was timely, coming as it did only six months after the Casey Review (2023), which concluded that the Metropolitan Police Service (MPS) was institutionally misogynistic, racist and homophobic. The Casey review had been established following the conviction of serving police officer Wayne Couzens for the abduction, rape and murder of Sarah Everard, whose misogyny, possession of extreme pornography and acts of indecent exposure towards women prior to murdering Sarah were overlooked by police leaders.

The work of Gordon Burn (1948–2009)

Gordon Burn was a trailblazing writer and a unique literary voice. Combining fact and fiction in his work, he interrogated the nature of fame, celebrity and media representations of violence and the individuals caught up in infamous criminal events. This constellation of crime, fame and the media are at the heart of works such as *Alma Cogan* (Burn, 2004a), *Fullalove* (Burn, 2004b) and *Best and Edwards: Football, Fame, and Oblivion* (Burn, 2007). In a series of non-fiction works and novels, Burn sought to dissect how the modern world of celebrity and the machinations of modern media which relies on violent crime for much of its content. In a flat, dislocating and fragmentary style, which contrasts markedly with tabloid-influenced true crime works, Burn avoids sensationalizing the brutality and violence he often documents. Relatedly, Burn reflects on the relationship between media, viewers and readers, arguing that the quest for understanding the motivations of killers and other violent subjects is a fig leaf that conceals darker drives such as our voyeuristic interest in graphic violence and what is done to victims. As such, Burn forces audiences to contemplate fundamental questions about the nature of violence and in so doing, he provokes a shift in 'gaze' from the violent individual/s, who have committed these acts, to those whose lives have been shattered by the loss of a loved one in dreadful circumstances.

Burn also unpicks the formulaic media reporting of murder events, revealing how narrative structure in crime reporting and fiction often overlap. The arc of this narrative begins with, for example, the report of a missing child and concludes with a criminal justice resolution involving the offender's arrest, trial and sentencing. As in fiction, the case is solved and order is restored – themes which have been explored in criminology by writers such as Sparks (1992), Young (1996) and Brown (2003). For Burn, this narrative formula reassures the viewer/reader but marginalizes the suffering and pain of victims' families. Likewise, he revealed how the world of modern celebrity was underpinned by a set of familiar tropes and a destructive relationship between the media, stars and fans.

Furthermore, Burn's novels and accounts of true crime predict the hyperreality which characterizes our media-saturated modern age. The trends that Burn examined, the dubious status of celebrity, the crafting of reality within media culture and the blurring of fact/fiction boundaries (Brown, 2003) and our fixation with pathological individuals and events (Seltzer, 2008; Yardley et al, 2019), have become more deeply entrenched in the age of social media. Indeed, Burn has become a hugely influential figure. The Gordon Burn Prize was established in 2013 to recognize writers who embrace Burn's approach to historical writing, social commentary, 'crossing genres and challenging expectations' (newwritingnorth.com). Burn has inspired modern writers including David Peace, Dan Davies, Ben Myers, Denise Mina and David Keenan, evident in their choice of subject matter, method and literary style.

Burn wrote two of the most influential English true crime works of the past forty years. *Happy Like Murderers*, his account of the crimes of Fred and Rosemary West, was described by the award-winning author Benjamin Myers as 'not merely a book: it is a haunted object; it is a helter-skelter ride down into Dante's inferno, an archaeological dig into an England previously unseen' (Myers, 2019). Consistent with the key concerns often evident in Burn's work, Myers argues that the Wests achieved a level of notoriety or fame that placed them in an elite tier of celebrity – where individuals are recognized by their first names alone. Burn covered the trial and, as Myers notes, his resulting book is even more harrowing than the news coverage of the West's kidnapping, torture and murder of at least 12 young women. Indeed, Burn offers a forensic examination of the long-term impact of the sexual violence, brutality and grinding rural poverty that forms the backdrop to the case – elements that tabloid reporting and more conventional true crime treatments downplayed or ignored. Consequently, Myers describes *Happy Like Murderers* as an experience to be 'survived'. Burn himself spoke openly about the traumatic effect the trial and writing the book had upon him. Despite the emotional and intellectual labour involved in the project, he could, nevertheless, offer no answers to the question of the Wests' motivation. Indeed, Colebrook (2012) notes that Burn acknowledged how despite his access to countless documents relating to the case and sitting through Rose West's trial, he could not explain the Wests' atrocities. The idea that writing and reading the book is a test of endurance places *Happy Like Murderers* in a unique category of true crime in terms of ethics, given that the usual critiques about true crime feeding voyeurism and the consumption of real suffering as entertainment do not apply in the same way here.

Somebody's Husband, Somebody's Son

Burn's true crime writing has been inspired by two classic American true crime works: Capote's *In Cold Blood* and Mailer's *The Executioner's Song*. He was reading Mailer when the news broke in January 1981 that a man had been arrested in connection with the Yorkshire Ripper murders. This drew Burn to the case to seek answers in the same way he was drawn to the Wests a decade later. Two days after Sutcliffe's arrest, Burn travelled to Bingley to begin research on the case. He was to spend three years in the town where Sutcliffe grew up to 'tell the story from the inside out' (Colebrook, 2012: 48). His immersion in Sutcliffe's community and culture, attention to detail and the rigour of his approach, which situates the case in its socio-cultural context, resembles social scientific ethnographic research. The subsequent book, *Somebody's Husband, Somebody's Son*, was published in 1984, The title of which derives from the police publicity campaign which included a leaflet asking for information from the public to catch the killer. Influenced by Truman Capote, Burn deploys the title ironically to interrogate how the wider culture had shaped Peter Sutcliffe. He uses a mixture of styles, memoir, realism and reportage, to construct his narrative and build a portrait of Sutcliffe and his hometown. In this sense, he is a bricoleur. Burn's eye for detail produces a compelling narrative that contrasts the apparent domestic normality of small-town Bingley with the serial murder and mutilation of women, the mythologizing of the killer and the climate of fear this created within local communities and beyond.

The research that informed *Somebody's Husband, Somebody's Son* exposed the misogyny and legitimation of violence against women at the heart of Sutcliffe's community – what might now be conceived of as 'toxic masculinity'. While these attitudes are not unique to Sutcliffe's community in Bingley or working-class masculinity more widely, Burn reveals the dynamics of problematic masculinity and the treatment of women in this social setting. For example, Sutcliffe's father was violent and abusive and would regularly humiliate his wife in front of their children. Burn also touches on how this community tolerated 'eccentricity' up to a point; alongside the social, psychological and, on occasion, physical cost to those deemed as 'different' – different in this setting effectively meaning anyone who was not part of a white married couple.

Certain infamous crimes become embedded in the popular and cultural imagination, with accounts of crimes and their investigation taking on the status of myth in the collective memory (Downing, 2013). Subsequently, true crime commentaries documenting extreme criminal events often present as crime fiction (Seltzer, 2008; Carrabine, 2008). Burn's work exhibits the conventions of literary fiction, reflected in its detailed scene setting and the drawing of characters in the story (Colebrook, 2012). For example, his work has been reviewed as if it were a novel or had the qualities of a novel. In his review, Colebrook (2012) refers to it as a novel throughout. Moreover, as if to emphasize its hybrid or liminal genre status, it was reviewed in the *London Review of Books* by the celebrated crime novelist Patricia Highsmith (1984). Notwithstanding, *Somebody's Husband, Somebody's Son*, nevertheless, demonstrates many of the features of the true crime genre. It is written after the arrest and conviction of Sutcliffe with the reader aware of the outcome and the identity of the perpetrator. As such, the events and interactions that Burn describes can be read as significant antecedents to Sutcliffe's violence (Rawlings, 1998). However, Burn uses the traditional true crime structure to subvert the conventions of the genre. The result is a cultural rather than a psychological autopsy of Sutcliffe and his crimes, told from the inside as opposed to a form of outsider analysis. The ambiguity of Burn's position is that he effectively remains an outsider, but the text provides such rich insights that the reader forgets this.

The attention to detail as well as the examination of the links between key events enables Burn to place these crimes in a broader, social, historical and cultural context, as well as embedding them in detailed descriptions of place (Myers, 2019). He achieves this by using a range of discourses including memoir and realism as well as a wide range of sources – interviews with family members, newspaper reports and, of course, his own field work notes. Burn eschews detailed descriptions of violence (which contrasts with his approach to the West case). This serves two purposes. It renders the violence that the readers know has occurred even more disturbing. It also demonstrates that the violence against women should be understood as being on a continuum – including the everyday use of misogynistic language, domestic abuse and femicide (Kelly, 1987). True crime presents violence as existing in normality but as being the result of individual aberration and pathology. In contrast, Burn connects Sutcliffe's violence to cultural attitudes and behaviour. Thus, in his hands, the title of the work possesses a double meaning.

Burn, fiction and the Sutcliffe case

In addition to true crime, the 'ripper myth' has inspired many fictional works. The Whitechapel murders brought about the first incarnation of the 'ripper' who went on to appear in various works of fiction across the 20th century. According to Caputi (1987), 'Jack the Ripper' began the 'age of the sex crime', involving the sexually motivated murder of women, who she argues become the object of loathing while male murderers are often celebrated within popular culture. Caputi argues that in the context of patriarchy, the sex crime formula, frequently invoking the ripper myth, forms the basis of numerous femicide narratives in drama and fiction from Hitchcock's *Psycho* to the 1970s slasher genre (Jenkins, 1994). For example, *The Lodger* (Belloc Lowndes, 1996) was first published in 1911 and is considered the first novel based on the Whitechapel murders. More recent, television dramas such as *Ripper Street* (2012–16) and *Whitechapel* (2009–13) continue to deploy the original Ripper myth as a draw for audiences. The former is set in Whitechapel in the late 1880s. Despite the title, which plays to a lazy invocation of the myth and its iconography, drawing on the original murders as a reference point, the series has been praised for its writing and character development (Raeside, 2016).

Returning to the Sutcliffe murders, in broad terms the lazy trope of the killer targeting prostitutes in liminal urban settings is frequently used in crime and detective drama and fiction. Mostly, this serves the killer's or the heroic detective's story and emphasizes the marginal and abject status of sex workers. However, there are several works of fiction that either refer to the Sutcliffe case specifically or bear a striking resemblance to it. For instance, Jennie Godfrey's (2024) *The List of Suspicious Things*, explores the murders from the point of view of a 12-year old girl, who along with her best friend, set out to identify the killer. Godfrey writes from the perspective of a childhood overshadowed by the murders, whose father worked with Sutcliffe. In common with Burn, she presents a picture of Northern England and a working-class community in the 1970s, and the positioning of the Ripper myth within that. Acclaimed crime writer Kate Atkinson uses the Sutcliffe case as a backdrop to her novel *Started Early Took My Dog*, which moves back and forth from the present day to 1970s Leeds, drawing on themes of missing and murdered girls and the Ripper's impact on the social and physical landscape through the climate of fear and its visibility via posters, police checks and roadblocks.

Two works of fiction and drama, which are not directly based on the case but explore the lives of working-class women involved in sex work and their vulnerability due to cultural indifference and oppressive policing, are the drama *Band of Gold* (1995–97) and Pat Barker's (1984) novel *Blow Your House Down*, which portrays the lives of four working-class women, three of whom are involved in street prostitution in a Northern English city where a serial killer is targeting sex workers. Barker denies the book is based on the Sutcliffe case; however, there are similarities – most notably an attack on a woman who survives bears a striking resemblance to Sutcliffe's attack on Olive Smelt in 1975. As Wattis (2018) argues in earlier work, Barker's novel does important cultural work in portraying poor, working-class women with depth and humanity and highlighting the lack of choices they face. This acts as a correction to the historical othering and hatred directed at sex workers originating in the Victorian era and reinforced by the Ripper myth. Moreover, Jouve (1986) asserts that it is only within Barker's fiction that Sutcliffe's victims are truly recognized and commemorated.

The novelist David Peace has spoken in depth about the influence of Gordon Burn on his work (Cummins and King, 2016). In his *Red Riding Quartet* of novels – 1974, 1977, 1980 and 1983 – which were subsequently adapted for television, Peace uses a mixture of reportage and individualistic prose style to explore themes of sexual violence, child abuse and police corruption. The years 1977 and 1980 also have the Yorkshire Ripper case at their centre. Peace's Yorkshire is a bleak and unforgiving place. It is amoral and corrupt, with public institutions including the police at the centre of power struggles where wrongdoing becomes an act of self-protection. The police in the *Red Riding* novels are also involved in pimping and pornography and extensively use violence and threats of violence.

In contrast to his major influence Burn, Peace's novels draw on the Ripper within a fictional narrative, whereas Burn's work is crime fact resembling literary fiction. Peace's novels contain brutal and graphic depictions of sexual violence for which Peace has been criticized. It is a criticism of his earlier work, particularly 1974, that he accepts (Cummins and King, 2016). However, this, nevertheless, raises questions about how writers, particularly male writers, use violence against women and the brutalized female body within their work. Indeed, returning to Gordon Burn, Jouve (1986) accuses him of reproducing misogyny by channelling the misogynist voices of Sutcliffe's family and peer group. As McRobbie (2007) has argued, representation and mediation of violence against women reproduce inequality and legitimate violence in patriarchal culture.

Notwithstanding, Peace's male characters, such as detectives Hunter and Molloy in 1980, are emblematic of masculine culture more broadly. Alongside the reader they are forced to confront the physical outcomes of extreme misogyny – femicide and the mutilated bodies of Sutcliffe's victims. They are both overwhelmed by the brutality, misery and degradation but share many of the attitudes that shape male violence against women and are themselves located within the same masculine culture, often defined by the contours of locality. This is the central link between Burn and Peace. Moreover, both writers show how crimes touch the lives and landscapes of all those involved. Also, in common with Burn, Peace examines how the media co-opts violent events and an important part of his work involves 'reclaiming' victims from the news media. He wants the audience to recognize women as mothers, daughters and sisters beyond their objectification as media victims, whose lives are only ever viewed through the prism of their brutal deaths or as a frozen image on a police poster. His work does not offer the traditional consolations of crime fiction; resolution and the restoration of the moral order do not feature in Peace's Yorkshire noir (Shaw 2012).

Conclusion

In a paper published 25 years ago, Grover and Soothill (1999) noted that the 'serial killing industry' was booming. This has proved to be something of an understatement. Boom hardly does justice to the continuing interest in true crime. An interesting feature of the true crime phenomenon is the continued interest in and power of what might be termed signature or iconic crimes (Biressi, 2001). Crimes such as the Moors Murders have an enduring fascination, and the Yorkshire Ripper case is similar in this regard. New pieces of information have appeared at various points since Sutcliffe was convicted. Stories about Sutcliffe's time in prison and Broadmoor or revelatory titbits about the case crop up in news coverage at regular intervals. For example, it was widely reported that Sutcliffe wrote to John Humble, the man convicted of the hoax letters and tape, after his conviction – blaming him for later murders (Robertson, 2019). This illustrates how serial killers have become part of the tawdry world of modern celebrity and a regular feature of modern mediascapes. At the same time, those whose lives they have destroyed become what Burn, in his novel *Alma Cogan*, refers to as a para-celebrity – a celebrity by association (Burn, 2004a: 106).

However, this chapter has noted how more recent cultural output examining the Sutcliffe case has moved away from exploitative images and details. Likewise, Burn's examination of the case, through a mixture of reportage and quasi-fiction, produced a true crime text which interrogates society's response to the most heinous crimes. Moreover, both Peace and Burn use true crime to explore diverse themes. These include the construction of masculinity, deindustrialization and the long-term impact of sexual violence, which they do without venerating the killer. The result challenges the cultural and media foundations upon which the serial killing industry is built. However, as Wattis (2020) notes, this still represents a male perspective on a male serial killer.

9

True Crime/*True Detective*

Introduction

One of the paradoxes of modern penal policy is that while it has become increasingly punitive, a wider scepticism in the institutions of the criminal justice system (CJS) has developed. The result is that several true crime books and podcasts have been produced in an attempt to overturn a wrongful conviction or challenge the established or official narrative. The most notable of these is the podcast *Serial*. In Baltimore in 1999, Hae Min Lee disappeared after school. A month later, her body was found in a city park. She had been strangled. Her 17-year-old ex-boyfriend, Adnan Syed, was arrested for the crime, and he was eventually sentenced to life in prison. This podcast examined the evidence that led to Syed's conviction. The series became a phenomenon. Recently Syed's conviction was overturned, and he was released from jail. As well as freeing the innocent, true crime has played a role in identifying the guilty. The American true crime author Michelle McNamara was convinced that a serial killer and rapist had committed a string of offences in California from the 1970s onwards. She published, posthumously, *I'll Be Gone in the Dark: One Woman's Obsessive Search for the Golden State Killer* (2018). The killer, Joseph James DeAngelo, was arrested and convicted after her death. These cases have positive outcomes but raise numerous ethical and legal issues that will be examined here.

Podcasts and the *Serial* phenomenon

If the podcast is the format that is now most associated with the true crime genre, then *Serial* is the leader in the format. The speed of modern media development means that it is something of a shock to realize that the iPod was released by Apple in 2001. Apple discontinued the iPod in 2022. It is estimated that over half a billion iPods were sold. Along with iTunes, the iPod was at the vanguard of changes in the way that we listen to music and audio. In 2005, podcast was named as word of the year by the New Oxford

American dictionary (Durrani et al, 2015). The podcast quickly established itself as a key format. Streaming services allow the listener to create their own schedules, following their own interests. They encourage binge listening. As has happened in the history of other new media formats, crime stories rapidly gained a prominent position. True crime as a genre and the podcast format are a match made in heaven – or hell given the focus on the darkest aspects of human behaviour. It is also a profitable enterprise. It is estimated that the hugely successful *My Favorite Murder* podcast generates over $15 million dollars a year for its hosts Karen Kilgariff and Georgia Hardstark.

Wakeman (2013) argued that podcasts played a key role in the development of true crime as a genre. The format saw the genre move from reproducing to challenging mainstream and hegemonic ideas about crime. One of the most interesting aspects of the podcast phenomenon is the way that episode and series are presented as 'deep dives' into cases. There is an implicit recognition here that the speed of the modern news media becomes a barrier to understanding. Cases and issues come to prominence and disappear so quickly that they cannot be examined in real depth. Changes in news media such as the decline in robust local journalism and detailed reporting of Courts are part of this increasingly fractured environment. True crime podcasts are something of postmodern oddity. They provide an immersive experience, which seems at odds with many other trends in popular culture and consumerism. The *True Murder* podcast hosted by Dan Zupansky – 'the godfather of true crime' – has been available since 2010 and there are now over 600 episodes. Each episode follows a similar format of an extended interview with a true crime author combined with crime reportage and journalism. The success of this podcast, which has a film noir aesthetic, highlights the wider attractions of the format. It gives the listener an insight into the process of writing true crime. Episodes released in 2024 include *Monster Mirror*, an interview with Dr Michael Caparrelli, a pastor who details his relationship with David Berkowitz – Son of Sam. Berkowitz has become a born-again Christian while in prison. The podcast as a format represents a push back against an online culture that is dominated by visual imagery. Most listeners are mobile (Sharon and John, 2019). The podcast can provide an escape from the online experience where there are always numerous potential distractions.

Yardley et al (2019), in exploring the true crime podcast as a form of popular criminology, note that the subject matter is similar to much of the previous work in this area. The construct of the ideal victim (Christie, 1986) is a powerful influence in the choice of cases. Yardley et al (2019) noted that none of the podcasts in their study covered cases where the victim was an adult male from an ethnic minority. Here the podcast is following well established patterns from mainstream media. However, as with all formats, there is the potential for more critical approaches. Yardley et al, (2019) use two examples where the podcast has been used as a way of exploring wider issues. The two examples move away from a traditional true crime narrative structure which focuses on the 'innocence' of the victim and their vulnerability as a way of generating audience sympathy. *Missing and Murdered* is a Canadian podcast. Season one is an eight-part podcast investigation that unearths new information and potential suspects in the cold case of a young Indigenous woman murdered in British Columbia in 1989. Gilchrist (2010) examined media reporting of the missing and murder cases of more than 500 Indigenous women that occurred in Canada from the 1980s onwards. These cases had been ignored by the press. The status of the missing women, who were from poor backgrounds, had histories of drug use and sex work mean that they were not seen as 'good'/'worthy' victims.

The construction of sex workers as 'the lesser dead' (Egger, 2002) is deeply embedded in media and popular cultures (Wattis, 2020) (see the previous discussion of the Yorkshire Ripper case). *Bowraville* is a podcast produced by *The Australian* newspaper. It is hosted by the crime reporter Dan Box. It chronicles the investigation into Australia's least-known serial killings. It tracks the case from the first disappearance of 16-year-old Colleen Walker-Craig on 13 September 1990. It becomes an extended examination of the racism in Australian society. *Missing and Murdered* explores hugely critical issues of gender, race and class. It places the case of Alberta Williams in the wider history of Canada as a colonial state. The true crime podcast presents personal and family stories that crystallize these issues. Both these podcasts are deeply critical of institutional failings. Yardley et al (2019) note that these podcasts engage with the audience's emotions in a way that academic criminology usually avoids. The podcasts clearly reach much wider audiences than any academic criminology paper will do.

Modern print media rarely covers criminal trials in depth. Some very high-profile trials will receive detailed coverage. In many cases, the coverage is restricted to opening and closing speeches, a key witness and then sentencing. Sentencing in very high-profile cases in England and Wales is now often televised. Thomas Cashman, 34, shot and killed nine-year-old Olivia Pratt-Korbel in August 2022. He was found guilty of murder at Manchester Crown Court in April 2023. The sentencing hearing, which Cashman refused to attend, was broadcast live (Sky News – Courts, 2023). The judge provided detailed reasoning for her decision not to impose a whole life sentence on Cashman.

In October 2023, Lucy Letby was convicted of murder and attempted murdered of babies at a neonatal intensive care unit where she worked as a nurse. In a weekly podcast produced by the *Daily Mail* (the podcast was hosted by a colleague of the author's at Salford University, and he appeared in one episode), listeners were able to follow the evidence. This trial was one of the longest and most complicated in recent legal history. The nature of the crimes and the fact that the victims were babies and Letby was a nurse generated huge interest. Following her conviction, the podcast explored the institutional failings in the case – these issues are discussed in more depth in Chapter 11. The enormous success of the podcast led to further series including coverage of the trial of two teenagers for the murder of Brianna Ghey. The award winning *The Trial* podcast once again demonstrates the adaptable nature of the true crime genre. The podcast format allows listeners to follow a case in real time. However, it will also attract listeners once a case has ended. High-profile cases generate huge publicity on conviction. Many of the legal restrictions no longer apply so there will be scope for further episodes. Listeners can then follow the completed case.

Serial

The New York Times reported in November 2014, that each episode of the *Serial* podcast was being downloaded over 1.5 million times (Durrani et al, 2015). Boling and Hull (2018) in discussing the subsequent true crime podcasting boom, which has continued and shows little sign of abating, outlined what they termed the '*Serial* effect'. The success of the first series inevitably led to many copies. The first series of *Serial* explores the conviction of Adnan Syed for the murder of his ex-girlfriend Hae Min Lee. Before the arrival of *Serial,* the case was not well known. In contrast, Season 2 of *Serial* covered a very high-profile case: the desertion of US soldier Bowe Bergdahl. Bergdahl left his base in Afghanistan and was taken prisoner by the Taliban. Bergdahl was a prisoner of the Taliban for five years. He was eventually released in a prisoner exchange with five Taliban leaders held Guantánamo Bay. Season 3 of *Serial* follows a year in a court in Cleveland. Seasons 2 and 3 of *Serial* were successful but did not match the impact of Season 1. Season 1 broke numerous records and won awards. It was the fastest ever podcast to reach five million downloads. It did this is in its first month. The spiralling success saw it reach 40 million downloads in two months. It was the number one download on the iTunes chart for three months. The host, Sarah Koenig, already a well-known broadcaster, was elevated to media superstar status. The podcast was the first to win a Peabody award. The citation for the award concluded: 'For its innovations of form and its compelling, drilling account of how guilt, truth, and reality are decided, *Serial* is honored with a Peabody Award' (Peabody Awards, 2014).

The murder of Hae Min Lee and the case against Adnan Syed

The first season of *Serial* is an investigation into the conviction of Adnan Syed for the murder of his former girlfriend. In 1999, Hae Min Lee, aged

18, a Baltimore high school student, disappeared at the end of the school day. Her body was found a month later buried in a park. She had been strangled. The police investigation led to the arrest of Adnan Syed. He was charged and pleaded not guilty. The prosecution case was based on the testimony of Jay Wilds, a friend of Syed's. Wilds gave evidence that he helped Syed to bury Lee's body. Phone records placed Syed near the park where the body was found. Syed was convicted and sentenced to life imprisonment for murder, robbery, kidnapping and false imprisonment. The case received comparatively little coverage until *Serial* propelled it into the national and international media spotlight. The podcast identified an alibi witness for Syed. Asia McClain stated that she was with him at a library at the time of the murder. She had been willing to testify, but Syed's lawyer, Maria Cristina Gutierrez, did not contact her. Gutierrez was disbarred in 2001 after a series of client complaints emerged. *Serial* also raised doubts about the phone evidence and revealed that evidence gathered in 1999 was never tested for Syed's DNA.

Serial led to an appeal. In 2016, Syed was granted a new trial. The state appealed the ruling. Throughout these legal processes the Lee family have opposed the appeal and remain convinced of Syed's guilt. A move for Syed to be released on bail was rejected. In 2018, a Maryland Court upheld the decision to grant a new trial. However, in 2019, Maryland's highest Court reversed this decision. The Court accepted the defence lawyer has been 'deficient'. In 2022 a new Maryland law allowed for the sentences of those convicted as juveniles and who had served 20 years to be modified. Syed was 17 at the time of his conviction and had been incarcerated for 23 years. He was released from prison. Syed was eventually cleared of all charges in September 2022, based on new DNA evidence. However, in March 2023, a Maryland appeals court reinstated Syed's conviction and sentence. The appeals court ruled that the lower court failed to give Young Lee, Ms Lee's brother, sufficient notice of the September 2022 hearing in which a judge vacated Syed's murder conviction and freed him from prison.

The *Serial* podcast format is now owned by *The New York Times*. It was originally produced by *This American Life*. *This American Life* is an America public radio institution. Hosted by Ira Glass, it is broadcast across over 300 radio stations in the USA. It has won numerous awards including a Peabody and a Pulitzer Prize.

Serial was clearly located in this tradition of public service broadcasting that seeks to inform, educate and entertain while illuminating the stories of individuals, families and communities which are often overlooked in the wider mainstream media. Sarah Koenig, the host of *Serial*, is an investigative journalist and producer on *This American Life*.

Koenig is an excellent and experienced broadcaster. *This American Life* established a particular style prior to *Serial*. This includes an informal but authoritative voice that helps to create a sense of intimacy with the audience. Koenig in gonzo journalism style centres herself in the story telling. She does this by sharing her own views and concerns. Each episode begins with the following.

Automated voice

> This is a Global-Tel link prepaid call from Adnan Syed an inmate at a Maryland Correctional facility …

This takes the listener to an environment that the majority will have had no direct contact with.

The introduction to Episode 1 captures Koenig's style perfectly:

> For the last year, I've spent every working day trying to figure out where a high school kid was for an hour after school one day in 1999 – or if you want to get technical about it, and apparently, I do, where a high school kid was for 21 minutes after school one day in 1999. This search sometimes feels undignified on my part. I've had to ask about teenagers' sex lives, where, how often, with whom, about notes they passed in class, about their drug habits, their relationships with their parents. And I'm not a detective or a private investigator. I've not even a crime reporter. But, yes, every day this year, I've tried to figure out the alibi of a 17-year-old boy.

Koenig seems to be both questioning her involvement but also engaging the audience – can anyone give an accurate account of what they were doing on a particular day? Koenig self-deprecatingly refers to herself as not a detective, investigator or 'even a crime reporter'. Koenig is aligning herself with the audience. There is a certain faux naivety here. She is clearly a highly skilled and experienced journalist with access to contacts and resources that the audience will not have. The gonzo journalism approach that influences Koenig exposes journalistic processes that are normally hidden.

One element of the success of *Serial* was the way that the audience felt that it was taking part in the investigation alongside with Koenig, rather than being presented with the story of a completed investigation. The *Serial* website has the tagline 'one story, told week by week'. This format allowed for and encouraged the fans forum where leads and ideas about the case were discussed. The narrative structure engages the audience, this includes cliffhangers and a 'season finale' (Engley, 2017; Baelo-Allue, 2019). These secondary elements all helped to create the *Serial* phenomenon. Koenig's technique and approach is akin to the New Journalism of the 1960s (Lindgren, 2016). The *Serial* audience, like other true crime formats, was overwhelmingly female. Boling and Hull (2018) noted that 73 per cent of the audience were women. Sixty-two per cent of the audience were aged 18–34. Sixty per cent of the audience had a college degree.

Serial and Koenig were criticized. The family of Lee remain totally convinced that Syed is guilty of the brutal abduction and murder of their loved one. In such cases, the privacy of victims and relatives is given little consideration (Cooper, 2019). Koenig has a series of prison phone conversations with Syed – hence the episode introductions. These give Syed a form of authorial voice that centres his experiences rather than the victim's. A podcast, particularly one enjoying the protection of the First Amendment, does not have to comply with evidentiary rules. Engley (2017) is concerned that there is a danger that crimes are tried via podcast rather than the Courts. There is no doubt that *Serial* was the key to Syed's conviction being overturned. There is little evidence that the case was being looked at before Koenig took it up. This is, of course, one of the reasons for a journalist to look at a case. Syed is no longer in prison, but he cannot escape *Serial*. This is true of others. In the HBO documentary *The Case Against Adnan Syed* (2019), Aisa McClain discussed the impact of appearing in *Serial* including criticisms she faced on social media. Hampton et al (2022) question the ethics and legacy of *Serial*. Their criticisms have echoes of many earlier criticisms of true crime. They suggest that the podcast trivialized a real crime – seeing it as a commodification of pain and suffering. Hampton et al (2022) also highlight the way that the podcast led to the identification of alternative suspects. The case of Adnan Syed gripped the public imagination in a way that the later seasons of *Serial* have not.

Season 1 of *Serial* is a modern version of a long-standing journalistic approach. As Hancock and McMurtry (2018: 83) put it 'bad thing happens, a crusading journalist investigates, interviews and discussion ensue'. Koenig helped to establish the true crime podcast as a form of 'gonzo journalism'. Gonzo journalism is associated with American writers such as Tom Wolfe, Hunter S. Thompson and Joan Didion. It is a style that places the journalist at the heart of the story. While traditional approaches focus on the objective reporting of facts, the gonzo style is much more personalized and impressionistic. As the story develops, the audience are given access to the thoughts of the reporter. Wolfe (1996), in outlining the approach of the New Journalism, highlighted the way that it used literary techniques: the construction of scenes, the use of dialogue and writing from a clear point of view as ways of producing a sense of place and character.

Thompson (2012) covered the 1972 US presidential election which saw Nixon win a landslide victory over the liberal McGovern. Thompson was clearly a McGovern supporter. He compared Nixon to a werewolf. He uses reportage to produce a portrait of the campaign and the wider society as well as his reactions to it. In *The White Album* Didion (1979a) uses a series of events from 1960s California to present a view of the counterculture of the period. Didion is not, in any sense, an impartial observer and makes no substantial claim to be one. In the essay, she discusses her own mental health struggles. She describes attending a recording by The Doors and meetings of the Black Panthers as well as meeting other key figures. Didion was an acquaintance of the actor Sharon Tate. Tate was murdered by followers of Charles Manson. In the essay, Didion discusses how these murders impacted the community of which she was part, painting a portrait of the fear and paranoia that took hold.

Citizen detectives

There is a long tradition of campaigning journalists seeking to expose wrongful convictions or other miscarriages of justice. Journalists are bound by a professional code of ethics as well as the law. They are employed by organizations or as freelancers. There is clearly a wide variety in news organizations in terms of sources, resources, wider influence and access. This puts them in a vastly different category to private individuals. There is barely an issue of the fortnightly satirical magazine *Private Eye*, which does not include an article that covers such a case. The late Paul Foot, a regular contributor to *Private Eye*, campaigned for decades on cases such as the Guildford Four, the Bridgewater Four and the Birmingham Six. In all three cases, the original convictions were overturned but only after the original defendants had spent over a decade in prison. The convictions of the Birmingham Six, who were convicted of Irish republican terrorist pub bombings in 1974, were overturned after a long campaign led by their families, community groups and journalist then Labour MP Chris Mullin. As part of the campaign, Mullin published a book, *Error of Judgment: The Truth about the Birmingham Bombings* (1986). The book reports Mullin's investigation of the case. It includes details of the violence and police brutality, to which the six men were subjected. The book also demonstrates that the positive results of the 'Greiss' explosives test, which along with their confessions, were the main basis of the prosecution case, were the result of residue from the men playing cards on the train before they were arrested.

In 1987, following the publication of Mullin's book and a series of documentaries for Granada TV's *World in Action*, the case went back to the Court of Appeal. This appeal was dismissed before the convictions were eventually overturned in 1991. Mullin's book and the Granada documentaries had a key role in exposing not only the police brutality but also the inadequacy of the forensic evidence. Mullin himself became something of a hate figure for the right-wing Tory tabloid press. He was portrayed as an Irish Republican Army (IRA) sympathizer. His work also raises questions about journalistic ethics. Mullin interviewed members of the IRA. In *Error of Judgement,* (Mullin, 1986), he states that he met the men who organized the bombings. He also states that he met the man who planted the bombs. The IRA member was at that time living in Dublin. The Birmingham Pub Bombings remains an open case. After a campaign by the bereaved families, an inquest was reopened into the deaths of the 21 victims. After the inquest, West Midlands Police took Mullin to court to make him reveal his sources. The Courts found in his favour.

The work of Chris Mullin in the Birmingham Six campaign is a classic example of a dogged journalist following a case. Mullin and Granada TV were one part of the successful campaign. Their work had a key role in discrediting the prosecution case. The wave of revulsion in the days after the bombing – which at the time was the biggest killing of civilians in British post-war history – meant that it was difficult for the facts of the case to be examined objectively. Press coverage had portrayed the Birmingham Six as members of an active IRA unit (Mullin, 1986). The men who became known as the Birmingham Six had no connection with terrorism. It would have been an unlikely crack terrorist cell that having planted two bombs in the centre of Birmingham got on the next train to make a connection to catch a ferry to Belfast. Mullin had the skills and resources of a journalist, alongside those that Granada provided. The result was that the case remained in the public eye and the appeal campaign was strengthened until its eventual success.

The appeal campaign for the Birmingham Six took place before the rise of social media. One of the features of the true crime podcast phenomenon has been the development of the 'websleuther' or 'citizen detective'. Detective fiction and dramas are full of amateur detectives who solve crimes that are beyond the local police. There is an often a class bias to these depictions. For example, Agatha Christie's Miss Marple is a middle-class woman of indeterminate independent means who is portrayed as using her superior intellect to solve crimes. Bruce Wayne is a wealthy industrialist. Witnessing the murder of his parents, leads him to become Batman, a superhero committed to tackling crime and bringing criminals to justice.

The rise of the true crime podcast has given a new boost to an existing trend which saw the greater involvement of citizens in law and order. Yardley et al (2018) highlight that true crime has become a form of 'infotainment'. Citizen detectives are the embodiment of crime infotainment. They not only respond to the drama but then become producers of it. Yardley et al (2018) draw on Seltzer's (2008) 'wound culture' to frame the practice of citizen detection. Much of true crime and, therefore, the involvement of citizen detectives, relates to violent crime. The development of the podcast as the key true crime format has been vitally important in the rise of the citizen detective. The roles of producer and consumer have become blurred and are often indistinguishable. This is a hugely significant development in the media's relationship with the media (Jewkes, 2019).

The dawn of the modern TV age saw the first call for assistance from the public. For example, *Police Five* first appeared in 1962. The programme asked for viewers to provide relevant information about recent crimes. The show became famous for the presenter Shaw Taylor's catchphrase asking viewers to be vigilant – 'Keep 'em peeled' accompanied with his gesture pointing at his eyes. The show ran on ITV until 1992. It was revived for Channel 5 in 2014. The BBC first broadcast *Crimewatch* in 1984. The programme was broadcast monthly. The show featured reconstructions of crimes and calls for information. The show included interviews with police officers leading cases and closed-circuit television (CCTV) of crimes. The show also included a wanted section. The programme at its peak had an audience of 14 million viewers. Sears (1995) noted that *Crimewatch* used fiction – that is, dramatic reconstructions – to present the details of real crimes which it hopes will be solved with the audience. Sears (1995) concluded that the appeals for public involvement mean that the programme contributed to a social good. The reality of crime in the hypermediated world is that the police on their own are unable to successfully tackle it. Police forces use social media outlets in investigations. *Crimewatch* reached its height of popularity during a period when the British legal system was facing a crisis. This was the result of the series of miscarriages of justice such as the cases of the 'Birmingham Six' and the 'Guildford Four'. *Crimewatch* and similar programmes emphasize the role that citizens can play in supporting the police in ensuring that justice prevails. These programmes also present the police as professionals committed to solving cases. One of the key aspects of any inquiry is a call for information from members of the public including access to new technological developments such as video or images from mobile phones, dashcam and ring doorbell footage, and personal CCTV (Nhan et al, 2015). The stark difference between these calls is the fact that the police themselves manage these processes.

The influence of the media on the construction of opinions about law and order and wider penal policy is not a new phenomenon. The criminal justice system (CJS) is a part of society that is both familiar and hidden. It is familiar in that a large part of daily news and television drama is devoted to it (Skolnick, 2011). The process of investigation is one the areas of the CJS that has been most hidden. The dramatic representation of policing and police investigation focuses like much media interest on the most violent crime. The schedules are full of dramas which depict psychologically damaged detectives trying to solve murders using clues left by the increasing bizarre modus operandi of killers. These cases are, of course, rare indeed. The representation of police investigation remains in thrall to the conventions of detective fiction. Crimes are solved by Holmesian insights and induction. Detection is a laborious process that involves officers gathering information.

Police officers view most procedural dramas as completely unrealistic full of errors (Cummins et al, 2014).

Reality TV and documentaries have gone some way to challenging the fictional representation of major police investigation. The relationship between the media representation of policing and crime has been a site of recurring debates throughout the history of modern policing (Reiner, 2010). From a conservative perspective, much media representation is seen as undermining the institutions of the CJS, particularly policing. In the past 20 years, these criticisms have shifted. The police have been subject to historically unusual levels of criticism from their traditional supporters on the right. For example, in 2023, the home secretary, Suella Braverman established a review into impartiality in the police (Home Office, 2023). This was part of a wider political campaign against so-called 'woke' influence in public institutions. Radical criminology argues that both news and drama are inherently conservative. News reports, by concentrating on violent crime, exaggerate legitimate concerns but also distort public perceptions about rates of crime (Simon 2007). Media representations also contribute to the rise of penal populism (Garland, 2001). Crime dramas, in particular, often present police officers as being bound by bureaucracy and legal restrictions, which restrict their ability to effectively fight crime and bring perpetrators to justice.

The social media age has seen an expansion of the role that members of the public can and do play in the investigation of crime. New forms of media allow for a different kind of relationship between the audiences and producers. Yardley et al (2018) explore 'web sleuthing'. It is important to note here that the public have always followed high profile cases and trials. However, the difference is that social media now provides a direct channel for not only responses to media reports but also active involvement in solving crimes. There are several ethical issues that result from 'citizen detectives'. As outlined previously, the public have a key role in supporting the police to solve cases and bring offenders to justice. De Rondo (2022) in their analysis of 'paedophile hunters' explore the motivations of these groups that seek to expose sex offenders. De Rondo (2022) outlines the way that these groups pose as children online waiting for predators to initiate sexual communications. If they have sufficient evidence of grooming, the hunters expose the predator in a livestreamed 'sting'. These stings take place in public where a predator has asked a child to meet him. De Rondo (2022) notes that the hunters are often driven by their own experience of abuse, but they also see themselves as heroes confronting evil. De Rondo (2022) argues that the hunters' narratives have echoes of superheroes such as Batman. They see themselves as tackling a social evil where the formal institutions of the CJS have failed or are complicit. The police are concerned by issues such as potential entrapment and the danger that these stings will hamper ongoing investigations. The hunters are not bound by evidential concerns. They obviously do not follow the Police and Criminal Evidence Act (PACE), which includes protections for vulnerable adults and juveniles.

Modern media provides many more opportunities to debate and analyse cases. This can play out in real time and a high-profile case receives an almost unmanageable amount of media coverage. On 27 January 2023, Nicola Bulley disappeared while walking her dog. Her body was found on 19 February. She had fallen into a river and drowned. There was no evidence of any crime and Lancashire Constabulary treated it as a high-risk missing person case. During the search for Ms Bulley, the police revealed details about her personal life and health. This was highly unusual. The release of this information only increased public and media focus on the case. The search for Ms Bulley became part of the 24-hour rolling news. The small village where she lived was soon full of reporters and TV crews. The College of Policing review (2023) highlights the huge media interest in the case. It suggests that on one day there were over 6,500 news articles worldwide about Ms Bulley's disappearance.

The case also attracted 'detectives' who descended on the village and posted content to social media. There were several completely baseless conspiracy theories including that Ms Bulley had been abducted or harmed by her partner. The College of Policing highlights that the police lost control of communications in the face of a media feeding frenzy. The fact that this was not a criminal investigation meant that reporting restrictions did not apply. There was an information vacuum that the police did not fill, resulting in uncontrolled media speculation.

The emergence of 'citizen detectives' is an area that requires further research. There is little known about the motivations for those taking part. The potential impact on the psychological well-being of the individuals is another area that needs to be examined. The relationship between the police and other CJS institutions is problematic. There is a danger of entrapment but also that these citizen detectives unintentionally obstruct police investigations and thus absorb resources. The role of the media in shaping narratives about crime and penal policy is vitally important. One of the underlying concerns is that the citizen detective is a form of vigilantism that supports a penal populist discourse that portrays the key CJS institutions as weak and ineffectual. This discourse has been a key driver of a more punitive approach over the past thirty years (Cummins, 2021).

Conclusion

True crime and the podcast represent a perfect coming together of form and content. The adaptability of true crime across genres has been perfectly illustrated by the development of the podcast. *Serial* – particularly Season 1 – can be viewed as a landmark in these processes. The success of *Serial* highlights many of the ongoing ethical issues associated with true crime. The gonzo aesthetic means that listeners are asked to care about the journalist as much, if not more sometimes, than the story. Podcast listening, unlike traditional radio listening, is an opt in choice as opposed to a listener coming across something in the radio schedules that captures their imagination and interest. A true crime investigation of a cold case or exploration of a miscarriage of justice creates a range of ethical and professional issues. There is a danger that citizen detectives act as vigilantes. Such individuals and groups may see themselves as acting in the community's best interests and supporting the police. However, they are not bound by evidentiary rules or legal processes designed to protect the most vulnerable in contact with the CJS. In addition, the activities of citizen detectives may obstruct the work of the police. The critical concern is that innocent individuals may be accused and then subject to trial by social media. The development of the true crime podcast has seen a more nuanced critical form appear. This has harnessed the potential for true crime to show the workings of the CJS, expose institutional failings and examine the experiences of marginalized victims in more depth.

10

True Crime and News Representations of a Femicide in Bulgaria: Narratives of Conspiracy and State Corruption

Katerina Gachevska

Introduction

This chapter examines a murder case that that took place in October 2018 in Ruse, a medium-sized Bulgarian city located at the country's northern border with Romania, by the Danube River. The brutally raped and mutilated body of a 30-year-old woman, Viktoria Marinova, a local TV personality whose last televised appearance was linked to an investigation of a case of corruption involving European Union (EU) funds, was found in the shrubs near the Danube riverbank at midday on 7 October 2018. Because of her profession and Bulgaria's past notoriety as a quasi-criminal state (Kavalski, 2003), the case was initially reported as politically motivated and sparked immediate global publicity with *The Guardian*, the BBC, *The Times*, DW, *Le Figaro*, CNN, *The Washington Post* and so forth framing the case as an attack on journalists and freedom of speech. For instance, in a BBC radio programme debating corruption in Bulgaria, the case was described as 'a reflection of corruption and crime penetrating the political structures' (BBC Radio 4, 2018). Many reports connected it to the previous murders of two journalists in Europe – Daphne Galizia in Malta and Ján Kuciak in Slovakia – and some went further noting the symbolism of the date which was the 12th anniversary of Russian investigative journalist, Anna Politkovskaya's assassination. News media narratives were also reflected on social media by outraged Western political leaders and EU officials. Frans Timmermans, an executive vice-president of the European Commission, tweeted: 'Again a courageous journalist falls in the fight for truth and against corruption' (Twitter, now X, 2018). UN Secretary

General António Guterres called for a transparent investigation of the 'grisly murder and rape' (AP, 2018), with The Council of Europe's Human Rights Commissioner Dunya Miyatovich calling for international scrutiny of the police investigation (Facebook, 2018). In Bulgaria, Viktoria's murder led to renewed political unrest in the form of anti-government protests motivated by perceived corruption, incompetence and systemic injustice. Vigils were organized in many Bulgarian cities with banners: 'No justice, no peace' (Неменски, 2018); a photograph of Viktoria in a t-shirt with the: 'The system is killing us' featured on multiple placards at the protests.

The chapter proceeds by discussing how the case played out as a true crime narrative due to its complex relationship to 'reality' (Seltzer, 2008). It begins with a discussion of a documentary television programme (also circulated online) which aired five years after Viktoria's murderer was apprehended on 9 October 2018. The investigation had swiftly determined that a 20-year-old man, named Severin Krasimirov, of Roma ethnic origin (although some media reported his ethnic identity as Turkish), was the perpetrator and he was arrested in Germany days after the body was found. No connections to political corruption, attempts to silence Viktoria or shady business deals related to her husband – the popular conspiracies that spread after her murder – were officially confirmed during the investigation. Severin admitted his guilt and received 30 years in prison due to a procedure that allowed for a reduced sentence when pleading guilty (thus avoiding a lifetime sentence). He is the subject of a 2023 true crime TV programme which revisits the murder and interviews Severin in prison. The programme is discussed here as a site of re-enacted public confession with no explanation offered for the murder beyond 'natural evilness'. The notion of 'truth' remains ambiguous and elusive in a manner typical for the true crime genre (Bruzzi, 2016), while the programme's format presents as one of truth-telling or the truth of collective trauma of a society-gone-wrong.

The ambiguity of the case is also rooted in the political circumstances which led to Viktoria's murder initially being interpreted as a conspiracy. This socio-political context is examined next to explore the reasons why her dead body is still difficult to disentangle from a discourse of systemic deformities. Instead of recognizing the case as gender-based violence, with clear race and class elements or even dwelling on the salacious detailed of a sexual femicide, the public's emotional responses centred on political conspiracy. This is not an untypical reaction in the so-called post-truth era, when 'opinions and feelings' play a key role in 'shaping what we think of as facts and truth' (McIntyre, 2018: 8). But conspiracies here do not just seek an alternative truth for Viktoria's murder, they serve to disrupt the flows of power or the official 'truth'-making machinery of the media-business-politics conglomerate that has captured Bulgarian public life since its transition from communism to neoliberal capitalism (Marionos, 2023). In other words, the chapter engages with this intricate play between a televised 'true crime' and what we might call a 'false crime' using Seltzer's notion (2007) of off-air conspiracy narratives and how both fail to shape a consensus on truth, or on cause and effect, yet nevertheless expose the fragility of institutionalized reality-making:

> This interestingly paradoxical relation between true and false crime points to the manner in which crime in modern society resides in that interval between real and fictional reality—that is, the uncertain and mobile, conditional, and counterfactual, reality of a 'reflexive modernity,' a modernity that includes the self-reflection of its reality as part of its reality, and as one of its defining attributes. That is, a reality bound up through and through with the reality of the mass media. (Seltzer, 2007: 17–18)

Methodology

The data for this piece was collected through fieldwork in 2018 in Ruse, which was initially presented at the European Criminology conference in Ghent, Belgium, in 2019. The data included media coverage of the case, interviews with local journalists, including Viktoria's former colleagues, casual conversations in personal social networks, and observations of the local and national public reaction to the case. Subsequent data was accumulated mostly through internet research of media coverage of the case. This diverse dataset which took place over seven years is approached using several types of analysis including narrative, content and discourse analysis. This methodological bricolage situates the case in the historical and political context of the contested post-communist 'transition' of Bulgarian society to a capitalist social and economic order: in itself a linguistic label which has been criticized for legitimizing the process of shifting wealth to new (and old) elites and justifying a new social stratification (Haynes, 1992; La Lane, 2005). The aim of the research is to understand the meanings created by and through this highly publicized murder which simultaneously challenges and conforms to power's construction of reality and truth. This is framed in a broad theoretical framework on 'truth' as shaped by power relations and historically determined structures of knowledge-making (Foucault, 1972, 1975, 2007).

The Genesis of Evil

The discussion of the case here deliberately works backwards and starts by looking at the most recent media coverage. The aim is to highlight how the case was closed with a focus on an individual offender and the randomness of the crime, and to then go back to the details which necessitated this resolution, namely reinstating order into the disorder of conspiracy and political drama. It is argued that in the contemporary media landscape in Bulgaria, 'true crime' stories serve the purpose of normalizing an unequal social order even as they raise questions or seek to subvert it (Browder, 2010). This is the effect of the two-part true crime programme based on an interview with Severin Krasimirov, convicted for Viktoria's murder in 2018, which was filmed by Nova Televizia and aired on 9 September 2023 (Нова Телевизия, 2023). It was also made available on the Nova's YouTube channel (with 197,940 views by August 2024). The programme was titled: *About Severin: The Genesis of Evil* and is part of the documentary series *Nichia Zemya*, or 'No-Man's Land', described on its YouTube channel as exploring 'no-man's places, no-man's memories, no-man's lives and no-man's people, who are forced to rely on themselves because the institutions have long abandoned them'. The programme sets out by stating that its aim is to 'find the roots of this extraordinary evil' born in a state of lawlessness. The message of the corruption of the human soul in the context of corrupt state runs throughout the storyline, and this is visualized through graphic images of violence depicting the murder which evolve into graphics of communist monuments towards the end of the programme. The choice of graphics, as research on representations of crime in graphic novels tells us, can be read as exploring the 'no-man's' space between law and justice (Giddens, 2015; Pégorier, 2024). In the case of Nova Televyzia's programme, it can be understood as an attempt on the part of the media to co-opt this space outside of the law and position itself as legitimate forum for justice, outside of the legal discourse of hard facts and established chronology and inside the depth of personal experiences, emotional trauma, psychologically exploration and even literary depictions of human destiny in a tough world.

The female presenter Daniela Trencheva sums up its central effort: to dissect the soul of a murderer. Yet *The Genesis of Evil* does not, in fact, find the true *roots of evil* but is more successful in demonstrating the difficulty in establishing truth. The programme takes an adversarial approach, centring on an interview with Severin in prison, with the camera facing him straight on and occasionally using a CCTV-styled angle from above. Daniela Trencheva as interviewer/interrogator, adopts the tone of a prosecutor, challenging Severin's responses with scorn and heightened disbelief. Placed in the spotlight, Severin, who in his own words agreed to give this interview to tell his truth, is expected to confess again, expose the depth of his violent soul, express remorse and accept the pains of imprisonment (Foucault, 1975). But while he confesses to the crime, Severin's story subverts some of the typical media constructs of the offender that portrays them as 'the other' who is not us (Jewkes, 2008). There are two major contradictions between the media and individualized offender narratives; one concerns the process of labelling and fixing criminal identity, and the other is the construct of innate and permanent criminality.

The central focus of *The Genesis* is Severin's rejection that it was he who killed Victoria because he claims not to be the same person he was when the murder took place. He attributes this to being under the influence of drugs and alcohol as he had attended a party the night before he killed Viktoria. In a final denouement, Severin claims he is *not a rapist and a murderer*, which is positioned as the shocking climax to the programme. This serves to confirm his pathological double deviance, captioned with 'The Dunning-Kruger effect', which implies a lack of insight to accurately evaluate one's own behaviour. But as Tabbert (2012) argues, linguistic constructions of offenders frequently conjoin the individual to the crime, such as *rape–rapist* which places him/her outside society and limits the information that the reader has on the case by pre-determining their views. Tabbert further suggests that this fixes the identity of the offender by facts or status rather than process, which closes down the potential for change and rehabilitation (Garland, 2001). This is reflected in the programme's use of time to construct the offender as unable to change – as pure evil. *The Genesis of Evil* uses links to footage from a previous edition which aired in 2018, shortly after Severin was apprehended (this is a programme based on an interview with Viktoria's ex-husband Svilen Maksimov and their family lawyer). Through this time loop, which is even more effective when the programme is watched online as both are linked in autoplay function, the story is constructed as fixed in time. This conveys that the perpetrator's character and wickedness is fixed. However, Severin's narrative of bodily change through regular exercise and his ambition to learn to read and write properly runs counter to that of a static offender personality. He captures his own identity-making by rejecting punishment in terms of retribution and 'just deserts'.

That said, the difficulty of establishing a firm culpability is absorbed in the overall narrative of the series because the master narrative is the accountability of the state even if this is only subtly implied. It starts with the following statement:

> This is a not a TV series, this is Bulgaria today. This is not an actor; this is not a film. This is the pure – gnawed by sadism and abjection – reality. The programme is not for children. Its only aim is to uncover the reasons why children become violent abusers. (Нова Телевизия, 2023)

The incompetence of the state is suggested in tabloid-infused accusations that convicted criminals have a nice life in prison, taking drugs, drinking alcohol, having access to a phone and staying connected on social networks. The journalist claims Severin has put his consciousness to sleep and is not accepting responsibility; his ambition to write and read is presented only as an attempt reduce his sentence. Additional content distances Severin the offender from the audience: footage from a prior interview with Victoria's ex-husband and a family lawyer (Нова Телевизия, 2018) and a discussion that explains his criminality is 'genetic', inherited from his recidivist father. Distrust and suspicion pierce the inability to extract truth and explain violence, which then remains a natural occurrence that has remained unsanctioned by the state. The implication being that every ordinary citizen of Bulgaria remains helpless at the hands of flawed institutions. This is a narrative constructed throughout the latest history of Bulgarian transition, and its foremost effect has been to shift blame from individuals to institutions but never to the capitalist system itself.

Crime and the media in Bulgaria

Victoria's murder took place in the age of media proliferation and commercialization, and a shift to more conservative and right-wing content (Marionos, 2023). On the one hand, the abundance of different television stations and various print press outlets, along with digital media and thriving social media platform, allow for different interpretations of news stories and remediation across different platforms (Horeck, 2019). But on the other hand, the Bulgarian media landscape is structured along international corporate ownership, often centralized in a few companies with political links. Nova Televyzia itself is part of series of media outlets in South-eastern Europe owned by United group, which also owns Vivacom, a major mobile and internet provider which has recently expanded into a national media conglomerate, acquiring national and local media and internet companies. As of the time of writing, Vivacom owns TVN, the network where Viktoria was an administrative director and a TV presenter (TVN was then owned by her former husband Svilen Marinov).

According to Spassov (2021), media independence in Bulgaria has deteriorated since the country joined the EU in 2007. This is based on the World Press Freedom index, compiled by Reporters without Borders (from 34th place in 2003 to 111th out of 180 countries with the most significant drop in 2018–20). Of all EU member states, Bulgaria now occupies the lowest place on the index of media independence. Spassov summarizes the issues as:

> [P]olitical pressure on media; media conformism and voluntary refusal to criticise the status quo; compliance with unofficial lists of politicians, parties and topics to be covered only in a positive light on the part of some editorial offices; allocation of money from public funds and European funds by the government and various municipalities to pro-government media (by means of contracts for advertising and media

coverage); strong dependence of regional print and online media on local government; lack of political will to tackle the problem of threatened media freedom. (Spassov, 2021: 78)

Although media freedom is protected by the law in Bulgaria, it is closely monitored with ruling political elites leaning on the media. This became especially apparent when journalists were beaten by police during intense protests in 2013, fuelled by long-standing political crisis. Relatedly, many journalists were also pressured by prosecutors to disclose the source of funding for investigative reports (Daskalova and Spassov, 2014). This 'pressure culture' aimed to align the media to a governmental agenda, and in the words of one local radio journalist interviewed as part of this research, the rise of news dissemination though social media in Bulgaria also aims to undermine professional news-making about local events through centralized and delocalized agents (author's personal fieldwork notes). The Bulgarian National Radio also reported the views of local journalists from Ruse that the national and global media coverage of Viktoria's murder shifted the focus from the male violence to her occupation as a media personality, with her labelled inaccurately as an 'investigative journalist' to weaken the prestige of the profession and undermine trust in how journalists define themselves and the *truth* they report on. In other words, the conspiracies that linked Viktoria's murder to other murders of investigative journalists are seen as a twisting of the truth and a public relations (PR) campaign for political reasons. In addition, journalists argued that the presentation of the case as a political assassination also marginalizes violence against women because it positions this as the murder of a journalist as opposed to a femicide where the victim could have been any woman on the grounds of being a woman (Wattis, 2018). However, the publicity around the case was generated by the highly politicized issue of corruption and distrust in state institutions (Bulgarian National Radio, 2018).

Crime reporting in Bulgaria is now commonplace and hardly distinguishable from tabloid-style crime journalism in most of the world. However, there are two notable exceptions that account for why crime is more politicized in Bulgaria. The first is the sudden appearance of crime in the public discourse after the end of communism in 1989 because social problems such as crimes were not publicly discussed during the authoritarian regime. Crime existed during the communist rule between 1945 and 1989, but the nature and extent of crime differed under communism. Crime rates were low before the 1990s due to separate ways of recording it but also due to full state ownership of the means of production and produce which meant that crimes against state ownership (such as embezzlement of state enterprises) were the predominant types of crime in existing statistics (Gachevska, 2009). The collapse of the state regime and the sharp economic crises that followed also meant a qualitative change in crime, which saw a sharp increase in interpersonal crime of approximately 300 per cent as crimes against private property emerged. While Bulgarians did not see stealing from the state as morally wrong, this ceased to be the case when they themselves were victimized by fellow Bulgarians. The early 1990s thus saw the emergence of the fear of crime and a period of intensive crime reporting by the newly emerging free media in the country. However, this discourse was soon married to political agendas related to the highly contested process of privatization of state assets, as discussed later.

The second change was related to the liberalization of party competition in the first years of transition to capitalism and democratic rule. The issue of crime became highly politicized. It was part of the agenda of the major political parties in their competition for power in a period of intense contestation over the nature of reform and the transition. Notably, crime was interpreted by the left-socialist party as a social ill stemming from rising inequalities and hence the need for a bigger state to provide social security; and, from the perspective of the right-liberals, crime was a result of delayed liberalization and privatization. The social-democratic union of pro-reform parties on the right, United Democratic Forces (UDF), were particularly active in exploiting the Mafia publicity that Bulgaria was gaining at home and abroad and linked this to the slow reform and privatization process. For example, *Capital*, a centre-right weekly broadsheet supporting UDF, published no fewer than 763 articles on organized crime in the period leading up to UFD coming to power in 1997 and interpreted it as stemming from the ongoing state ownership of major enterprises (Gachevska, 2009). This rhetoric was effective in linking crime and corruption to the lack of privatization which created support for market reports and selling off of state assets.

The debate between left and right on the just distribution of resources was thus reframed as a debate about the moral imperative of fighting crime, two decades after 'Policing the Crisis' established a similar ideological shift the UK under Thatcher (Hall et al, 2017). It must also be noted that in conditions where the state controls many assets, political messages would consolidate under non-economic agendas, and for the Bulgarian public, personal security and the subsistence from emerging small businesses was vital. Yet, the specific nature of the crime discourse in Bulgaria was how it linked to the functioning of the state as part of the process of transformation into a EU member state. The EU had its own political dynamic for exporting its anti-crime security agenda onto third states and used enlargement as a way of constructing a neoliberal criminal justice order (Nieto, 2012; Edwards and Gill, 2002). This will not be discussed in detail but suffice to say that in this process Bulgaria was singled out and labelled as a state with unresolved crime problems. Concepts such as 'state capture' by the Mafia (Hellman,

Jones and Kaufmann, 2000) became popular in explaining the Bulgaria's botched transition to a market economy and democracy. The juxtaposition between the individual and the 'Mafia' was endorsed by major media outlets too, in increasingly right-wing and populist media narratives and as a shortcut to blame institutional incompetence as opposed to systemic failure. In this context, the shortcut explanation for the murder of Viktoria in 2018 was that she was killed by the state.

'The system is killing us'

The Bulgarian public were split over the resolution of the case, and many – particularly the citizens of Ruse, as fieldwork revealed – did not accept that the perpetrator was Severin. Conspiracy theories were quickly spreading about a contract killing, a botched job by the police, a cover-up by the government, or even her ex-husband or someone involved in his business operations, as the killer. A petition was signed by thousands calling for the EU to investigate the case directly (signed by 75,876 people by the time of writing):

> We call for full and independent investigation into the murder of the Bulgarian investigative journalist Victoria Marinova. She was brutally raped, beaten, and strangled while investigating corruption involving EU funds at the highest echelons of Bulgarian power structures. We believe that the investigation by the Bulgarian authorities is biased and will serve the interests of the corrupted Bulgarian officials. We call for complete withholding of all EU investments in Bulgaria until such investigation is completed. (Change.org, 2018)

The poor reputation of the Bulgarian investigative mechanisms has been built up by the European Commission itself. There have been widespread assumptions in Western capitals that Bulgaria was a corrupt country where Mafia-rule is the norm. Bulgaria was not allowed to join the EU with the rest of the central European former communist states in 2004. Together with Romania, its entry was delayed until 2008, and it was seen as lagging on criminal justice reforms and the lack of resolution for over 1,040 contract killings. The year before Viktoria's murder marked the 10th anniversary of Bulgaria's accession to the EU, during which period Romania and Bulgaria were monitored by the EU under the so-called Cooperation and Verification Mechanism (CVM) for their progress on achieving benchmarks in the fight against corruption and organized crime (respectively). The CVM was meant to be in place for a few years post enlargement, but in 2017 it issued its 10th anniversary report, which stated that Bulgaria had not at this stage achieved the necessary benchmarks. For the Commission, who defined the benchmarks at the time of the accession, this meant institutional and legislative measures which were felt 'in practice' and allowed citizens to feel confident in the rule of law and to trust Bulgarian institutions, including the media, which as stated, was not perceived as independent (European Commission, 2017b: 2–3). This surveillance and distrust on part of the EU is mirrored in public opinion which supported the continuation of the CVM: 'In Bulgaria, just over seven in ten (72%) of those polled found that the CVM action should continue until convergence with other Member States had been achieved' (European Union, 2017). The CVM mechanism to observe new member states was a new experimental tool for governance that avoids direct interference but imposes an agenda from a distance (Chandler, 2014). It aims to create satisfied citizens but does not resolve social problems.

The EU's main offer to ordinary citizens of its member states is so-called Europeanization – domestic change toward an improved lifestyle because of European integration, with criminal justice high on the agenda for problem areas in poor South-eastern Europe. Constant institutional improvements under observation by a centralized supranational structure is seen as fitting with the modern globalized and knowledge-based societies, where resilience supports constant change. Such supranational technocratic governance through observation is seen as superior to representational democracy. Yet through this observation mechanism crime appears divorced from its context of structural inequalities and identities in conflict; it is no longer used to measure the success of economic and social policies but is transformed into a tool for measuring satisfaction through citizen feedback, that is, a narrative for resilience not transformation (Chandler, 2014). Thus, it can be argued that crime in Bulgaria is 'watched' in more ways than in the media and this discourse similarly constructs a reality of different relations between actors. In the winter of 2013, Bulgaria was frozen by a series of protests triggered when the centre-right government hiked up the cost of electricity and hot water. The protest spread to 30 cities and led to the resignation of the government. They were led by the motto 'Citizens against the Mafia' and turned into a mass non-partisan movement against the ruling political elite throughout the whole period of neoliberal 'transition' to market economy, prompted by the fall of the communist regime in 1989.

The role of the EU in mediating an image of a Mafia state in the case of Bulgaria is undeniable. In its reducing crime to the functional failure of state institutions, the EU facilitated the redefinition of the role of the state from redistributor of resources to that of a manager of social discontent (Wacquant, 2009b). It is thus understandable that conspiracies around Viktoria's murder found a receptive public. The vigil and protests were marked by the slogan and photos taken from a campaign Viktoria was involved with, related to disadvantaged children: 'The system is killing us' (the children) but re-interpreted here as the system, or *the state*, having had killed Viktoria. This dangerous assumption that undermined political elites in Bulgaria necessitated a swift neutralization through competing narratives focusing on the individual offender.

Severin himself reflects on his fate as one of corrupt justice in *The Genesis of Evil*. When accused of breaking discipline in prison, the journalist cites a list of occasions when he had done so, he says: 'They can write whatever they want. This is only pen and paper' (Нова Телевизия, 2023, part two). He states that he has been a victim of violence by prison guards, and he will one day be killed by either Viktoria's ex-husband Svilen Maximiv or the prison guards, whom he refers to as 'the State'. He goes on to claim that in Bulgaria there is no justice and no care for accused, which is why he and his mother initially asked to be tried in Germany, where he was arrested. In a 'citizen against the Mafia' discourse, systemic failures to protect both Viktoria as a murder victim, and Severin as an offender, are explained by institutional corruption, a narrative that is set and maintained by the EU, and in which other forms of systemic injustice which are facilitated by capitalist and patriarchal order are swiftly dissolved.

Marginalized discourses: class, race and gender

The conspiracy and counter-conspiracy reporting on Viktoria's murder constructs the case as one of individualized and brutal violence, either organized by Mafia figures or committed by a man with uncontrollable sexuality, respectively. The case's striking juxtapositions of social identities fail to leave a mark on either discourse. Viktoria made a better victim as a journalist than as a woman (and her rape is marginalized) or her misfortune is linked to attractiveness and poor luck to be in the wrong place at the wrong time. Her murderer Severin's ethnicity is read as either corruptibility (he is paid to admit the murder as a poor Roma man) or his ethnicity is sexualized as a representative of a badly integrated ethnic group whose animalistic urges prevent their socialization. There is a mutually reinforced 'blind spot' in both the media and off-air conspiracies scripts in that they both marginalize issues of class, race and gender.

The random encounter of Victoria and Severin is reconstructed by the Nova's programme through a map of their movements on the day of the murder, but the map is not read as the text of class–race disparity which it so clearly speaks of: Viktoria, a young and healthy woman going for her daily run by the river in an area 'frequented by so many people' (personal fieldwork notes), encounters unwholesome Severin who is only there because he is crossing the area to reach his home in the Roma ghetto, coming back from a drug and alcohol-infused party in another segregated Roma community. The media's conservative message locates the crime inside Severin as a criminal 'type', albeit in the context of his belonging to a wrecked and socially isolated Roma community. In addition, class is also hidden in the media discourse. While Viktoria's freedom to go anywhere is, on the one hand, apparent. She is a wealthy woman who lives in the big house and runs by the river, enjoying the mobility that accompanies wealth and status (her former husband is one of the wealthiest people in the region and the family also owns the only private plane in the region). She is, however, also a woman, whose spatial and temporal movements are circumscribed by fear, risk and the threat and actuality of male violence (Stanko, 1993). At the same time, bound by ethnicity and poverty, the river is not a place where Severin should have been either. His movements are restricted to Roma neighbourhoods, which have emerged historically in decades of social isolation, deprivation, restriction of property rights (Ivancheva, 2015a) – and with this the constraints placed on movement, employment and access to resources which have exacerbated in the neoliberal age (Wacquant, 2009a).

Indeed, the 'bare life' status of many in the Roma communities in Bulgaria is accepted as the sacrificial social 'killing' of those unfit for society and not a result of decades of racist treatment of by successive Bulgarian governments (Agamben, 1995). This life can exist on drugs and crime, or corruption and exploitation, if it remains within its geographical and social boundaries. And the use of gender performativity as another marker of exclusion is also notable here. While Viktoria is presented as the mother of a seven-year-old daughter and further humanized by references to charitable work for disabled children, and references to good relations with her former husband, Severin's mother is presented in Nova's racist gaze as a woman who gave birth to eight children but 'only to give them away' (Нова Телевизия, 2023). Moreover, Severin's relationships with women are pathologized as his personal life is presented as dysfunctional (he had no civil marriage with his so-called 'wife' but had a child with a former girlfriend). The Roma women's victimhood and double oppression is marginalized and worse – they are implicated in the story as 'enablers' of crime. The intersectional complexity of the case involving inter-ethnic gendered violence is not explored as it would contradict the media and conspiracy narratives of pure evil and systemic corruption.

Equally, the issue of gender-based violence hereby is supressed. While Bulgarian's socialist history had elevated the social position of women particularly in employment, post-socialism has exposed many deep structural issues in gender inequality which have been deeply embedded but hidden in Bulgarian society (Ivancheva, 2015b). While socialism was based on more formal equalities, the private sphere of gender relations was left out of institutional and legal arrangements. Data on domestic violence and sexual abuse is sparse for that period, and for much of procommunism the problem had remained barely recognized in public debates. The Bulgarian National Statistical Institution first published data on gender-based violence in 2022 (НСИ, 2022), as part of an EU project for data harmonization, which showed that gender abuse is common. The data shows that 11.9 per cent of women between the age of 18 and 74 have experienced at least one occasion of physical or sexual violence in their lifetime; 20.5 per cent had experienced persistent psychological, sexual or physical abuse by an intimate partner; and every third woman, or 36.3 per cent of women aged between 18 and 29 has been abused by a current or former partner (НСИ, 2022). The statistics for 2023 show only 181 people have been sentenced for sex-related crimes, of which only 28 were for rape (НСИ, 2023). Violence against women received more publicity in 2023 but only after a brutal case of domestic violence came to light. The case involved an 18-year-old woman, who was cut 400 times with a carpenter's knife by an ex-partner who remained out of custody because the law considered the mutilation to be a light form of bodily harm which is only investigated when the victim presses charges (Радио Свободна Европа, 2023). Another case which also triggered feminist protests in Bulgaria was related to the problematic definition of stalking which is only legally recognized if the victim has been in an intimate relationship with the perpetrator. Such cases provoke public outrage and protest for legal change, but at the time of writing, the envisaged changes to the law of domestic violence had not yet taken place.

Back in 2018, Viktoria's murder was not placed in the wider context of gender-based violence by media coverage in the initial weeks following the murder as the discourse focused on political violence. The analysis of the narratives and structure of news coverage of the case covering print, online and radio news (performed as part of fieldwork on the case in 2018/19) demonstrates a masculinist discourse that runs through the mediated stories of the case. Viktoria's mutilated and sexually assaulted body was not read as a text of gender-based violence, an open wound in Bulgarian society. On one hand, she was described as 'the pretty face on TV', a popular media personality, not a 'fallen woman' to whom a victim blaming discourse can be more easily attached by the media. She was an ideal female victim in terms of class, appearance and respectability (Wattis, 2017).

The news value of Viktoria's murder was her profession and her social status. As some of the journalists and police representatives revealed during interviews: such murders 'happen all the time but do not make the news' (fieldwork research notes). Hence the case as a shocking global news piece got its resolution once a proper identification of a perpetrator had been made. The masculine drive to put randomness into order, to construct a linear narrative, had thus been completed. But equally, the narratives of conspiracy of politically motivated murder or a cover up, also distract from systemic gender violence. It is easier to believe that Viktoria was a victim of a paid assassin, sent from abroad, maybe from a former Soviet republic notorious for its violent thugs, in the words of her former husband (Нова

Телевизия, 2018), or even killed by the government, than being a victim of femicide in the context of patriarchy, exacerbated by the deteriorating social relations and rising inequalities of post-communism.

Conclusion

The debates about media and power, and their convergence, present an obsession of neoliberal governance which seeks to define a functioning democracy as one of transparent, legitimate and trusted government able to maintain property relations and a functioning market. But such a discourse, as appealing as it may be even for critics of power, marginalizes the core problem of social inequalities exacerbated by a liberalized market and weakened ability of the state to redistribute resources. Inequality also determines access to 'truth' along classed, race and gendered lines. While on one hand, conspiracies emerge to close such gaps and make sense of contradictions and indeed disrupt power's veil to truth (West and Sanders, 2003). On the other, they foreclose debates about inequality and ways to contest it beyond denying 'sanctioned truth'. In the words of Bulgarian thinker Ivan Krustev (2017), conspiracies have replaced ideologies and construct new types of identities, built around shared conspiracies, and:

> an identity based in conspiracy theories subverts the need for self-criticism [and] when political identities are based on shared conspiracy theories, people are committed not to finding truth but to revealing secrets. The idea of truth appeals to our common sense. The seductiveness of conspiracy theories is that they appeal to our imaginations.

The 'true crime' and its counter-narrative of political conspiracies took this murder case out of the locality, where the authorities were eager to keep it, and to the level of political developments which have impacted Bulgaria over the past 30 years. Both can be read as an attempt to disrupt power's function in making knowledge and controlling the discourse. Despite the structural inequalities along class, gender and race lines that intertwine here, most interpretations link to the public outrage directed at institutional incompetence and corruption. This outrage was also desperately seeking to internationalize its appeal for help because it perceives the Bulgarian state as incompetent to protect the safety of citizens. Thus, Viktoria's murder case channelled a micro-discourse of individualized violence (as reflected in Nova's programme) but also a macro-discourse of 'state failure' popularized in Western-European political circles as a shortcut to state classification along lines of state institutional (in)efficiency.

This model is then replicated by the complex web of internationally owned media networks and reproduced in a similar logic of the construction of the individualized pathology of Severin Krasimirov. Yet the truth remains elusive, and the discussion here detected multiple points of resistance to 'truth'-telling. If neoliberalism relied on the truth of the market as the successful route to a harmonious and well-functioning society (Foucault, 2007), a brutally disrupted life in the small Bulgarian border town of Ruse emerged as a counter-truth of a botched-up transition to democracy, loss of trust in those in power and a new level of disengagement with social change from below. In the final words of the *Genesis of Evil* presenter: 'he told his story; and what truth is and which part of it you believe is another matter'.

11

Lucy Letby: The Vanilla Killer

Introduction

To say that the case of Lucy Letby caught the imagination of the British public would be somewhat of an understatement. Letby, aged 33 at the time of her conviction, is the most prolific child serial killer in modern British history (Coffey, 2023). On 18 August 2023, Letby received multiple whole life terms for the murder of seven babies and attempting to kill six infants at The Countess of Chester Hospital, UK, between June 2015 and June 2016. Details of the methods used emerged during the trial which lasted from October 2022 to August 2023. These included injecting infants with insulin and air, force-feeding with milk and physical abuse. She also falsified patient records and removed confidential nursing handover sheets from the hospital (Coffey, 2023). The Cheshire Constabulary expressed a suspicion that Letby may have committed further crimes. At Liverpool Women's Hospital two infants died during Letby's stay there as a trainee (O'Donoghue and Moritz, 2023). Letby maintained her innocence throughout the trial and pleaded not guilty on all counts and refused to appear for sentencing. In May 2024, Letby was denied permission to appeal against her convictions (Halliday, 2024), and in June 2024 a retrial of one of the original cases resulted in a further conviction (Moritz and Coffey, 2024).

Only three other women in UK history have been given multiple life terms: the high-profile cases of Myra Hindley and Rose West and Joanna Dennehy, who killed three men and dumped their bodies in ditches, the so-called Peterborough Ditch Murders (Press Association, 2013). This chapter will explore a number of themes present in the Letby case, which are pertinent to the study of true crime. First, it is a classic example of mediatized murder (Greer, 2004) and the symbiotic relationship between the mass media and serial killers (Haggerty, 2009). This will be discussed in relation to the works of a number of articles on the subject and also via a case study within a case study, namely a BBC *Panorama* documentary broadcast on the evening of Letby's sentencing, and by examining a number of examples of rolling news broadcasts and podcasts covering the case. Media interest (some might say obsession) with such cases brings celebrity status to the serial killer (Cummins et al, 2019) and a guaranteed place in popular culture.

In sentencing Letby, Mr Justice Goss described Letby's action as being contrary to normal human instincts of nurturing and caring and a gross breach of public trust (Halliday, 2023). This statement feeds into the stereotypical view of nurses as 'angels', linked to this is the particular status and perception of the female serial killer and the way in which they are represented in the media. The notion of 'evil' is also a common theme in the literature on true crime. The female serial killer is seen as doubly transgressive (Wilde, 2016), something which is implied in Mr Justice Goss' comment on 'nurturing and caring'. A case such as Letby's inevitably raises the eternal 'why did she do it?' question and the quest for explanations, the production of typographies of serial killers. This will be explored in relation to this case.

Finally, the apportioning of blame. We would argue that the Letby case, while not unique in terms of raising questions about safeguarding in large institutions, has placed a great emphasis on naming key figures in the hospital management team, outlining the way in which suspicions about Letby's behaviour were dismissed and demands for an institutional response, perhaps going further than in previous cases in this respect.

Mediatized murder

In Chapter 1, Haggerty's (2009) argument that there is a symbolic relationship between the media and serial killers and the notion of mediatized murder (Greer, 2004) are explored. One of the key features of modernity, Haggerty (2009) argues, is the role of mass media and celebrity culture and that this has given rise to the serial killing industry. This is not to suggest that media coverage is the cause of serial killing, only that it has a part to play in the creation of the category of serial killer. TV channels are now filled with documentaries about historic serial killers, their names become familiar to the public and so they become part of modern celebrity. With the emergence of a new serial killer such as Lucy Letby, old tropes and themes are revived, as documented throughout this chapter, and the killer obtains celebrity status gained via notoriety. Pictorial representations of the killer form an important part of this. The public can put a face to a name, a face that is splashed all over newsstands. A 'nickname' given to the serial killer has also become part of this celebrification.

In Letby's case a description of Letby as a 'beige nurse' by Professor David Wilson, a true crime celebrity himself, became worked up by the tabloid media into 'The Vanilla Killer'. In an article in *The Guardian* Wilson

(2023: 2) argues that Letby did not display the 'red flags' that have been identified in cases where nurses kill in hospital settings. There has been much work in academic settings, which we would argue is also part of the serial killing industry, in which attempts are made to identify typologies of serial killers based on previous cases and therefore identify the 'red flags' that Wilson speaks of in his article (Yardley and Wilson, 2016; Menshaway and Menshaway, 2023). The usefulness of this work is contested but it tends to feed into the tabloid feeding frenzy that occurs around the trial of serial killers. Because Letby did not fit these typologies, was seen as 'ordinary' or 'beige' by colleagues, the label has stuck.

There are two key photographs of Lucy Letby used to accompany news stories about the case. One, where she is wearing her nursing scrubs, smiling and holding up a baby, is used to emphasize her ordinary 'girl next door' nature, contrasting with her actions. The second, a mugshot, where she is staring into the camera looking depressed, is akin to the famous Hindley mugshot and, as such, usually features in the stories which contain 'evil' in the headline.

Leszkewiecz (2023) writing in *The Spectator* draws on Haggerty's (2009) ideas in discussing the Lucy Letby industry describing it as a prime example of 'True Crime entertainment' (Leszkewiecz, 2023: 4). She outlines the numerous ways the modern media has latched onto the case after the trial with endless newspaper coverage, hours of rolling broadcasts, a *Panorama* documentary broadcast on the evening of the verdict (discussed elsewhere in this chapter) and multiple podcasts. She singles out the *Daily Mail*'s weekly *Nurse on Trial* (Cheetham and Hull, 2023) podcast in particular as a good example of the Letby industry and the use of true crime as entertainment. She describes the style of the journalists Liz Hull and Caroline Cheetham as 'pious concern masking voyeuristic excitement' and 'furrowing one's brow while licking one's lips' (Leszkewiecz, 2023: 4). 'The hand rubbing tone' she adds, 'is a deeply uncomfortable listen' (Leszkeweicz, 2023: 4). The first episode has all the hallmarks described by Leszkeweicz (2023) describing the trial as 'one of the most anticipated', an interesting use of the term 'anticipated', mainly used to describe media products such as Hollywood blockbusters, the next season of a Netflix serial or the dropping of a new album by Beyoncé but consistent with academic literature on the way in which murder trials have become a 'dystopian spectacle' (Bolton, 2005: 4). One of the opening statements of the podcast which discusses how the case has 'caught the attention of millions of people around the world' is similarly consistent. From the outset the journalist presenters are keen to present themselves as being at the centre of the spectacle, a good example of the way in which the media feeds off itself and becomes part of the news story (et alet al, 2019), and this also applies to the *Panorama* documentary (Coffey, 2023) discussed later in the chapter. For example, Liz Hull tells the listeners that Chester is her hometown, goes into great detail about the town and reveals that her own children were born at the Countess of Chester Hospital. Later, we are told that the media will be in an annexe at the magistrates' court for the trial, emphasizing public interest, and, in subsequent podcasts, great play is made of their positioning, this implied importance to the process. It also features an interview with consultant Ravi Jayaram who first raised suspicions about Letby and who we learn has already appeared on two popular magazine TV shows, *This Morning* and *The One Show*, thus becoming what Gordon Burn (1984: 106) called 'a para-celebrity – a celebrity of association'.

The final podcast *Over to You* is split between discussing the verdict of the trial and a studio Q and A in which the presenters discuss questions sent in by listeners. There are good examples of Leszkeweicz's (2023), 'pious concern masking voyeuristic excitement' as the presenters tell us that they have 'just come from inside court 4' and repeat the phrases already used frequently by the tabloid press, 'most prolific baby killer' and 'worst serial killer of modern times'. While the second half is ostensibly a Q and A, much of the time is devoted to a discussion of why and how the journalists decided to produce a podcast and goes into details of obstacles and legal issues faced and the impact, they feel that reporting on the trial has had on them, once again positioning themselves at the centre of the spectacle.

Lucy Letby: The Nurse Who Killed

This BBC *Panorama* documentary provides another prime example of the symbiotic relationship between the media and true crime, mediatized murder (Greer, 2004) in action. The fact that it was broadcast on the evening of the trial verdict says something about the nature of modern news media with a reporter waiting outside the court and announcing the verdict as it happens.

Seal (2014) outlines a shift at the beginning of the 20th century from the spectacle of punishment, for example public hanging, to the spectacle of the trial itself and public consumption of sensationalist trials, where 'murder became a staple of popular culture' (Seal, 2014: 56). The trial of Ian Brady and Myra Hindley at Chester Assizes in 1966 can be seen as an important landmark, the first such spectacle in the TV age and a template for subsequent coverage. Pamela Hansford Johnson who attended the trial on behalf of *The Daily Telegraph* to write about her impressions of the event stated, 'there is no disguising the fact that a part of me was titillated. I wanted to know all the details not solely because it was my job to do so, but because there was in them an element of repulsive stimulation' (Hansford Johnson, 1967: 60).

The trial as a 'dystopian spectacle' (Bolton, 2005: 4) where public fascination with serial killing focuses on the intersection between the ordinary and the extraordinary, what Peelo (2006: 64) describes as 'the shock of ordinariness invaded by the brutal and corrupt' provides the central plank for the BBC documentary on the Letby case, the trial of 'Britain's most unlikely serial killer', according to the documentary.

Overall, the documentary is not without its merits. It gives voice to the victims' families and includes a number of interviews in which they obviously express sorrow, raise the issue of 'evil' and also disbelief. One mother tells the reporter that she could not believe that Lucy Letby was the perpetrator. 'Not nice Lucy, I thought' and others describe how Letby had seemed 'normal' and 'ordinary' and how she had comforted them on their loss. One parent describes extensively how Letby bathed and dressed their baby following the child's death. A close friend of Lucy Letby is also interviewed and tells how her and Lucy's other close friends still believe that she is innocent. 'I will never believe that she is guilty' is her final statement.

The documentary also outlines the facts of the case and a timeline of events, including Operation Hummingbird, an investigation commencing in May 2017, when the police were finally called in. There is a discussion of handwritten notes, discovered at Letby's home, containing contradictory statements. One, 'I haven't done anything wrong'. Others: 'I killed them', 'I'm evil I did this' are contradictory as is much of the documentary evidence found in her home. Letby kept notes and diaries documenting her actions, a common feature of serial killer behaviour (Cummins et al, 2019). For example, it was the discovery of documents relating to the murder of Lesley Ann Downey (photographs and a tape recording of her torture and murder) in a suitcase in a left luggage locker at Manchester Central Station that cemented Ian Brady's conviction in 1966 (and Hindley's voice on the tape was a key factor in tying her to the crimes). Despite much documented evidence the police's final statement in the closing is 'we don't know why'.

The documentary also gives space to the story of the institutional response, previously discussed, through an extensive interview with Dr Susan Gilbey, who replaced Tony Chambers, following his resignation as chief executive officer (CEO) of the Countess of Chester Hospital in 2018 (Gilbey remained as CEO until 2022 and is now suing for constructive dismissal). When questioned by the *Panorama* reporter about the 'cover up' she states that protecting the reputation of the institution was a big factor guiding the processes that took place. Dr Stephen Brearey, a consultant at the Countess of Chester, is also interviewed throughout the documentary and reflects on the whistleblowing process and the responses of senior management.

In many ways, then, the documentary provides an accurate report of events and processes leading to Letby's conviction. However, it is the foregrounding and centrality of the BBC reporter, Judith Moritz, which draws us back to writings of Seal (2014), Bolton (2005), Peelo (2006) and Hansford Johnson (1967) on the dystopian spectacle of the trial and public titillation, as she seems to revel in the position of the media ringmaster. The production of the documentary becomes a key feature of the documentary itself. Moritz talks to the camera. We see her sitting in the van ('this is my office') drinking coffee, busying herself, working with technicians to put the programme together ('how long have I got to do this voiceover?'). She emphasizes the drama unfolding in the courtroom behind her ('today is the moment we get to see her; she will be just on the other side of this wall'). The atmosphere created seems at odds with the seriousness of the subject matter. The clichéd tabloid statements are all present, 'beyond imagination'. This phrase was applied by Williams in his book *Beyond Belief* (Williams, 1967) to Brady and Hindley, 'a hateful human being'.

The crescendo comes towards the end of the documentary. Following a voiceover announcing that the jury is expected to give their verdict that day, we see a shot of the TV outside broadcast van then Moritz speaks to camera. 'You can feel the tension here every day. No one knows if this (emphasized) will be the day the jury returns its verdict.' Shots of other reporters and cameramen outside the court are shown and a voiceover announces that the jury has reached their verdict. Cue Moritz running out of the court, piece of paper in hand. She comes up to the camera for a close up: 'She's guilty, the jury's found Lucy Letby guilty of murdering seven babies and attempting to murder another six ... they've clearly found that she's one of Britain's most notorious killers'. The documentary ends with Moritz asking the eternal question 'what turned a likeable fun-loving nurse into a serial killer'. No answer is forthcoming, and the final word goes to a mother of one of the victims: 'I think its summat that we'll never know and as a family I think we need to make our peace with that.'

Angels of death

There is an emerging body of work on health care serial killers (Yardley and Wilson, 2016; Menshawey and Menshawey, 2023) triggered by a number of high-profile and highly mediatized cases over the last 30 years, in particular, Beverley Allitt (Davies, 1993), Harold Shipman (Peters, 2005) and Charles Cullen (Ramsland, 2007). The term 'angel of death', once reserved specially for female health care serial killers, has now started to be used more widely in reference to all those who kill in a health care setting (Yardley and Wilson, 2016). However, an early definition by Kelleher and Kelleher (1998: 15) states that an angel of death is 'a woman who systematically murders individuals who are in her care' and Hickey (2013) has argued that the term is more likely to be applied to a female killer. Mr Justice Goss' comments on Letby at her sentencing, discussed previously, certainly draw on the double transgression of the female who kills, with specific reference to the idea of nurses as 'angels'. A popular BBC drama broadcast in the 1970s about nurses in a hospital setting was called *Angels* (Milne, 1975).

Representations of female serial killers

Gender is obviously a key issue in the reporting of the female serial killer. Wilde (2016) has argued that this is a result of deeply ingrained patriarchal attitudes, this being in reference to the case of Myra Hindley who, arguably, is still seen as the benchmark in terms of evil women who kill and certainly provides a good example of the way in which women who kill, particularly who kill children, are seen as doubly deviant, transgressing feminine norms and a perversion of the female role as mother and nurturer. The bizarre hierarchy of female killers has no real logic. Rose West partnered her husband, Fred, and was convicted of ten murders (Burn, 2011). Letby acted alone and it will be interesting in the longer term to see how she is viewed, particularly as she murdered babies and infants. The coverage of the Letby case and the public outrage at her actions are similar to those in the Hindley case, tightly bound to gendered notion of how women should and should not behave. Women are perceived to be the 'softer' sex, biologically programmed to be 'good' mothers, nurturing and kind (Wilde, 2016). Women are far less likely to commit violent crimes than men. Women who commit murder are statistically rare (Cummins et al, 2019). The 'mad' or 'bad' debate is one that punctuates much discussion of true crime, particularly in relation to serial killing. While Hindley's partner in crime, Ian Brady, was eventually diagnosed as a psychopath and spent the majority of his sentence at Ashworth Special Hospital, there was no suggestion that Hindley was 'mad', and the issue was not a factor in the Letby case. Storrs (2004) has argued that in cases such as that of Brady and Hindley or Fred and Rose West, where crimes are committed jointly, it is the women who bear the burden of responsibility while Gavin (2019: 13) notes that in such cases 'it is the women who fascinate and repel us'.

Evil persists as a key theme in the reporting of crime, especially when women are involved (Arendt, 1963). Hindley again provides the benchmark here, persistently referred to as 'the most evil woman in Britain' in the tabloid press, from the moment of conviction, throughout her attempts to gain parole and in the reporting of her death in 2002 (Cummins et al, 2019). Indeed, the arrangements for Hindley's funeral provide a powerful example of the way in which the link between serial killers, particularly female serial killers, and evil is conceptualized (no controversy existed around the funeral of Fred West, for example). Lee (2010: 22) describes Hindley's funeral as 'a gothic soap opera', held in secret without mourners on a rainy night. She documents the fear of contamination by proximity to evil thus: 'But in death it was as if her power to terrify and repulse was multiplied – as if mere nearness to her corpse would contaminate the bystander' (Lee, 2010: 17). Previously, funeral directors had refused to take the job, no one wanted to drive the hearse, while everything contained in her room in which she died was burned and the room redecorated (Lee, 2010). After the funeral, Bernard McHale, secretary of British Cremation Authorities, assured the public that all traces of dust and ash were removed and the cremator cleaned. Writing in *The Guardian*, Adderley (2002: 2) states: 'It is not entirely clear what particular contaminating power of Hindley's the undertakers most feared – perhaps that microscopic traces of Hindley's dust might accidently become mixed with that of future customers or that her restless spirit might … pop up from behind the catafalque during someone else's funeral.'

The use of the term 'evil' is a shorthand for the fear and a lack of understanding as to why someone would commit such crimes. It also suggests that the endless TV documentaries, podcasts and academic typographies which seek to explain such events fail to do so. Dalton (2023) points out that a handwritten note found at Letby's home by the police which stated, 'I am evil I did this' (a document extensively quoted by the media) is totally at odds with Letby's eventual not guilty plea and her refusal to admit that she committed the crimes that she was accused of.

The use of the term 'evil' applied extensively in media coverage of the case, again illustrating, perhaps, that all other explanations have failed and most powerfully illustrated in an interview in the BBC *Panorama* documentary (Coffey, 2023) with the mother of one of the victims who states, 'I am horrified that someone so evil exists'.

A Google search using the term 'Lucy Letby evil' brought up ten video clips and well over 100 articles from newspapers and magazines, including those with a target audience of women and those containing religious content. *The Daily Mirror* on 19 September had the headline 'Lucy Letby's "chilling" post it note confession that exposed her as evil baby killer' (Dalton, 2023) and a story covering the police's discovery of documentary evidence and handwritten notes at Letby's home, with particular reference to the 'I am evil I did this' note. She is also described as 'cold-blooded killer'. *Take a Break* on 19 September 2023, a populist publication (and it is interesting that the case had become so embedded in the public imagination that such a magazine would run the story), went with the headline 'The Real Lucy Letby – the EVIL – nurse who killed innocent babies' (evil in capitals for emphasis) (Rowland, 2023). The article focuses on the ordinary nature of Letby, a key theme to emerge throughout coverage of the trial, with a quote from forensic psychiatrist Dr Soham Das: 'She somehow managed to compartmentalise her dark and twisted emotions and could divorce her actions from the rest of her everyday normal life' (Rowland, 2023: 1).

A good example of the way in which the public seem to have been gripped by the whole affair is that an episode of ITV's *Loose Women* broadcast the day after Letby's sentencing, contained a panel discussion on 'Can you be born evil?' A similarly populist endeavour, *Talk TV*, ran an interview with a former Met police officer, Peter Bleksley, who described Letby as a 'truly evil piece of garbage', again the discussion focussing on the 'vanilla' nature of Letby, with the interviewer stating that she was 'not what you would imagine evil looks like'. On a subsequent programme on the same channel, an interview with Dr Dewi Evans, an independent medical witness brought in by the prosecution, was introduced as 'the man who took down evil Lucy Letby', and his interview takes place against a backdrop of a picture of Letby and the caption 'Angel of Death'. 'The unexpected force of evil' is a headline from an article in the magazine *Prospect* (McDonald, 2023). Again, the emphasis is on the 'ordinary' nature of Letby and the idea that evil is not always that easy to spot (the article also, as you would expect, contains a theological discussion on good and evil), and it concludes with the statement 'sometimes the monster is a vanilla nurse who had dance lessons'. Letby provides a contrast, it is argued, to other examples of evil (Hitler, Brady and Hindley), that in these cases evil is easier to see. There is an attempt to explain the reason for a public yearning to be able to spot evil. 'If evil has a face, a form, a body, then perhaps it helps give us a sense of control over it' (McDonald, 2023: 1).

Polly Toynbee in *The Guardian* (18 August 2023) again tackles the issue of the public's need for a rational explanation under the headline 'Faced with evil like Lucy Letby's we yearn for a rational explanation. Sometimes there is none.' It is an interesting piece, but evil is foregrounded once again and Toynbee concludes with: 'We will never know what evil or insanity could have induced Lucy Letby to sweep away the lives of seven babies' (Toynbee, 2023: 1) and her description of Letby's actions as 'monstrous deeds' draws on tropes from coverage of previous female serial killers such as Myra Hindley and Rose West. Collier (2023) in *The Daily Star* points out that 'Baby killer Lucy Letby joins the list of Britain's most evil medical murderers', rehashing coverage of the Beverley Allitt and Harold Shipman cases.

As time moves on from the trial, journalists move on to look at other angles of the case which continues to keep it in the public eye. In October 2023, Brooks et al (2023) writing in *The Daily Express*, ran a story under the headline 'Lucy Letby inseparable with evil new pal behind bars who killed baby with painkillers'. They go on to describe Lucy Letby's friendship with Michelle Smith who was convicted of killing her baby with painkillers in 2007 and also with Shauna Hoare, jailed in 2015 for her part in the murder of Becky Watts. The tone is one of horror and indignation, particularly as the three are reported to have spent movie and karaoke nights together.

The articles quoted from here are just a handful of the multitude produced, particularly in the aftermath of the trial verdict and sentencing, but provide good examples of the way in which the idea of 'evil' and serial killing is inextricably linked in media coverage of true crime and the way in which true crime has increasingly become part of the entertainment industry. Cummins et al (2019), with particular reference to the case of the Moors Murderers, have discussed the way in which stories relating to serial killers are kept alive by the news media, often digging into the archives and regurgitating old texts.

Institutional responses

The institutional responses to suspicions raised by medical staff and what are seen as perceived failings by senior managers at the Countess of Chester Hospital has featured as a prominent theme in media reporting of the case. The fact that suspicions raised about Lucy Letby's behaviour and presence at the unusual number of deaths in the Countess of Chester Neonatal Unit, were raised as early as mid-2015 are in the public domain.

Chakrovarty (2023: 1) writes:

> The case of Lucy Letby killing innocent babies in a neonatal unit has yet again shaken the healthcare professionals … is the abject failure of leadership to heed concerns raised (whistleblowing) and actions that may be considered collusive or protectionism towards Lucy Letby, who did not have the 'face of a killer.'

The Thirwell Inquiry, which began in September 2024, was established to examine these issues. The inquiry is examining how Letby was able to murder, how the hospital managed concerns and will also look at the wider issue of National Health Service (NHS) culture (O'Donoghue and Moritz, 2023). The NHS whistleblowers group (a group made up of health professionals from a variety of disciplines) applied to contribute to the inquiry, determined to have their voices heard (Buchanan, 2023). Members of the senior management team at the Countess of Chester Hospital (none of whom are now employed there), namely, Tony Chambers, former CEO, Ian Harvey, former medical director, Alison Kelly, former director of nursing and Sue Hodkinson, former HR director, have been named as core participants in the inquiry.

Consultant Stephen Breary was interviewed as part of the BBC *Panorama* documentary (Coffey, 2023) and describes how he had raised concerns about the unusual number of deaths on the neonatal unit in 2015. These were dismissed by senior management. He then discussed how, in February 2016, Dr Ravi Jayaram came to him with concerns about Lucy Letby after he had found her standing over an incubator, and he suspected that she had been interfering with a breathing tube. In all, seven consultant paediatricians had raised concerns about Letby and the fact that she had been on shift when baby deaths had occurred up to that point. Breary tells the interviewer how he demanded an urgent meeting, which did not happen until May 2016. Again, concerns were dismissed. In June 2016, two of three triplets in the unit died. Letby was on shift again. At that point Breary asked senior management to stop Letby from working. This was initially refused but she was later assigned to admin duties and the deaths stopped. The group of senior consultants all expressed concerns in emails to the CEO and asked that the police be called in. Instead, CEO Tony Chambers requested an inquiry by the Royal College of Paediatrics and Child Health and the consultants were told that all emails regarding Letby were to stop forthwith, and that if they did not there would be consequences. Chambers later claimed that this had been taken out of context. However, the consultant group were forced to write an apology to Letby and two were put into face-to-face mediation with her after she took out a grievance. However, two months after the apology, the police were finally called in. Operation Hummingbird, an investigation of Lucy Letby, was launched in May 2017, and she was arrested in July 2018.

Dr Susan Gilbey who replaced Chambers as CEO (she resigned in 2018 and accepted a post elsewhere) was also interviewed for the *Panorama* documentary (Coffey, 2023). When asked by the reporter if she thought there was a cover up, she states that there seemed to be a strong narrative at work which was about not involving the police, and that senior management were really concerned with 'how it would look' and protecting the reputation of the institution. This obviously had serious and tragic consequences. The reporter concludes that senior management went out of their way to protect Letby and the fact that, as Chakrovarty (2023: 1) states, she 'apparently did not have the face of a killer' seems to have been a factor. Stephen Breary admits that as his suspicions grew, he thought surely 'not nice Lucy', but he also adds that his being forced into mediation sessions with Letby was 'a way of delaying action and investigating those concerns'.

Chakrovarty (2023: 1) states 'established systems for raising concerns were blatantly defeated by the actions of leaders' and adds that the beigeness of the perpetrator and her failure to meet any of the criteria outlined in the typologies of healthcare serial killers previously discussed was a major factor. The attempt to silence whistleblowers in this case has once again raised this as a major concern for those working in the healthcare sector. It has also rekindled a debate about the way in which concerns about treatment raised by parents/relatives and the proposed implementation of 'Martha's Rule', triggered by the case of 14-year-old Martha Mills who died in 2021 after her parents' concerns about her worsening condition were ignored by staff. The proposed implementation suggests that patients, family and next of kin should have the opportunity to raise concerns directly and demand an independent clinical review (Dyer, 2023).

Conclusion

The Thirwell Inquiry to examine the institutional response and attempt to unravel the processes that led to Letby's actions going undetected for so long began in September 2024. Letby is also due for a retrial on another count of murder that the jury were unable to reach a verdict on at the original trial (Dowling, 2024). These events will galvanize the serial killing industry into action once again and the themes discussed in this chapter will once again be revived and pored over in both media and populist tabloid circles. At the time of writing, an article by Rachel Aviv (2024) in the *New Yorker*, unavailable in the UK due to it being considered contempt of court, has found its way onto X (formerly Twitter). Aviv (2024) goes through each of Letby's convictions and argues that the circumstantial evidence should not have been enough to convict her. Maher (2024) outlines how this case may set up a showdown between England's justice system and the magazine but what is more interesting in the context of this chapter, are the multitude of responses to the article, extremely polarized, many in agreement with Aviv's (2024) analysis, others questioning how anyone can possibly think that evil Letby is innocent. The case of the Vanilla Killer, then, provides a good example of the way in which the serial killing industry and mediatized murder operates and the public's appetite for true crime stories. It has certainly caught the imagination of the British public, journalists and academics, and will continue to do so for some time to come.

12

Conclusion

True crime's trajectory and the current true crime moment

This volume offers a sense of the shape of true crime in the current digital media moment while also recognizing how its distinct form was forged in the recent past of late modernity. We note how cultural narratives of murder and violence and public fascination with criminal subjects and murder events have a long history. Cultural production chronicling crime and criminals in the 17th and 18th centuries took a variety of formats documenting the lives of criminals, justice proceedings and executions with a growth in longform biographies of criminals in the 18th century (Rawlings, 1998; Macmillan, 2016). The modern phenomena of the mass media and crime 'sensation'/detective fiction emerged in the 19th century (Brown, 2003; Flanders, 2011), alongside the production of broadsides and penny dreadfuls aimed at the working classes.

With increasing urban populations, murder rates spiked as the cultural production of crime spectacle proliferated amidst public anxiety and fascination with grisly and macabre murder narratives in the Victorian period which shaped modern understandings of crime (Flanders, 2011; Motion, 2011). Judith Flanders identifies how playing with historical fact by fictionalizing it, was evident in the work of Collins and Dickens who demonstrated an increasing interest in the criminal subject as opposed to the criminal event across fact/fiction divides. The Whitechapel murders of 1888 brought forth the ultimate criminal subject in the figure of Jack the Ripper and a media and cultural frenzy that continued long into the 20th century. Indeed, this was a key moment that introduced the media/cultural figure of the serial killer as a figure of modernity into popular culture (Downing, 2013; Linnemann, 2015), spawning a raft of 'fact'/fiction hybrids across the 'ripper' industry, as well as the misogynist true crime pseudo-science of Ripperology whose main concern was to identify the still unknown killer.

However, the longform murder narrative (Murley, 2008), based on actual crime events, but resembling a work of fiction which often plays with truth, came into its own and established the true crime genre in the late 20th century. As we have discussed, the serial killer's cultural prominence is bound up with how true crime became established at this time. Although, his 'invention' of the genre is disputed (Voss, 2011), Capote's (1966) literary treatment of the real-life mass murder of a family in rural North America, came to define the genre of crime fact written in the style of longform literary fiction. However, as Jenkins (1994) observes, the Federal Bureau of Investigation (FBI), informed by a political agenda justifying its own existence and to secure future funding, identified/invented the serial killer as a new criminal type and threat to the nation in the 1970s, and positioned itself as the only organization with the expertise to deal with the serial killer problem in the United States. Drawing on Phillip Jenkins' (1994) work on the cultural construction of the serial killer, Linnemann (2015) argues that following the London Whitechapel murders in1888, the FBI's adopting of the serial killer to promote itself in the 1970s was the other key moment in the history of true crime, serial murder and the making of the serial killer industry.

The FBI's classification of the serial killer as a specific criminal type coincided with the reality of rising violence and a set of high-profile serial murder cases in the US in the 1970s and 1980s which attracted huge amounts of news coverage and became the subject matter of much true crime output. Echoing this, Murley (2008) notes how true crime's popularity increased alongside spikes in violence in the US in the 1970s and 1980s and 'became the dominant form of non-fiction murder narration' (Murley, 2008: 4). Likewise in Britain, news media and popular criminology fixated on a selection of macabre cases involving serial murder: the Moors Murders, the so-called Yorkshire Ripper, Dennis Nilsen and Fred and Rosemary West. As Biressi (2001) observes, the content generated by cases such as these, accounts for the growth of true crime in the 1970s and 1980s, its association with serial murder and gratuity, and assumptions about its low-brow status in the form of pulp novels, low-budget documentaries and their forerunner, the true crime magazine. The symbiotic relationship between true crime and serial murder, and murder narratives more broadly, was fixed, establishing both the genre and, with the help of fictional portrayals, creating a recognizable character in the figure of the serial killer. Indeed, popular culture bestowed serial killers with a set of distinctive features that rendered him at once compelling, fascinating, in some cases attractive (Jenkins, 1994) and taking on the status of 'dubious infamy' as celebrities in postmodern culture (Schmid, 2008).

Reading history and culture through true crime

Recent work by Wattis (2022, 2023, 2024c) has stressed that the true crime genre is far more diverse than media commentaries and, indeed, many academic analyses would have us believe. Wattis argues that true crime, in fact, explores a wide range of compelling criminal figures, cases, criminological issues and also performs ethical and activist work in exposing injustice and the harms of violence across a wider range of formats. Digital and online culture have transformed social life and social practices and have played a key role in diversifying the true crime genre, as well as revisiting and continuing to dwell on the serial killer. Horeck (2019) identifies the role of digital culture in propelling true crime's current popularity, arguing that the arrival of new formats and the fact that true crime content now resides across multiple platforms means that audiences can now actively engage with content across a range of online spaces that offers immediacy in dispensing just justice and offering the emotional fix often associated with true crime.

However, a lot of the time, discussions in this book reside in a different space at a different time in the history of popular culture, true crime and the history of the murder narrative. There is something of a retro feel to the discussions, which include British New Wave cinema, the place of Ian Brady and Myra Hindley in the British cultural landscape of the 1960s, gonzo journalism and a focus on three cases from the 1970s and their cultural treatment. However, chapters on the murderer Gary Gilmore (more accurately Mailer's work on the case), the prolific cultural output on Ted Bundy, which continues in contemporary culture, and the focus on Gordon Burn's insights on media and popular culture, violence and celebrity, form a set of case studies which capture some of the main cultural work performed by true crime and the role it plays in bringing forth the serial killer.

For instance, as we highlight, the 'empirical events' (Brown, 2003) of Gary Gilmore's crimes and their representation in Mailer's *Executioner's Song* kicked off debates about ethics, punishment and the death penalty in the US and the public and media/cultural life of the murderer. Gilmore's relationship with punishment, justice and media is an important example of how the celebrity killer can come into being, given Gilmore's overnight infamy and the fan mail he received following his refusal to appeal the death sentence. Sheila Brown (2003) points to how crime fiction acts as a lens that refracts history, crime and culture and the way that works of crime fiction should thus be regarded as valuable historical and sociological documents. This could equally apply to the *Executioner's Song*, which reveals the lived experience of the poor working-class in the US, and the history of politics, violence and punishment within the US at a specific juncture given how the case and the novel links to liberal politics and its occurrence on the cusp of Reaganism and the ushering in of law and order politics and the era of mass incarceration.

The book is a powerful account of the place of violence in American culture, offering a reckoning with violence and its consequences. As such, it highlights how works of popular criminology contribute to and enhance criminological epistemology and imagination, offering alternative emotional and immersive takes of crime and violence (Rafter, 2007; Wakeman, 2013; Wattis, 2018).

Likewise, Gordon Burn's insights on violence, popular culture and celebrity continue to resonate in our encounters with crime and true crime narratives in digital culture. For instance, Burn maintains how voyeuristic drives, as opposed to a need to comprehend motivation, account for the current popularity of true crime as murder event across popular culture. Furthermore, Burn's prescient concerns with the shallow nature of celebrity, the crafting of reality in media culture and the collapse of fact/fiction boundaries are increasingly salient in true crime's current online eco-system (Sherrill, 2020).

Femicide and true crime

More than any other figure, Ted Bundy exemplifies the serial killer as attractive, compelling and heroic, aligning with the idea of him as the dubious celebrity of late modern culture (Schmid, 2008). This supports Downing's (2013) analysis of murder as a path to masculine transcendence and hero worship which confirms the misogyny of a 'murder worshipping culture' (p 113). This path is never available to the female killer. The discussion of the media framing of Lucy Letby in Chapter 11 shows that the focus was on how ordinary she was. This led to her being referred to as 'beige' or 'vanilla'. Echoing Downing (2013), other feminist work on serial murder (often involving a sexual motivation), masculinity and femicide identifies how popular culture, via true crime texts and news media, celebrates and elevates men who murder women while victims become background figures serving the killer's story. Either that or female victims become hyper-visible objects of voyeurism as texts dwell on mutilated bodies and disregard victims' humanity (Walkowitz, 1982; Caputi, 1989; Wattis, 2018).

As Jane Caputi (1987) observes, the Whitechapel murders involving five poor and marginalized women in 1888, which invoked the ripper myth, set the template for sex crime across the 20th century. For Caputi, men's murder and degradation of women should be understood as political acts in the wider context of patriarchy, where the killer is elevated to the 'ultimate man' (p 62). At times, Caputi's analysis does lack nuance and ignores differing typologies and representations of the serial killer, the existence of male victims and the diversity and popularity of violent masculine subjects beyond the sexually motivated serial killer. Cameron and Frazer (1989) fill in some of these gaps, condemning psychological explanations that focus on individual pathology and identifying this criminal subject as a product of misogyny and masculinity while also recognizing that misogyny cannot account for male victims and sometimes male killers are constructed as abject and Other in news and true crime discourses. Cameron and Frazer get round the fact that misogyny does not always figure in serial murder by drawing attention to the links between masculinity, transcendence and exceptionality: the idea that practising domination and cruelty renders the male subject special. Downing (2013) notices this earlier work and concludes that a culture in thrall to the male killer is misogynist. This is explicit in victim-blaming and the abjection of victims linked to sex work. Indeed, writing about the Whitechapel murders, Walkowitz (1982) notes how commentators at the time deemed the 'lifestyle' of the Whitechapel victims more sinful than their murder and mutilation. The Yorkshire Ripper murders attracted similar indifference to victims evident in songs, jokes and the adoption of the myth into local folklore and football culture (Caputi, 1987; Smith, 2013; Wattis, 2018).

There are many examples of culture fetishizing the male killer, but Ted Bundy stands out in terms of the quantity of true crime content devoted to him and the nature of the discourse that surrounds him. The earlier discussion in Chapter 7 identifies the breadth of true crime output devoted to Bundy and how it has persisted into true crime's digital era. His acts of femicide are overshadowed by a preoccupation with his physical appearance and disavowed as he is elevated from ordinary man to a criminal genius who managed to evade capture. This is evident in the way women who attended his trial were labelled 'groupies' and the judge who sentenced him lamented the wasted potential of a man who kidnapped, raped and murdered up to 30 women and more. As Wattis (2024: 91) highlights in earlier work, 'the true crime oeuvre on Bundy has curated the figure of the charming and attractive killer of women, whose victims are of little consequence'. Furthermore, the way culture elevates Bundy and overlooks his rape and murder of women, also exposes true crime's problematic relationship to race. As Murley (2008) points out, historically, the victims who feature in true crime have been white, which inverts the reality of the risk of violence and fatal violence faced by Black communities. Likewise, 'traditional' true crime features white perpetrators, but race/ethnicity is not deployed to understand their criminality. Indeed, as Wattis (2023) observes, 'Bundy's education, demeanour, respectability and appearance present him as a figure of white respectability which stands in stark contrast to Black criminality and helps make sense of the way he is accepted and romanticized in popular culture' (p 83).

Even as true crime has diversified in the realm of digital culture, the cult of the serial killer persists, with Bundy continuing to be a popular choice for content creators and audiences. The turn to victims in the post #MeToo era has produced more sensitive and victim-centred treatments such as the docuseries *Falling for a Killer* (Wood, 2020), but other productions continue to rely on Bundy's appearance, charisma and supposed high-level intellect, placing him at the centre of the story and indulging the ego and voice of the killer, as is the case with *Conversations with a Killer: The Ted Bundy Tapes* (Berlinger, 2019a). Indeed, even the transgressive post MeToo podcast *My Favorite Murder* has at times defaulted to Bundy as the star turn at one of their live shows (Hoffman and Hobbs, 2021). It is also evident that attempts by documentary makers to create content that challenges the conventions of true crime based on serial killers, still rely upon accepted tropes and risk disappointing audiences if they do not deliver standard true crime formulas (McCabe, 2022).

True crime and digital culture

Digital culture has transformed the way we communicate with one another, how we consume media and the types of culture/media we engage with. In addition, it has also led to active consumers who respond to, produce and create content for themselves (Yardley, 2017; Yardley et al 2018). The expansion of digital technology has played a key role in true crime's current popularity as podcasts and documentaries on streaming platforms have become the preferred formats for audiences. Horeck (2019) identifies network culture as the perfect vehicle for true crime because it offers interaction across multiple platforms, connection and the opportunity for active and emotive participation. This leads Horeck (2019: 4) to single out true crime as 'an exemplary genre for the digital, multi-platform era'. Audiences can listen to a podcast, seek out related content, join a forum to discuss the podcast or the case and follow and comment on social media. Along the way, content may provoke opinions emotional responses which are validated across platforms in online interactions. Moreover, podcast listening represents an immersive and private experience with the potential for closer and more personal engagement with subjects (Greer, 2017).

The true crime genre has diversified as it has evolved in the digital era. Pulp novels are still readily available, low-brow documentaries reconstructing historical cases still exist on dedicated channels and murder narratives and serial killers still make much up much podcast content. However, other narrative forms such as 'injustice narratives' (Larke-Walsh, 2020), that claim a higher purpose in exposing miscarriages of justice and corrupt criminal justice actors, have come to prominence. As we discuss in Chapter 9, the award-winning first season of the podcast *Serial* was a pioneer of the injustice narrative and represented a departure for the genre as a piece of quality investigative journalism which resembled the gonzo style associated with esteemed literary figures, defined by a personal style and point of view. *Serial*'s premise was to revisit a specific case and challenge a murder conviction by questioning the evidence. According to Doane et al (2016), Koenig creates a safe space from which to tackle provocative issues by asking questions of her audience and not making claims to objective truth. In this sense, Doane et al (2016) view her method as feminist, especially as her work focuses on injustice and social justice. Other work observes the social justice and feminist potential of a range of podcasts that examine violence against women and missing and murdered women, and expose how power and inequality shape this violence (Horeck, 2019; Pâquet, 2021; Slakoff, 2021). Moreover, looking at screen media, a new genre of true crime has emerged in the form of the victim-centred documentary which examines sexual violence and abuse from the perspective of the victim and in so doing reveals the harms of sexual violence and the victim/survivor experience more fully (Wattis, 2024d).

Digital culture and the rise of the podcast has also led to gender-specific content which demonstrates gendered sensibilities which appeal specifically to male and female audiences. As we explore in Chapter 3, women-led podcasts revisit and discuss 'murder events' (Murley, 2008) but combine this with comedy and therapy, fostering a sense of community among audiences and a grounding in popular feminism that acknowledges male violence against women and women's relationship to fear and of male violence in the wake of #MeToo. As we further note, the male audience has been overlooked in debates about the significance of true crime's current popularity. However, as Wattis (2020, 2023, 2024a, 2024b, 2024c, 2024d) points out, if we go beyond the murder narratives and serial murder that have come to define the genre, male audiences, who are more interested in different criminal subjects, such as men with a reputation for serious violence and organized crime, come into view. Prior to the onset of digital culture, this type of true crime primarily took the form of biographies and memoirs of gangsters and hardman, but there now exist numerous podcast titles focused on hardman stories that adhere to a specific masculine aesthetic, offer an ambivalent position on criminality and court a male audience.

Wattis (2024c) contrasts the differing cultural work performed by podcasts that appeal to men and women. For example, shows popular with female listeners offer a sense of community, therapeutic and empathetic elements, and escape and reassurance via engagement with familiar murder narratives (Yardley et al, 2019). Rodgers (2022: 3050) argues that in the context of the online space, *My Favorite Murder* and shows like it, offer emotional engagement and connection with content, as well as a political space 'for the collective condemnation of the cultural attitudes and social conditions that lead to the victimization of women and girls'.

In contrast, the 'digital hardman' invites audiences to engage with a history of violence and criminal culture, alongside a hegemonically violent masculine aesthetic. Hardman podcasts follow a different premise and narrative, involving a host who interviews a variety of guests who recount life stories and/or significant life events. The shows do not focus solely on organized crime and the hardman, also hosting sporting figures and those with a story to tell. That said, this type of violent individual and narrative is a consistent feature across the genre. Moreover, as with true crime in digital culture more generally, podcasts exist in an interconnected 'ecosystem' of social media pages, accounts and subreddit forums (Horeck, 2019; Sherrill, 2020; Rodgers, 2022). As such, the podcasts share a specific masculine aesthetic and connect to a variety of male-centred content, some of which may promote misogyny and right-wing ideologies.

As we discuss in Chapter 3, the ethics of true crime have become more complex and pressing in late capitalism and digital culture. Exploiting real violence and trauma, turning it into spectacle and making heroes out of serial killers – defining features of old-style true crime – have continued alongside more insidious harms and practices, with the ethical questions of newer genres less clearcut. Audiences have assumed a more active role in digital culture and in their engagement with true crime which present a new set of ethical problems.

For example, documentaries and podcasts that claim to seek truth and justice and uncover corruption within the criminal justice system also manipulate audiences and risk demeaning formal legal and justice processes in the way they invite audiences to decide on guilt and truth (Engley, 2017; Bruzzi, 2016). As we point out in Chapter 9, in spite of claims to justice and ethics and official recognition through awards, the *Serial* podcast, and specifically the first series that made its name, nevertheless resorted to trivializing murder and disregarding the victim and her family, operating in a commercial mediascape where money and careers are made from the stories of actual suffering (Yardley et al, 2019).

This is even more pronounced in the case of web sleuths whose active engagement and interference with criminal cases can have real-world consequences (Yardley et al 2018; Rondo, 2022). There is, of course, the critically lauded version of the 'citizen detective' evident in Michelle McNamara's account of her obsessive and meticulous on and off-live investigation of *the Golden State Killer* who raped and murdered at least 13 victims in California in the 1970s and 1980s. In *I'll Be Gone in the Dark: One Woman's Obsessive Search for the Golden State Killer*, McNamara offers a sensitive and insightful reflection on her decades-long involvement and obsession with the case. McNamara humanizes victims and offers a strong sense of history and place, as well as ensuring the reader is aware of the damage wrought by the perpetrator in this case. Moreover, McNamara gathered evidence, organized large volumes of information and drew media and popular attention to the case. All of which contributed to police apprehending the killer in 2018. And, as we highlight in Chapter 6, in the pre-digital era, by involving themselves and intervening in cases, investigative journalists have carried out important activist and justice work in overturning wrongful convictions and exposing police brutality and corruption, albeit not without its own ethical dilemmas.

However, as Yardley et al (2018) point out, the rise of the web sleuth in network culture exemplifies Seltzer's (2007) notion of the pathological public sphere or 'wound culture' where individuals gather online to pick at and pore over violence and trauma. The harms and ethical problems linked to web sleuthing relate to the further exploitation of suffering in digital true crime, the compromising of criminal and missing persons investigations and the way in which amateurs assume roles which they are not qualified to carry out fuelled by a sense of individualistic entitlement as a key feature of the neo-liberal mindset in the context of late capitalism. Numerous cases involving web sleuth interference illustrate this in action. For example, the wrongful identification of suspects and wilful meddling and disruption of missing person investigation as happened in the Nicola Bulley case which hindered the police investigation and caused the family further distress and anguish. The harms of sleuthing also came to the fore following the broadcast of Netflix's *Baby Reindeer* in 2024, which was based on comedian Richard Gadd's experiences of stalking and sexual abuse. Web sleuths took it upon themselves to identify the female stalking perpetrator, sparking a legal and ethical storm regarding the vulnerability of the perpetrator, the 'truth' of personal stories and the afterlife of stories beyond the original narrative (Thorpe, 2024).

Taken together, all of this begs the question as to whether true crime can ever be ethical. This may be more clearcut when it comes to fetishizing serial killers, but digital and network culture poses a wider array of moral dilemmas for the genre. Moreover, as we propose in Chapter 3, drawing on a deviant leisure framework which argues that in the of context neo-liberal, late capitalism, a coherent ethical social order simply does not exist. As such, does this render futile any consideration of the ethical possibilities of true crime?

Final reflections

Arguably, the most important chapters in this volume are the ones examining the Lucy Letby case and the femicide of a Bulgarian journalist. We concede that much of this volume deals with true crime's standard subject matter – historic and notorious cases of murder and serial murder which have shaped what we think we know about this type of violence and the true crime genre (Biressi, 2001). The fact that for a long time a collection of infamous cases came to define the true crime genre (Murley, 2008), as well as marking out how news media responds to and represents necessitates this focus. Moreover, even as technology and the internet have transformed social life and popular culture, and true crime's diversity has become apparent, digital culture has reinforced the cult of the killer and offered new ways to consume and engage with serial killer narratives.

With this in mind, the case of Lucy Letby presents an opportunity to reflect on how news and true crime media approach a high-profile serial murder case in the networked digital era. Looking at the media's treatment of the case, it is clear that the media serial killer relationship still retains many of its original elements. For instance, the centring of the trial as 'dystopian spectacle' (Bolton, 2005), which was a key feature of high-profile 20th century cases such as the Moors Murders and the Sutcliffe case. The Letby case also demonstrates the overlap between celebrity and the serial killer as a figure of 'dubious infamy', as well as significant individuals connected to the case who take on the mantle of 'para-celebrity' (Burn, 1984). Indeed, the positioning of the serial killer in celebrity and mainstream culture is evident in the tone of the public conversation about the case and the media spaces where these conversations take place – the morning and evening magazine shows and the women-led panel where hosts and guests debate Lucy Letby. Thus, we see familiar patterns of representation applied to the case, alongside coverage in several podcasts and across multiple connected platforms as the serial killer industry expands and adapts in contemporary network culture. Unsurprisingly, the female serial killer whose victims were children reignites familiar media discourses concerned with the nature of evil and femininity, and the way gender shapes the framing of the serial killer (Jewkes, 2019).

If the Lucy Letby case highlights how the familiar tropes of the serial killer industry remain intact in contemporary digital mediascapes, Gachevska's examination of the rape and murder of broadcast journalist Viktoria Marinova in the Bulgarian city of Ruse in 2018 highlights how, when we move beyond true crime's Western lens, alternative narratives on murder emerge. As a brutal sexual femicide, Viktoria's murder fits a typical true crime murder narrative. Invoking the perpetrator as *evil* and as racialized criminal Other resembles familiar true crime representational territory. As Gachevska shows, however, the importance of context beyond Western experiences is fundamental to how media and public discourse understood the murder. Shaped by a post-communist relationship to crime and fear of crime, linked to perceived state corruption and incompetence, and organized crime, the belief that Viktoria was a victim of political corruption and state violence dominated. The case, and Gachevska's analysis of it, demonstrate that future studies of true crime will be much enriched by adopting a global, intersectional approach.

This volume has traced the development of true crime highlighting that it is now deeply embedded in popular culture and daily life, driven in no small part by digital shifts and advances. True crime also increasingly preoccupies academic audiences across disciplines, who appreciate that along with other genres of popular criminology, studying true crime offers a lens onto crime and culture beyond academic epistemology. This is in spite of, and indeed because of, its ethical ambiguities, which as we point out, have become more complex in the digital era. Indeed, true crime's popularity shows no sign of abating, and there is much more to say about popular culture, crime and representation, especially as the sands of technology, politics and violence continue to shift.

References

Bulgarian language sources

НСИ (2023) Осъдени лица по глави от наказателния кодекс и някои видове престъпления и по наложени наказания. Национален Статистически Институт, available at https://www.nsi.bg/bg (accessed 18 August 2024).

НСИ (2022) Насилие, основано на пол. Национален Статистически Институт, available at https://infostat.nsi.bg/infostat/pages/module.jsf?x_2=348 (accessed 18 August 2024).

Неменски, Н. (2018) Защо беше убита млада журналистка в Русе. Работи се по всички версии, като според адвокат Марин Марковски, убийството няма общо с работата на жертвата. Вести, available at https://www.vesti.bg/bulgaria/incidenti/bdenie-za-ubitata-zhurnalistka-iskat-otgovori-6087224 (accessed 15 December 2018).

Нова Телевизия (2018) 'Ничия земя': Недоизказани факти за убийството на Виктория Маринова. 20 November 2018, available at https://www.vbox7.com/play:3c8e744e37 (accessed 15 December 2018).

Нова Телевизия (2023) За Северин: Генезиса на злото. Програма *Ничия земя*, available at https://www.youtube.com/watch?v=Kue1TmhDF0U (accessed 15 August 2024).

Радио Свободна Европа (2023) '400 шева бяха направени'. Жена е обезобразена в Стара Загора. Обвиняемият й бивш приятел е на свобода. 23 юли 2023, available at https://www.svobodnaevropa.bg/a/nasilie-zhena-prebita-naryazana-napadatel/32524019.html (accessed 15 August 2024).

Abbott, J. (1981) *In the Belly of the Beast: Letters from Prison*. Random House.

Adams, M. (2024) From Des and Angie's marriage breakdown to Tracy's Murder confession, the soap two-handers that changed everything. *Metro*, available at metro.co.uk (accessed 10 June 2024).

Adderley, E. (2002) Why did local undertakers refuse to cremate Myra Hindley? *The Guardian*, available at www.theguardian.com/uk/2002/nov/21/ukcrime.estheraddley (accessed 6 February 2025).

Agamben, G. (1995) *Homo Sacer: Sovereign Power and Bare Life*. Stanford University Press.

Alexander, M. (2010) The war on drugs and the New Jim Crow. *Race, Poverty & the Environment*, 17(1), pp 75–7.

Amirante, S.L. and Broderick, D. (2011) *John Wayne Gacy: Defending a Monster*. Simon and Schuster.

Anderson, L. (1963) *This Sporting Life*. Rank Organisation.

Anderson, M. (2003) 'One flew over the psychiatric unit': Mental illness and the media. *Journal of Psychiatric and Mental Health Nursing*, 10(3), pp 297–306.

AP (2018) The latest: UN's Gutteres notes violence against journalists. Associated Press, available at https://apnews.com/general-news-eb1229cfe4004ffea79a6d22dc63485f (accessed 12 December 2024).

Arendt, H. (1963) *Eichmann in Jerusalem*. Penguin.

Arnold, L. (2020) *Des*. ITV.

Arnold, L. (2023) *The Long Shadow*. ITV.

Atkins, S. and Schiller, L. (1970) *The Killing of Sharon Tate*. New American Library.

Atkinson, R. (2019) From edge work to death drive: The pursuit of violence and the denial of harm in a leisure society, in T. Raymen and O. Smith (eds) *Deviant Leisure: Criminological Perspectives on Leisure and Harm*. Palgrave, pp 215–37.

Atkinson, R. and Rodgers, T. (2016) Pleasure zones and murder boxes: Online pornography and violent video games as cultural zones of exception. *The British Journal of Criminology*, 56(6), pp 1291–307.

Aviv, R. (2024) A British nurse was found guilty of killing seven babies. Did she do it? *New Yorker*, 30 May 2024, pp 2–6.

Baelo-Allué, S. (2019) Transhumanism, transmedia and the serial podcast: Redefining storytelling in times of enhancement. *International Journal of English Studies*, 19(1), pp 113–31.

Baldwin, J. (1988) *The Black Boy Looks at the White Boy: Collected Essays*. Library of America.

Bandura, A., Ross, S.A. and Ross, D. (1963) Imitation of film-mediated aggressive models. *Journal of Abnormal Psychology*, 66(1), pp 3–11.

Banet-Weiser, S. and Higgins, K.C. (2022) Television and the 'honest' Woman: Mediating the labour of believability. *Television & New Media*, 23(2): pp127–147.

Barker, M. and Petley, J. (eds) (1997) *Ill Effects: The Media/Violence Debate*. Routledge.

Barker, P. (1984) *Blow Your House Down*. Virago.

Bartkowski, J.P., Kohler, J. and Hoffmann, J.P. (2023) The legacy of blood atonement? Gauging Mormon support for the death penalty. *Religions*, 14(208), pp 1–13.

Bauman, Z. (1989) *Modernity and the Holocaust*. Cornell University Press.
Bauman, Z. (1993) *Postmodern Ethics*. Blackwell.
BBC Radio 4 (2018) The world this weekend, Sunday 7 October 2018.
Beale, V. (2015) Too close to Ted Bundy. *New Yorker*, available at https://www.newyorker.com/books/page-turner/too-close-to-ted-bundy (accessed 9 April 2025).
Becker, G. (1968) Crime and punishment: An economic analysis. *Journal of Political Economy*, 78, pp 169–217.
Belloc-Lowdnes, M. (1996) *The Lodger*. Introduction by Laura Marcus. Oxford University Press.
Benioff, D. and Weiss, D.B. (2011–2019) *Game of Thrones*. HBO.
Bentham, A. (2015) Fatal attraction: The serial killer in American popular culture. *Violence in American Popular Culture*, 1, pp 203–22.
Berlinger, J. (2019a) *Conversations with a Killer: The Ted Bundy Tapes*. Radical Media.
Berlinger, J (2019b) *Extremely Wicked, Shockingly Evil and Vile*. COTA Films.
Bilton, M. (2003) *Wicked Beyond Belief: The Hunt for the Yorkshire Ripper*. Harper Collins.
Biressi, A. (2001) *Crime, Fear, and the Law in True Crime Stories*. Palgrave Macmillan.
Biressi, A. (2004a) 'Above the below': Body trauma as spectacle in social/media space. *Journal for Cultural Research*, 8(3), pp 335–52.
Biressi, A. (2004b) Inside/out: Private trauma and public knowledge in true crime documentary. *Screen*, 4(Winter), pp 401–12.
Blacklock, M. (2015) *I'm Jack*. Granta Publications.
Boling, K.S. and Hull, K. (2018) Undisclosed information—*Serial* is my favorite murder: Examining motivations in the true crime podcast audience. *Journal of Radio & Audio Media*, 25(1), pp 92–108.
Bolter, J, and Grusin, R. (1999) *Remediation: Understanding New Media*. MIT Press.
Bolton, Z. (2005) Entertainment and dystopia film noir, melodrama and Mildred Pierce, available at http://www.conneculture.com/contents-articles-spring05-mildred%20pierce.html (accessed 3 January 2025).
Bonn, S. (2014) *Why We Love Serial Killers: The Curious Appeal of the World's Most Savage Murderers*. Skyhorse.
Boudreau, K. (2006) *The Spectacle of Death: Populist Literary Responses to American Capital Cases*. Prometheus Books.
Bourdieu, P. (1977/1972) *Outline of a Theory of Practice*. (R. Nice, Trans) Cambridge University Press.
Bourgois, P. (1995) *In Search of Respect: Selling Crack in El Barrio*, Cambridge University Press.
Bowman, P. (2020) In toxic hating masculinity: MMA hard men and media representation. *Sport in History*, 40(3), pp 395–410.

Bridle, J. (2019) *New Dark Age: Technology and the End of the Future*. Verso.
Bronte, E. (1847) *Wuthering Heights*. Thomas Couthey Newby.
Brooks, C., Rowlands, S. and Annett, J. (2023) Lucy Letby 'inseparable' with evil new pal behind bars. *Daily Express*, available at express.co.uk/news/uk/1827690/lucy-letby-evil-new-friend-prison.baby (accessed 9 April 2024).
Browder, L. (2010) True crime, in C. Nickerson (ed) *The Cambridge Companion to American Fiction*, Cambridge University Press, pp 121–34.
Brown, J.K. (2019) *The Perversion of Justice: The Jeffrey Epstein Story*. Blackstone.
Brown, S. (2003) *Crime and Law in Media Culture*. Open University Press.
Brown, S. (2006) The criminology of hybrids: Rethinking crime and law in techno social networks. *Theoretical Criminology*, 10(2), pp 223–44.
Browder, L. (2006) Dystopian romance: True crime and the female reader. *The Journal of Popular Culture*, 39(6), pp 928–53.
Bruzzi, S. (2016) Making a genre: The case of the contemporary true crime documentary. *Law and Humanities*, 10(2), pp 249–280.
Bryant, J. and Thompson, S. (2002) *Fundamentals of Media Effects* (1st edn). McGraw-Hill Higher Education.
Buchanan, M. (2023) Letby inquiry: NHS staff want their voices heard, BBC, available at bbc.co.uk-england-merseyside-68620678 (accessed 9 April 2024).
Buford, B. (1983) Granta 8 dirty realism, available at https://granta.com/dirtyrealism/ (accessed 9 April 2025).
Bulgarian National Radio (2018) Журналисти от Русе: Фокусът се измества и някой се опитва да си направи ПР от трагедията с Виктория Маринова [Journalists from Ruse: The focus is shifted and someone is trying to turn the tragedy with Viktoria Marinova into a PR case], available at https://bnr.bg/post/101028988/jurnalisti-ot-ruse-fokusat-se-izmestva-i-nakoi-se-opitva-da-si-napravi-pr-ot-tragediata (accessed 9 April 2025).
Burn, G. (1984) *Somebody's Husband, Somebody's Son*. Faber and Faber.
Burn, G. (2004a) *Alma Cogan*. Faber and Faber.
Burn, G. (2004b) *Fullalove*. Faber and Faber.
Burn, G. (2007) *Best and Edwards: Football, Fame, and Oblivion*. Faber and Faber.
Burn, G. (2011) *Happy Like Murderers*. Faber and Faber.
Burns, S. (2011) *The Central Park Five: A Chronicle of a City Wilding*. Random House.
Byford, L. (1981) *The Yorkshire Ripper Case: Review of the Police Investigation of the Case* by Lawrence Byford, Esq., C.B.E., Q.P.M., Her Majesty's Inspectorate of Constabulary. Home Office.
Cain, J.M. (1934) *The Postman Always Rings Twice*. Alfred A. Knopf.
Cameron, D. and Frazer, E. (1987) *The Lust to Kill: A Feminist Investigation of Sexual Murder*. New York University Press.
Cantor, D. (2003) *Mapping Murder Walking on Killers' Footsteps*. Virgin Books.

REFERENCES

Capote, T. (1966) *In Cold Blood: A True Account of a Multiple Murder and Its Consequences*. Penguin.

Caputi, J. (1987) *The Age of the Sex Crime*. Bowling Green State University Popular Press.

Caputi, J. (1989) The sexual politics of murder. *Gender & Society*, 3(4), pp 437–56.

Carlen, P. (1992) Women, Crime, Feminism, and Realism, in J. Lowman and B. MacLean (eds) *Realist Criminology: Crime Control and Policing in the 1990s*. University of Toronto Press, pp 203–220.

Cameron, D. and Frazer, E. (1987) The Lust to Kill: A Feminist Investigation of Sexual Murder. New York University Press.

Carrabine, E. (2008) *Crime, Culture, and the Media*. Polity.

Carver, R. (2009) *What We Talk About When We Talk About Love* Vintage Classics.

Casey, Baroness (2023) An independent review into the standards of behaviour and internal culture of the Metropolitan Police Service, available at (https://www.met.police.uk/SysSiteAssets/media/downloads/met/about-us/baroness-casey-review/update-march-2023/baroness-casey-review-march-2023a.pdf) (accessed 10 April 1025).

Chakrovarty, I. (2023) The case of Nurse Letby: Systems failure in safeguarding patients. *Sushruta Journal of Health Policy and Opinion*, 15(3), pp 1–8.

Chandler, D. (2014) *Resilience: The Governance of Complexity*. Routledge.

Change.org (2018) For independent EU investigation into the murder of Bulgarian journalist Victoria Marinova. Petition, available at https://www.change.org/p/eu-high-commission-for-independent-eu-investigation-into-the-murder-of-bulgarian-journalist-victoria-marinova (accessed 10 April 2025).

Cheetham, C. and Hull, L. (2023) *Nurse on Trial*. Daily Mail Podcast.

Chibnall, S. (1977) *Law and Order News: An Analysis of Crime Reporting in the British Press*. Tavistock.

Childs, T. (1975) *The Sweeney*. Euston Films.

Christie, N. (1986) The ideal victim, in I. Anttila (ed), *From Crime Policy to Victim Policy: Reorienting the Justice System*. Palgrave Macmillan UK, pp 17–30.

Clarke, G. (2006) *Capote: A Biography* Abacus.

Clayton, J. (1959) *Room at the Top*, British Lion Films.

Clear, T.R. (2009) *Imprisoning Communities: How Mass Incarceration Makes Disadvantaged Neighborhoods Worse*. Oxford University Press.

Cleaver, E. (1968) *Soul on Ice*. Delta.

Coffey, J. (2023) *Panorama. Lucy Letby: The Nurse Who Killed*. BBC TV. 18 August 2023.

Cohen, S. (2011) *Folk Devils and Moral Panics*. Routledge.

Colebrook, M. (2012) The edgier waters of the era: Gordon Burn's *Somebody's Husband, Somebody's Son*, in C. Gregoriou (ed), *Constructing Crime: Discourse and Cultural Representations of Crime and 'Deviance'*. Palgrave Macmillan UK, pp 48–61.

College of Policing (2023) *Independent external review of Lancashire Constabulary's operational response to reported missing person Nicola Bulley*, available at https://assets.college.police.uk/s3fs-public/2023-11/Nicola-Bulley-independent-external-review.pdf (accessed 19 June 2025).

Collier, A. (2023) Baby killer Lucy Letby joins list of Britain's most evil murderers. *Daily Star*, available at dailystar.co.uk/latest-news/baby-killer-lucy-letby-joins-30735250 (accessed 9 April 2024).

Connell, R.W. (2005) *Masculinities* (2nd edn). University of California Press.

Conquergood, L.D. (2002) Lethal theatre: Performance, punishment, and the death penalty. *Theatre Journal*, 54(3), pp 339–67.

Cooper, K.-L. (2019) Is our growing obsession with true crime a problem? BBC News, 1 April, available at www.bbc.com/news/world-us-canada-47474996 (accessed 19 June 2025).

Crabbe, T. (2006) From the terraces to the boardrooms: Reviewing theories and perspectives on racism in football. *International Review of Modern Sociology*, 32(2), pp 241–56.

Creeber, G. (2015) Killing us softly: Investigating the aesthetics, philosophy, and influence of Nordic Noir. *Journal of Popular Television*, 3(1), pp 21–35.

Crimecon (2024) *Crimecon: London 2024*, available at www.crimecon.co.uk/london-2024 (accessed 19 June 2025).

Culver, J.H. (1985) The states and capital punishment: Executions from 1977–1984. *Justice Quarterly*, 2(4), pp 567–78.

Cummins, I. (2018) From hero of the counterculture to risk assessment: A consideration of two portrayals of the 'psychiatric patient'. *Illness, Crisis & Loss*, 26(2), pp 111–23.

Cummins, I. (2020) Mass incarceration and neoliberal penality: A response to Lloyd and Whitehead's *Kicked to the Curb*. *International Journal of Law, Crime and Justice*, 62, p 100408.

Cummins, I. (2021) *Welfare and Punishment: from Thatcherism to Austerity*. Policy Press.

Cummins, I. and King, M. (2014a) Happy like profilers: Gordon Burn, modernity and serial killing. *International Journal of Criminology and Sociological Theory*, 7(3), pp 1–11.

Cummins, I. and King, M. (2014b) The violences of men: David Peace's 1974. *Culture, Society and Masculinity*, 6(1), pp 91–108.

Cummins, I. and King, M. (2016) 'Oh Manchester so much to answer for …' exploring society's fascination with violent crime: An interview with David Peace. ESRC Festival of Social Science.

Cummins, I. and King, M. (2017) 'Drowning in here in his bloody sea': Exploring TV cop drama's representations of the impact of stress in modern policing. *Policing and Society*, 27(8), pp 832–46.

Cummins, I., Foley, M. and King, M. (2014) '… And after the break': Police officers' views of TV crime drama. *Policing: A Journal of Policy and Practice*, 8(2), pp 205–16.

Cummins, I., Foley, M. and King, M. (2019) *Serial Killers and the Media: The Moors Murders Legacy*. Springer.

Dalton, N. (2023) Lucy Letby's 'chilling' post it-note confession that exposed her as evil baby killer, *Daily Mirror*, available at www.mirror.co.uk/news/uk-news/evil-lucy-letbys-harrowing-post-30718891 (accessed 10 June 2023).

Daskalova, N. and Spassov, O. (2014) *Balkan Media Barometer: Bulgaria 2014*.

Davies, N. (1993) *Murder on Ward Four: The Story of Bev Allitt and the Most Terrifying Crime Since the Moors Murders*. Chatto and Windus.

Davis, J. (2005) *Criminal Minds*. CBS.

Death Penalty Information Center (2024) Executions by State and Region since 1976, available at https://deathpenaltyinfo.org/executions/executions-overview/number-of-executions-by-state-and-region-since-1976 (accessed 9 April 2025).

Dekle Sr, G.R. (2011) *The Last Murder: The Investigation, Prosecution, and Execution of Ted Bundy*. Bloomsbury Publishing USA.

DeLisi, M. (2023) *Ted Bundy and the Unsolved Murder Epidemic: The Dark Figure of Crime*. Springer Nature.

Denzin, A.J. and Lincoln, Y. (2000) *Handbook of Qualitative Research* (2nd edn). Sage.

Derrida, J. (2013) *The Death Penalty, Volume I (The Seminars of Jacques Derrida)*. University of Chicago Press.

De Rondo, M. (2022) What I learned from paedophile hunters, available from https://www.jbs.cam.ac.uk/2022/what-i-learned-from-paedophile-hunters/ (accessed 10 April 2025).

Didion, J. (1968) John Wayne: A love song, in *Slouching Towards Bethlehem: Essays*. Farrar, Strauss, and Giroud, pp 29–41.

Didion, J. (1979a) *The White Album*. Simon & Schuster.

Didion, J. (1979b) I want to go ahead and do it. *New York Times*, available at https://archive.nytimes.com/www.nytimes.com/books/97/05/04/reviews/mailer-song.html (accessed 10 April 2025).

Didion, J. (1991) Sentimental journeys, available at https://www.nybooks.com/articles/1991/01/17/new-york-sentimental-journeys (accessed 10 April 2025).

Dietz, P. (1986). Mass, serial, and sensational homicides. *Annals of the NY Academy of Medicine*, 62, pp 477–491.

Doane, B., McCormick, K. and Sorce, G. (2016) Changing methods for feminist public scholarship: lessons from Sarah Koenig's podcast *Serial*. *Feminist Media Studies*, 17(1), pp 119–21.

Ditton, J., Chadee, D., Farrall, S., Gilchrist, E. and Bannister, J. (2004) From imitation to intimidation: A note on the curious and changing relationship between the media, crime and fear of crime. *British Journal of Criminology*, 44(4), pp 595–610.

Dowling, M. (2024) Lucy Letby: Retrial to begin on attempted baby murder charge. *Chester Standard*, available at www.chesterstandard.co.uk (accessed 10 June 2024).

Downing, L. (2013) *The Subject of Murder*. University of Chicago Press.

Duncan, P. and Müller, J. (2024) *Film Noir*. Taschen.

Durkheim, E. (1972) *Emile Durkheim: Selected Writings*. Cambridge University Press.

Durrani, M., Gotkin, K. and Laughlin, C. (2015) Serial, seriality, and the possibilities for the podcast format. *American Anthropologist*, 117(3), pp 593–6.

Duru, N.J. (2003) The Central Park Five, the Scottsboro Boys, and the myth of the bestial Black man. *Cardozo Law Review*, 25, pp 1315–64.

Duvernay, A. (2016) *13th*. Netflix, available from https://www.netflix.com/gb/title/80091741 (accessed 21 September 2024).

Duvernay, A. (2019) *When They See Us?*, available from https://www.netflix.com/gb/title/80200549 (accessed 10 October 2024).

Dyer, C. (2023) Martha's Rule: What could the proposed changes mean for doctors?. *BMJ*, 382, p 2067.

Ebert, R. (1997) *M.* movie review and film summary, available at www.rogerebert.com (accessed 15 April 2024).

The Economist (2023) Nicola Bulley and the era of the social media sleuth: The case of a missing Briton illustrates a big challenge for the police, available at https://www.economist.com/britain/2023/02/21/nicola-bulley-and-the-era-of-the-social-media-sleuth (accessed 10 April 2025).

Edwards, A. and Gill, P. (2002) The politics of 'transnational organized crime': Discourse, reflexivity, and the narration of 'threat'. *British Journal of Politics and International Relations*, 4(2), pp 245–70.

Egger, S.A. (2002) *The Killers Among Us: An Examination of Serial Murder and Its Investigation*. Prentice Hall.

Elton, A. (1938) *Housing Problems*. British Commercial Gas Association.

Engley, R. (2017) The impossible ethics of *Serial*: Sarah Koenig, Foucault, Lacan, in E. McCracken (ed), *The Serial Podcast and Storytelling in the Digital Age*. Routledge, pp 87–100.

Esquinazi, D.S. (2016) *Southwest of Salem: The Story of the San Antonio Four*. Motto Pictures and Naked Edge Films

European Commission (2017a) Commission outlines conditions for ending Cooperation and Verification Mechanism on judicial reform, corruption, and organised crime. Press release, available at https://ec.europa.eu/commission/presscorner/detail/en/IP_17_129 (accessed 10 April 2025).

European Commission (2017b) Report from The Commission to The European Parliament and The Council on Progress in Bulgaria under the Co-operation and Verification Mechanism SWD (2017) 24 final, available at https://eur-lex.europa.eu/legal-content/EN/TXT/PDF/?uri=CELEX:52017DC0043&from=BG (accessed 10 April 2025).

European Union (2017) Flash Eurobarometer 445: The Cooperation and Verification Mechanism for Bulgaria and Romania – third wave, available at https://data.europa.eu/data/datasets/s2128_445_eng?locale=en (accessed 11 September 2017).

Facebook (2018) Council of Europe Commissioner for Human Right post, available at https://www.facebook.com/CommissionerHR/photos/a.127151594127426/1100449100130999/?type=3&theater&_rdr (accessed 12 December 2018).

Fanning, S.E. and O'Callaghan, C. (2023) *Serial Killing on Screen: Adaptation, True Crime and Popular Culture*. Palgrave Macmillan.

Farrands, D. (2021) *Ted Bundy: American Boogeyman*. 1428 Films and Green Light Pictures.

Feifer, M. (2009) *Bundy: An American Icon*. Barnholtz Entertainment.

Fernández-Morales, M. (2023) *Survivor Memory and Rape Memoir: Chanel Miller's Know My Name*. Life Writing, online first.

Ferrell, J. (1998) Criminology verstehen, in J. Ferrell and M. Hamm (eds) *Ethnography on the Edge*. Northeastern University Press, pp 18–38.

Fincher, D. (2007) *Zodiac*. Warner Bros.

Finley, L.L. (2024) *The Death Penalty as State Crime: Who Can Kill?*. Taylor & Francis.

Fish, S. (1980) *Is There a Text in This Class? The Authority of Interpretive Communities*. Harvard University Press.

Flanagan, E. (2012) Death penalty discourses and the UK polity: A critical analysis. *Journal of Language and Politics*, 11(4), pp 521–42.

Flanders, J. (2011) *The Invention of Murder: How the Victorians Revelled in Death and Detection and Created the Modern Crime*. Thomas Dunne.

Fleischer, R. (1971) *10 Rillington Place*. Columbia Pictures

Foucault, M. (2007) *Security, Territory, Population: Lectures at the Collège de France, 1977–78*. Springer.

Foucault, M. (1972) *Archaeology of Knowledge*. Routledge.

Foucault, M. (1975) *Discipline and Punish*. Vintage Books.

Friedman, M. (2016) Capitalism and Freedom, in R. Blaug and J. Schwarzmantel (eds), *Democracy: A Reader*. Columbia University Press, pp 344–9.

Gachevska, K. (2009) *Building the New Europe: Soft Security and Organised Crime in EU Enlargement*. Unpublished PhD thesis. University of Wolverhampton, available at https://wlv.openrepository.com/bitstream/handle/2436/77554/Gachevska_PhD%20thesis.pdf?sequence=1&isAllowed=y (accessed 10 August 2024).

García, A.N. (2020) 'Tell me, what are you becoming?' Hannibal and the inescapable presence of the grotesque. *Horror Studies*, 11(1), pp 83–100.

Garland, D. (1996) The limits of the sovereign state: Strategies of crime control in contemporary society. *The British Journal of Criminology*, 36(4), pp 445–71.

Garland D. (2001) *The Culture of Control: Crime and Social Order in Contemporary Society*. Oxford University Press.

Garland, D. (2010) *Peculiar Institution: America's Death Penalty in an Age of Abolition*. Oxford University Press.

Garland, D. (2021) What's wrong with penal populism? Politics, the public, and criminological expertise. *Asian Journal of Criminology*, 16(3), pp 257–77.

Gastón-Lorente, L. and Gómez-Baceiredo, B. (2022) Fiction as an ally to make journalism more believable: rape, trauma, and secondary victimization in the Netflix miniseries 'Unbelievable'. *Feminist Media Studies*, 11(5), pp 134–51.

Gavin, H. (2009) 'Mummy wouldn't do that' the perception and construction of the female child sex abuser, in *Evil, Women and the Feminine*, 1–3 May, (Unpublished) available at https://eprints.hud.ac.uk/id/eprint/9222/7/HG_EWF2.pdf (accessed 19 July 2024).

Gibson, D.C. (2006) *Serial Murder and Media Circuses*. Bloomsbury Publishing USA.

Giddens, T. (ed) (2015) *Graphic Justice: Intersections of Comics and Law*. Routledge

Gilchrist, K. 2010. 'Newsworthy' victims? Exploring differences in Canadian local press coverage of missing/murdered Aboriginal and White women. *Feminist Media Studies*, 10(4), pp 373–90.

Gilmore, M. (1994) *Shot in the Heart*. Doubleday.

Gilmore, L. (2017) *Tainted Witness. Why We Doubt What Women Say About Their Lives*. Columbia University.

Giroux, H. (1995) Racism and the aesthetic of hyper-real violence: Pulp fiction and other visual tragedies. *Social Identities*, 1(2), pp 333–54.

Giroux, H. (2011) Neoliberalism and the death of the social state: Remembering Walter Benjamin's angel of history. *Social Identities*, 17, pp 587–601.

Godfrey, J. (2024) *The List of Suspicious Things*. Cornerstone.

Gottlieb, G. (2005) *Theater of death: Capital punishment in early America, 1750–1800*. University of Pittsburgh.

Graham, M. and Pharoah, A. (2008) *Ashes to Ashes*. Kudos Film and Television.

Grealish, S. and Goodwin, H. (2023) Killer nurse Lucy Letby is struck off and stripped of all nursing credentials after being jailed for life for murdering seven babies, available at www.mirror.co.uk (accessed 10 June 2024).

Greer, A. (2017) Murder, she spoke: The female voice's ethics of evocation and spatialisation in the true crime podcast. *Sound Studies*, 3(2), pp 152–64.

Greer, C. (2004) Crime, media, and opportunity: Grief and virtual engagement in later modernity, in J. Ferrell, K. Hayward, W. Morrison, and M. Persdee (eds) *Cultural Criminology Unleashed*. Cavendish, pp 123–32.

Greer, C. (2010) *Crime and Media: A Reader*. Routledge.

Grover, G. and Soothill, K. (1999) *British Serial Killing Towards a Structural Explanation*. The British Criminology Conferences: Selected Proceedings. Volume 2. Papers from the British Criminology Conference, Queens University, 15–19 July 1997.

Haggerty, K. (2009) Modern serial killers. *Crime, Media, Culture*, 5(2), pp 168–87.

Haggerty, K. and Ellerbrok, A. (2011) The social study of serial killers: Kevin Haggerty and Ariane Ellerbrok examine the cultural and historical context of serial killing. *Criminal Justice Matters*, 86(1), pp 6–7.

Halberstam, J, (1995) *Skin Shows: Gothic Horror and the Technology of Monsters*, Duke University Press.

Hall, S. (1986) Popular culture and the state, in Tony Bennett, Colin Mercer and Janet Woollacott (eds) *Popular Culture and Social Relations*. Open University, pp 22–49.

Hall, S. (1997) *Representation: Cultural Representations and Signifying Practices*. Sage.

Hall, S. (2006) Popular culture and the state. *The Anthropology of the State: A Reader*, 9, p 360.

Hall, S., Critcher, C., Jefferson, T., Clarke, J. and Roberts, B. (2017) *Policing the crisis: Mugging, the state, law, and order*. Bloomsbury Publishing.

Halliday, J. (2023) Lucy Letby sentenced to whole life term after murdering seven babies, *The Guardian*, 21 August.

Halliday, J. (2024) Lucy Letby loses attempt to appeal against baby murder convictions, *The Guardian*, 24 May, available at www.theguardian.com/uk-news/article/2024/may/24/lucy-letby-loses-attempt-to-appeal-against-baby-convictions (accessed 10 June 2024).

Hamerton, C. and Hobbs, S. (2022) *Privatising Criminal Justice: History, Neoliberal Penality and the Commodification of Crime*. Routledge.

Hammond, P. (1970) *Spring and Port Wine*. Anglo-Amalgamated.

Hampton, R., Rosario, D. and Lavoi, R. (2022) Should we thank Serial for Adnan Syed's release?, available at https://slate.com/culture/2022/09/serial-legacy-adnan-syed-sarah-koenig.html (accessed 13 October 2024).

Hancock, D. and McMurtry, L. (2018) 'I know what a podcast is': Post-serial fiction and podcast media identity, in R. Llinares, N. Fox and R. Berry (eds), *Podcasting: New Aural Cultures and Digital Media*. Palgrave Macmillan, pp 81–105.

Haney-López, I. (2014) *Dog Whistle Politics: How Coded Racial Appeals Have Reinvented Racism and Wrecked the Middle Class*. Oxford University Press.

Hanley, D. (2011) *The British New Wave and Its Sources*, Offscreen, 15(6), July, available at https://offscreen.com/view/british_new_wave (accessed 17 April 2024).

Hansford Johnson, P. (1967) *On Iniquity*. MacMillan.

Hanson, H. (2005) *Bones*, 20th Century Fox Television.

Harcourt, B.E. (2018) *The Counterrevolution: How Our Government Went to War Against Its Own Citizens*. Basic Books.

Hardey, M. and James, S.J. (2022) Digital seriality and narrative branching: The podcast *Serial*, season one. *Communication and Critical/Cultural Studies*, 19(1), pp 74–90.

Harris, T. (1988) *The Silence of the Lambs*. Random House

Hayek, F.A. and Caldwell, B. (2014) *The Road to Serfdom: Text and Documents: The Definitive Edition*. Routledge.

Haynes, M. (1992) Class and crisis – the transition in Eastern Europe. *International Socialism*, Spring 1992, pp 45–104.

Helgeland, B. (2011) *Legend*. Universal Pictures.

Hellman, J., Jones, G. and Kaufmann, D. (2000) Seize the state, seize the day: State capture, corruption, and influence in transition. SSRN, available at https://ssrn.com/abstract=240555 (accessed 15 August 2024).

Hersey, J. (1946) Hiroshima. *New Yorker*, available at https://www.newyorker.com/magazine/1946/08/31/hiroshima (accessed 15 August 2024).

Hess, A. (2018) The transgressive appeal of the comedy murder podcast. *New York Times*, 16 February.

Hickey, E.W. (2013) *Serial Murderers and Their Victims* (6th edn). Wadsworth.

Hinton, E., Henderson, L. and Reed, C. (2018) An unjust burden: The disparate treatment of Black Americans in the criminal justice system. *Vera Institute of Justice*, 1(1), pp 1–20.

Hitchens, P. (2010) *PACE versus Gene Hunt*, available at https://hitchensblog.mailonsunday.co.uk/2010/04/pace-versus-gene-hunt.html (accessed 27 May 2024).

Highsmith, P. (1984) Fallen *Women*, available at https://www.lrb.co.uk/the-paper/v06/n11/patricia-highsmith/fallen-women (accessed 27 May 2024).

Hoffman, M. and Hobbs, S. (2021) 'Stay sexy and don't get murdered': Depictions of female victimhood in post-Me-Too true crime, in M. Mellins and S. Moore (eds) *Critiquing Violent Crime in the Media*. Palgrave Macmillan, pp 21–53.

Holmes, R.M. and Holmes, S.T. (2009) *Serial Murder*. Sage.

Home Office (1985) *Police and Criminal Evidence Act 1984*. HMSO.

Home Office (2023) Update on our activism and impartiality in policing inspection, available at https://hmicfrs.justiceinspectorates.gov.uk/publication-html/update-on-activism-and-impartiality-in-policing/ (accessed 19 June 2025).

Hooper, T. (2012) *Les Misérables*. Universal Pictures.

Horeck, T. (2019) *Justice on Demand: True Crime in the Digital Streaming Era*. Wayne University Press.

Horeck, T. (2024) I'll be gone in the dark: Feminism and the adaptation of true crime in the #MeToo era, *New Review of Film and Television Studies*, 22(1), pp 337–59.

Horeck, T. and Negra, D. (2021) Reconsidering television true crime and gendered authority in Allen v. Farrow, *Feminist Media Studies*, 22(6), pp 1564–9.

Horvath, I. (1984) *Murder: No Apparent Motive*. Rainbow Broadcasting Co.

Huesmann, L.R. (2007) The impact of electronic media violence: Scientific theory and research. *Journal of Adolescent Health*, 41(6), pp 6–13.

Ingebretsen, E.J. (1998) Monster-making: A politics of persuasion. *Journal of American Culture*, 21(2), pp 25–34.

Ivancheva, M. (2015a) From informal to illegal: Socialist housing for Roma in Sofia. Centre for Advanced Study Sofia, available at https://www.academia.edu/16825426/Housing_for_Roma_in_post_socialist_Bulgaria (accessed 12 July 2024).

Ivancheva, M. (2015b) The spirit of the law: Mobilizing and/or professionalizing the women's movement in post-socialist Bulgaria, in Andrea Krizsan (ed) *Mobilizing for Policy Change: Women's Movements in Central and Eastern European Domestic Violence Policy Struggles*. Central European University, pp 45–84.

Jarecki, A., Durst, R., Jarecki, A. and Napoli, G. (2013) *The Jinx: The Life and Deaths of Robert Durst*. HBO.

Jarrold, I., March, J. and Tucker, A. (2009) *The Red Riding Trilogy*. Resolution Films.

Jarrold, J. (2011) *Appropriate Adult*. ITV.

Jarvis, B. (2007) Monsters Inc: Serial killer and consumer culture, *Crime, Media, Culture*, 3, pp 326–44.

Jena, S. (2023) Ann Rule's *The Stranger Beside Me*: A curious work of criminal biography. *The Criterion*, available at https://www.the-criterion.com/V14/n6/AM05.pdf (accessed 19 August 2024).

Jenkins, P. (1994) *Using Murder: The Social Construction of Serial Homicide*. Routledge.

Jennings, H. (1942) *Listen to Britain*. Crown Film Unit.

Jewkes, Y. (2008) *Offending Media: The Social Construction of Offenders, Victims, and the Probation Service*. London Willan Publishing

Jewkes, Y. (2019) The construction of crime news (2004), in C. Greer (ed), *Crime and Media*. Routledge, pp 215–27.

Jiwani, Y. and Young, M.L. (2006) Missing and murdered women: reproducing marginality in news discourse. *Canadian Journal of Communication*, 31, pp 895–917.

Jones, C. (2017) Jack the Ripper and the commodification of sexual violence, available at https://theconversation.com/jack-the-ripper-and-the-commodification-of-sexual-violence-87232 (accessed 27 May 2024).

Jouve, N.W. (1986) *'The Streetcleaner': The Yorkshire Ripper Case on Trial*. Marion Boyars Publishers.

Katz, I. (2017) Ann Rule, a high life of crime. *The Guardian*, available at https://www.theguardian.com/books/2017/dec/19/ann-rule-author-high-life-of-crime-archive-1994 (accessed 13 October 2024).

Katz, Z. (1988) *Seductions of Crime: Moral and Sensual Attractions in Doing Evil*. Basic Books.

Kaufman, E. (2019) Fact check: Are violent video games connected to school shootings?. *CNN*, 5 August.

Kavalski, E. (2003) Bulgaria: The state of chaos, *Southeast European Politics*, 4(1), pp 69–90.

Kelleher, M.D. and Kelleher, C.L. (1998) *Murder Most Rare: The Female Serial Killer*. Praeger. Angels.

Kelton, E. (1991) The Myth of the Mythical West. *Western American Literature*, 26(1), pp 3–8.

Kendall, E. (2020) *The Phantom Prince: My Life with Ted Bundy*. Abrams.

Keppel, R.D. and Birnes, W.J. (2010) *The Riverman: Ted Bundy and I Hunt for the Green River Killer*. Simon and Schuster.

Kesey K. (2005) *One Flew Over the Cuckoo's Nest*. Penguin.

Kincheloe, J.L. (2001) Describing the bricolage: Conceptualising a new rigor in qualitative research. *Qualitative Inquiry*, 7(6), pp 679–92.

Kincheloe, J.L. (2005) Onto the next level: Continuing the conceptualisation of the bricolage. *Qualitative Inquiry*, 11(3), pp 323–50.

King, M. (2013) *Men, Masculinity, and the Beatles*. Ashgate.

King, M. and Cummins, I. (2013) 'Dead cities, crows, the rain and their ripper, the Yorkshire ripper': The Red Riding Novels (1974, 1977, 1980, 1983) of David Peace as Lieux d'horreur. *International Journal of Criminology and Sociological Theory*, 6(3), pp 43–56.

King, M., Foley, M. and Cummins, I. (2016) The strange case of Ian Stuart Brady and the mental health tribunal. *The Internet Journal of Criminology*, available at e-space.mmu.ac.uk (accessed 10 June 2024).

Kinnell, H. (2008) *Violence and Sex Work in Britain*. Willan.

Krustev, I. (2014) *Shifting Obsessions: Three Essays on the Politics of Anticorruption*. Central European University Press.

Krustev, I. (2017) The rise of the paranoid citizen. *New York Times*, 16 March 2017, available at https://www.nytimes.com/2017/03/16/opinion/the-rise-of-the-paranoid-citizen.html (accessed 10 December 2018).

LaChance, D. and Kaplan, P. (2019) The seductions of crimesploitation: The apprehension of sex offenders on primetime television. *Law, Culture and the Humanities*, 15(1), pp 127–50.

Laclau, E. (2006) Why constructing a people is the main task of radical politics. *Critical Inquiry*, 32(4), pp 646–80.

Lake, P. (1990) Puritanism, Arminianism, and a Shropshire axe-murder. *Midland History*, 15(1), pp 37–64.

La Lane, D. (2005) Revolution, class, and globalisation in the transition from state socialism. *European Societies*, 7(1), pp 131–55.

Landsel, D. (2024) Jack the Ripper's face finally revealed – here's what AI thinks the notorious prostitute killer looked like, *New York Post*, available at: https://nypost.com/2024/02/16/lifestyle/heres-what-jack-the-ripper-looked-like-according-to-ai/ (accessed 19 June 2025).

Lang, F. (1931) *M*. Nero-Film A.G.

Larke-Walsh, G.S. (2019) 'The King's Shilling': How 'Peaky Blinders' uses the experience of war to justify and celebrate toxic masculinity. *Journal of Popular Television*, 7(1), pp 39–56.

Larke-Walsh, G.S. (2020) Injustice narratives in a post-truth society: Emotional discourses and social purpose in Southwest of Salem: The story of the San Antonio four. *Studies in Documentary Film*, 15(1), pp 89–104.

Larsen, R.W. (2019) *Bundy: The Deliberate Stranger*. Simon & Schuster.

Langford, B. (2003) Revisiting the 'Revisionist' Western. *Film & History: An Interdisciplinary Journal of Film and Television Studies*, 33(2), pp 26–35.

Latif, L. (2023) Surviving R. Kelly part III: The Final Chapter review – this glorious series has helped to make history, *The Guardian*, 3 April.

Lee, C.A. (2010) *One of Your Own: The Life and Death of Myra Hindley*. Mainstream Publishing.

Lennon, J.M. (2013) *Norman Mailer: A Double Life*. Simon and Schuster.

Leskewiecz, A. (2023) *The Lucy Letby Industry*, New Statesman, 45, pp 1–7.

Leung, R. and Williams, R. (2019) #MeToo and intersectionality: An examination of the #MeToo Movement through the R. Kelly scandal. *Journal of Communication Inquiry*, 43(4), pp 349–71.

Leyton, E. (1986) *Hunting Humans: The Rise of the Modern Multiple Murderer*. McClelland & Stewart.

Levi Strauss, C. (1972) *The Savage Mind* (2nd edn). Weidenfeld and Nicholson.

Lincoln, Y. (2001) An emerging new bricoleur: Promises and possibilities. A reaction to Joe Kincheloe's 'Describing the Bricolage'. *Qualitative Inquiry*, 11(3), pp 350–72.

Linder, M. and Chao, S. (1988–2021) *America's Most Wanted*. Fox.

Linders, A. (2002) The execution spectacle and state legitimacy: The changing nature of the American execution audience, 1833–1937. *Law & Society Review*, 36(3), pp 607–55.

Lindgren, M. (2016) Personal narrative journalism and podcasting. *The Radio Journal: International Studies in Broadcast & Audio Media*, 14(1), pp 23–41.

Linebaugh, P. (1977) The ordinary of Newgate and his account, in J.S. Cockburn (ed) *Crime in England 1550–1800*. Taylor and Francis, pp 246–269.

Linebaugh, P. (1991) *The London Hanged: Crime and Civil Society in the Eighteenth Century*. Penguin.

Linedecker, C.L. (1993) *The Man Who Killed Boys: The John Wayne Gacy, Jr Story*. Basingstoke Macmillan.

Linnemann, T. (2015) Capote's ghosts: Violence, media and the spectre of suspicion. The *British Journal of Criminology*, 55(3), pp 514–33.

Lloyd, A. and Whitehead, P. (2018) Kicked to the curb: The triangular trade of neoliberal polity, social insecurity, and penal expulsion. *International Journal of Law, Crime and Justice*, 55, pp 60–9.

Loving, J. (2016) From solitary to the city: Norman Mailer's bet on Jack Henry Abbott. *The Mailer Review*, 10(1), pp 129–35.

Mackay, F. (2015) *Radical Feminism: Feminist Activism in Movement*. Palgrave Macmillan.

MacMillan, K. (2016) True crime reporting in Early Modern England. *Oxford Research Encyclopedia of Criminology*, available at https://oxfordre.com/criminology/view/10.1093/acrefore/9780190264079.001.0001/acrefore-9780190264079-e-164 (accessed 8 January 2025).

Maher, B. (2024) New Yorker defies contempt risk to Publish Lucy Letby story in UK print edition. Media Law, available at pressgazette.co.uk (accessed 18 May 2024).

Mailer, N, (1985) *The Prisoner of Sex*. Little Brown.

Mailer, N. (2007) *Oswald's Tale: An American Mystery*. Random House.

Mailer, N. (2012) *The Executioner's Song*. Hachette UK.

Mailer, N. (2017) The white Negro, in L. Wilson and M. Keunen (eds), *On Bohemia: The Code of the Self-Exiled*. Routledge, pp 185–94.

Mailer, N. (2018a) *The Naked and the Dead*. Penguin UK.

Mailer, N. (2018b) *The Armies of the Night: History as a Novel/The Novel as History*. Penguin Modern Classics.

Mangan, L. (2019) *Conversations With a Killer: The Ted Bundy Tapes* review – harrowing, but pointlessly so, *The Guardian*, 24 January, available at: www.theguardian.com/tv-and-radio/2019/jan/24/conversations-with-killer-ted-bundy-tapes-review (accessed 19 June 2025).

Mangan, L. (2020) *Des* review: David Tennant excels as a perfectly ordinary serial killer. *The Guardian*, available at https://www.theguardian.com/tv-and-radio/2020/sep/14/des-review-david-tennant-excels-as-a-perfectly-ordinary-serial-killer#:~:text=Rare%20it%20is%20to%20watch,would%20surely%20have%20hated%20it. (accessed 23 May 2024).

Mangan, L. (2021) *Football's Darkest Secret* review: Spare & unrelenting. *The Guardian*, available at https://www.theguardian.com/tv-and-radio/2021/mar/22/footballs-darkest-secret-review-spare-and-unrelenting (accessed 18 February 2025).

Marinos, M. (2021) The media in South-East Europe after 1989, in N. Daskalova and H. Sittig (eds), *Three Decades Later: The Media in Southeast Europe after 1989*. University of Illinois Press.

Marionos, M. (2023) *Free to Hate: How Media Liberalization Enabled Right-Wing Populism in Post-1993 Bulgaria*. University of Illinois Press.

Martinson, R. (1974) What works? Questions and answers about prison reform. *The Public Interest*, 35(2), pp 22–54.

Masters, B. (1985) *Killing for Company*. Arrow Books.

Matera, D. (2021) *Ed Kemper: Conversations with a Killer: The Shocking True Story of the Co-Ed Butcher*. Union Square & Co.

Mayr, A. (2012) Chopper: From the inside: Discourses of the 'celebrity' criminal Mark Brandon Read. *Language and Literature*, 21(3), pp 260–73.

McCabe, R. (2022) Conversations with a killer: The Ted Bundy tapes and affective responses to the true crime documentary. *Studies in Documentary Film*, 16(1), pp 38–54.

McCann, B.J. (2021) Duplicity and the depraved uncanny in mediations of Ted Bundy. *Women's Studies in Communication*, 44(3), pp 340–59.

McClain, A. (2019) *The Case Against Adnan Syed*. HBO.

McDonald, C. (2023) The unexpected face of evil. *Prospect*, available at prospectmagazine.co.uk (accessed 9 April 2024).

McGowen, R. (1994) Civilizing punishment: The end of the public execution in England. *Journal of British Studies*, 33(3), pp 257–82.

McIntyre, L. (2018) *Post-Truth*. MIT Press.

McNamara, M. (2018) *I'll Be Gone in the Dark: One Woman's Obsessive Search for the Golden State Killer*. Faber & Faber.

McRobbie, A. (2009) *The Aftermath of Feminism: Gender, Culture and Social Change*. Sage.

Mead, R. (2017) Norman Mailer's Snarling Encounter with Feminism, Restaged in Trump's America. *New Yorker*, available at https://www.newyorker.com/culture/cultural-comment/norman-mailers-snarling-encounter-with-feminism-restaged-in-trumps-america (accessed 12 July 2024).

Meili, T. (2003) *I Am the Central Park Jogger: A Story of Hope and Possibility*. Simon and Schuster.

Meindl, J.N. (2017) Mass shootings: The role of the media in promoting generalized imitation. *American Journal of Public Health*, 107(3), pp 368–70.

Menis, S. (2021) The deceased accused and the victim as a commodity: Jimmy Savile as a case study to examine the role of the real-crime documentary in reproducing violence as entertainment, in M. Mellins and S. Moore (eds) *Critiquing Violent Crime in the Media*. Palgrave Macmillan, pp 21–53.

Menshaway, R. and Menshaway, E. (2023) Brave Clarice: Healthcare service killers, patterns, motives. *Forensic Science, Medicine, and Pathology*, 19, pp 452–63.

Menual, C. (2005) *See No Evil: The Moors Murders*. Granada TV.

Merrick, I. (1977) *The Black Panther*. Alpha Films.

Messing, J.T., AbiNader, M.A., Pizarro, J.M., Zeoli, A.M., Loerzel, E., Bent-Goodley, T. and Campbell, J. (2023) Femicide in the United States, in *The Routledge International Handbook on Femicide and Feminicide*. Routledge, pp 288–97.

Michaud, S.G. and Aynesworth, H. (2000) *Ted Bundy: Conversations with a Killer*. Authorlink.

Millett, K. (1970) *Sexual Politics*. Doubleday.

Mills, C.W. (2000) *The Sociological Imagination*. Oxford University Press.

Milne, P. (1975) *Angels*. BBC TV.

Mishra, S. and Shewan, K. (2023) Surviving R. Kelly: A budding space for Black feminist discourses? *Feminist Media Studies*, 24(7), pp 1465–81.

Motion, A. (2011) The Invention of Murders by Judith Flanders – review. *The Guardian*, 8 January, available at www.theguardian.com/books/2011/jan/08/invention-of-murder-judith-flanders-review (accessed 6 January 2025).

Moritz, J. and Coffey, J. (2024) Lucy Letby: Courtroom drama, a failed appeal, and battles over the truth. BBC News, available at bbc.co.uk/news/articles/c727jgdm7r40 (accessed 4 July 2024).

Morrison, B. (2003) The killing suit. *The Guardian*, available at www.theguardian.com/books/2003/mar/15/featuresreviews.guardianreview8 (accessed 6 June 2024).

Mullin, C. (1986) *Error of Judgment: The Truth about the Birmingham Bombings* Chatto.

Mumford, G. (2016) *Making a Murder*. The Netflix documentary beating TV drama at its own game. *The Guardian*, available at www.theguardian.com/tv-and-radio/tvandradioblog/2016/jan/07/making-a-murderer-the-netflix-documentary-beating-tv-drama-at-its-own-game (accessed 12 July 2024).

Murley, J. (2008) *The Rise of True Crime: Twentieth Century Murder and American Popular Culture*. Routledge.

Myers, B. (2019) Fred and Rose: Gordon Burn's journey to the grubby heart of England. *The Guardian*, available at www.theguardian.com/books/2019/sep/26/gordon-burn-england-happy-like-murderers-fred-rose-west (accessed 27 May 2024).

Nelson, R. (1970) *Soldier Blue*. Embassy Pictures.

Newburn, T. and Jones, T. 2005. Symbolic politics and penal populism: The long shadow of Willie Horton. *Crime, Media, Culture*, 1(1), pp 72–87.

Newson, E. (1994) *Video Violence and the Protection of Children, Report of the Home Affairs Committee*. HMSO.

Newman, S. (1963) *Dr Who*. BBC TV.

Nhan, J., Huey, L. and Broll R. (2015) Digilantism: An analysis of crowdsourcing and the Boston Marathon bombings. *British Journal of Criminology*, 57(2), pp 341–61.

Nichol, A. (2024) My sister was murdered thirty years ago: True crime repackages our pain as entertainment. *The New York Times*, available at (www.nytimes.com/2024/01/08/opinion/movies-books-true-crime.html) (accessed 21 May 2024).

Nicholson, R. (2019) Making a murderer: Part 2 review – Netflix's grisly mystery continues to enthral. *The Guardian*, available at www.theguardian.com/tv-and-radio/2018/oct/19/making-a-murderer-season-2-review (accessed 1 August 2024).

REFERENCES

Nieto, D. (2012) Neoliberalism, biopolitics, and the governance of transnational crime. *Colombia Internacional*, 76, pp 137–65.

Nora, P. (1989) Between memory and history: Les lieux de memoire. *Representations*, 26, pp 7–24.

Nozick, R. (1974) *Anarchy, State, and Utopia*. Basic Books

NPCC (2024) *Violence Against Women and Girls*, available at https://www.npcc.police.uk/our-work/violence-against-women-and-girls/ (accessed 19 June 2025).

Nuttall, N. (2009) Cold blooded journalism: Truman Capote and the non-fiction novel, in H. Bloom (ed) *Truman Capote*. Chelsea House, pp 173–88.

NY Times (1973) Aide to Washington's Governor posed as student in Foe's camp, 30 August, available at www.nytimes.com/1973/08/30/archives/aide-to-washingtons-governor-posed-as-student-in-foes-camp.html (accessed 19 June 2025).

O'Donoghue, D. and Moritz, J. (2023) The Lucy Letby inquiry, BBC News, available at bbc.co.uk/news/uk-england-merseyside-67488797 (accessed 9 April 24).

O'Hagan, A. (1995) *The Missing*. Picador.

Oleson, J.C. (2005) King of killers: The criminological theories of Hannibal Lecter, part one. *Journal of Criminal Justice and Popular Culture*, 12(3), pp 186–210.

Oleson, J.C. (2006) Contemporary demonology: The criminological theories of Hannibal Lecter, part two. *Journal of Criminal Justice and Popular Culture*, 13(1), pp 29–49.

Osborne, J. (1956) *Look Back in Anger*. Faber and Faber.

Pâquet, L. (2018) Literary forensic rhetoric: Maps, emotional assent, and rhetorical space in *Serial* and *Making a Murderer*. *Law and Humanities*, 12(1), pp 71–92.

Pâquet, L. (2021) Seeking justice elsewhere: Informal and formal justice in the true crime podcasts *Trace* and *The Teacher's Pet*. *Crime, Media, Culture*, 17(3), pp 421–37.

Patterson, J. (2012) Why *The Black Panther* can hold its head up high. *The Guardian*, available at omp.guardian.com (accessed 15 May 2024).

Pavelko, R.L. and Myrick, J.G. (2019) Murderinos and media effects: How the *My Favorite Murder* podcast and its social media community may promote well-being in audiences with mental illness. *Journal of Radio & Audio Media*, 27(1), pp 151–69.

Peabody Awards (2014) Serial, available at: https://peabodyawards.com/award-profile/serial/ (accessed 19 June 2025).

Peace, D. (2008a) *1974*. Serpent's Tail.

Peace, D. (2008b) *1977*. Serpent's Tail.

Peace, D. (2008c) *1980*. Serpent's Tail.

Peace, D. (2008d) *1983*. Serpent's Tail

Peelo, M. (2006) Framing homicide narratives in newspapers: Mediated witness and the construction of virtual victimhood. *Crime Media Culture*, 2(2), pp 159–75.

Pégorier, C. (2024) Graphic narrative as alternative jurisdiction. *Law and Literature*, pp 1–25.

Pelot-Hobbs, L. (2023) *Prison Capital: Mass Incarceration and Struggles for Abolition Democracy in Louisiana*. UNC Press Books.

Penfold-Mounce, R. (2010) *Celebrity Culture and Crime: The Joy of Transgression*. Palgrave Macmillan.

Penfold-Mounce, R. (2016) Corpses, popular culture, and forensic science: Public obsession with death. *Mortality*, 21(1), pp 19–35.

Penfold-Mounce, R. (2020) Value, bodily capital, and gender inequality after death. *Sociological Research Online*, 25(3), pp 490–506.

Petridis, A. (2017) 'Columbine destroyed my entire career': Marilyn Manson on the travails of being the lord of darkness. *The Guardian*, available at https://www.theguardian.com/music/2017/sep/21/columbine-destroyed-my-entire-career-marilyn-manson-on-the-perils-of-being-the-lord-of-darkness (accessed 6 August 2024).

Peters, C. (2005) *Harold Shipman: Mind Set on Murder*. Carlton Books.

Platten, D. (2022) Damaged goods? The edginess of true crime. *Crime Fiction Studies*, 3(2), pp 140–58.

Plimpton, G. (1966) The story behind a nonfiction novel. *The New York Times*, 16 January, available at https://archive.nytimes.com/www.nytimes.com/books/97/12/28/home/capote-interview.html?r=1 (accessed 18 June 2025).

Prejean, H. (1993) *Dead Man Walking: An Eyewitness Account of the Death Penalty in the United States*. Random House.

Prejean, H. (2006). *The Death of Innocents: An Eyewitness Account of Wrongful Executions*. Hymns Ancient and Modern Ltd.

Presdee, M. (2000) *Cultural Criminology and the Carnival of Crime*. Routledge.

Press Association (2013) Woman admits murdering three men found stabbed to death in ditches. *The Guardian*, available at www.guardian.com (accessed 10 June 2024).

Presser, L. (2008) *Been a Heavy Life: Stories of Violent Men*. University of Illinois Press.

Punnett, I.C. (2018) *Toward a Theory of True Crime Narratives: A Textual Analysis*. Routledge.

Rackstraw, E. (2023) *When Reality TV Creates Reality: How 'Copaganda' Affects Police, Communities, and Viewers*. SSRN, available at: https://ssrn.com/abstract=4592803 (accessed 19 June 2025).

Raeside, J. (2016) Ripper Street: a ridiculously underrated Victorian crime thriller, The Guardian, 14 October, available at: www.theguardian.com/tv-and-radio/tvandradioblog/2016/oct/14/ripper-street-a-ridiculously-underrated-victorian-thriller (accessed 19 June 2025).

Rafter, N. (2007) Crime, film, and criminology: Recent sex-crime movies. *Theoretical Criminology*, 11(3), pp 403–20.

Rafter, N. and Brown, M. (2011) *Criminology Goes to the Movies: Crime Theory and Popular Culture*. New York University Press.

Ramey, J. (2004) The bloody blonde and the marble woman: Gender and power in the case of Ruth Snyder. *Journal of Social History*, 37(3), pp 625–50.

Ramsland, K. (2007) *Inside the Minds of Healthcare Serial Killers: Why They Kill*. Bloomsbury.

Rangan, P, and Story B. (2021) Four propositions on true crime and abolition, in Alexandra Juhasz and Alisa Lebow (eds) *World Records*, Vol. 5, Article 16. https://worldrecordsjournal.org/category/volume-5/ (accessed 18 February 2024).

Rawlings, P. (1992) *Drunks, Whores, and Idle Apprentices: Criminal Biographies of the Eighteenth Century*. Routledge.

Rawlings, P. (1998) True crime. *British Criminology Conferences*, Vol. 1, available at www.britsoccrim.org/volume1/010.pdf (accessed 10 October 2023).

Ray, L. (2018) *Violence and Society*. Sage.

Raymen, T. and Smith O. (2019) Introduction, in T. Raymen and O. Smith (eds) *Deviant Leisure: Criminological Perspectives on Leisure and Harm*. Routledge, pp 1–19.

Redhead, S. (2010) Lock, stock and two smoking hooligans: low sport journalism and hit-and-tell literature. *Soccer & Society*, 11(5), pp 627–42.

Reiner, R. (2010) *The Politics of the Police*. Oxford University Press.

Reisz, K. (1961) *Saturday Night and Sunday Morning*. Woodfall/Bryanston Films.

Renck, J. (2019) *Chernobyl*. HBO/SKY UK.

Ressler, R.K., Burgess, A.W., Douglas, J.E., Hartman, C.R. and D'Agostino, R.B. (1986) Sexual killers and their victims: Identifying patterns through crime scene analysis. *Journal of Interpersonal Violence*, 1(3), pp 288–308.

Ricciardi, L. and Demos, M. (2015) *Making a Murderer*. Netflix and Synthesis Films.

Richards, D. (2000) *This Is Personal: The Hunt for the Yorkshire Ripper*. Granada TV.

Richardson, T. (1959) *Look Back in Anger*. Warner Bros.

Richardson, T. (1960) *The Entertainer*. Woodfall/Bryanston Films.

Richardson, T. (1961) *A Taste of Honey*. British Lion Films.

Richardson, T. (1962) *The Loneliness of the Long-Distance Runner*. British Lion Films.

Ricks, C. (2008) Norman Mailer's *The Executioner's Song*. *The Mailer Review*, 2(1), pp 483–94.

Rios, S.B. (2020) Rebalancing the extra-judicial scales: Documentary aesthetics and the legacy of the Central Park Five. *Synthesis: An Anglophone Journal of Comparative Literary Studies*, (13), pp 70–92.

Roberts, L. (2008) The question of space: A renew essay, *Humanities*, 7(42), pp 1–8.

Roberts, L. (2018) Spatial Bricolage: The art of poetically making do. *Humanities*, 7(43). https://doi.org/10.3390/h7020043

Robertson, R. (2019) The shocking letter Yorkshire Ripper Peter Sutcliffe wrote to Wearside Jack hoaxer John Humble in prison, *Sunderland Echo*, available at www.sunderlandecho.com/news/crime/the-shocking-letter-yorkshire-ripper-peter-sutcliffe-wrote-to-wearside-jack-hoaxer-john-humble-in-prison-491142 (accessed 19 June 2025).

Rodgers, K. (2022) 'F★cking politeness' and 'staying sexy' while doing it: Intimacy, interactivity and the feminist politics of true crime podcasts. *Feminist Media Studies*, 23(6), pp 3048–63.

Rojek, C. (2001) *Celebrity*. Reaktion.

Rowland, A. (2023) The real Lucy Letby: The evil nurse who killed innocent babies. *Take A Break*, 19/01, pp 15–16,

Rubenhold, H. (2019) *The Five: The Untold Lives of the Women Killed by Jack the Ripper*. Houghton Mifflin.

Ruffert, C. (2019) Instrument of social enquiry: The British documentary film movement of the 1930s. *Research in Film and History*, 2, pp 1–10.

Rule, A. (2000) *The Stranger Beside Me*. First published in 1980. Norton.

Saltzman, R.H. (1995) 'This buzz is for you': Popular responses to the Ted Bundy execution. *Journal of Folklore Research*, 32(2), pp 101–19.

Sawyer, M. (2014) *Serial* review: The greatest murder mystery you will ever hear. *The Guardian*, available at https://www.theguardian.com/media/2014/nov/08/serial-review-greatest-murder-mystery-ever-hear) (accessed 19 July 2024).

Schiller, L. (1970) *The Killing of Sharon Tate*. Signet.

Schlesinger, J. (1962) *A Kind of Loving*. Anglo-Amalgamated.

Schmid, D. (2006) Idols of destruction: Celebrity and the serial killer, in S. Homes and S. Redmond (eds) Framing Celebrity: New Directions in Celebrity Culture. Routledge, pp 295–310.

Schmid, D. (2008) *Natural Born Celebrities: Serial Killers in American Culture*. Routledge.

Schlesinger, J. (1963) *Billy Liar*. Warner-Pathe.

Seal, L. (2014) *Capital Punishment in Twentieth Century Britain: Audience, Justice, Memory*. Routledge.

Sears, J. (1995) 'Crimewatch' and the rhetoric of verisimilitude. *Critical Survey*, 7(1), pp 51–58.

Seltzer, M. (1998) *Serial Killers: Death and Life in America's Wound Culture*. Routledge.

Seltzer, M. (2004) The crime system. *Critical Inquiry*, 30(3), pp 557–83.

Seltzer, M. (2007) *True Crime: Observations on Violence and Modernity*. Routledge.

Seltzer, M. (2008) Murder/media/modernity. *Canadian Review of American Studies*, 38(1), pp 11–41.

Seltzer, M. (2013) *Serial Killers: Death and Life in America's Wound Culture*. Routledge.

Serisier, T. (2018) *Speaking Out: Feminism, Rape and Narrative Politics*. Palgrave Macmillan.

Shankman, A. (2007) *Hairspray*. Ingenious Media.

Sharon, T. and John, N.A. (2019) Imagining an ideal podcast listener. *Popular Communication*, 17(4), pp 333–47.

Shaw, K. (2012) (Dis)locations: Post-industrial gothic in David Peace's Red Riding Quartet. *The Review of Contemporary Fiction*, 32(3), pp 62–72.

Shelden, R.G. and Vasiliev, P.V. (2017) *Controlling the Dangerous Classes: A History of Criminal Justice in America*. Waveland Press.

Sherrill, L.A. (2020) The '*Serial* effect' and the true crime podcast ecosystem, *Journalism Practice*, 16(7), pp 1473–94.

Siegal, D. (1971) *Dirty Harry*. Warner Bros.

Simon, J. (2007) *Governing Through Crime: How the War on Crime Transformed American Democracy and Created a Culture of Fear*. Oxford University Press.

Simon, J. (2014) *Mass Incarceration on Trial: A Remarkable Court Decision and the Future of Prisons in America*. The New Press.

Simpson, O.J. (1995) *I Want to Tell You: My Response to Your Letters, Your Messages, Your Questions*. Little, Brown Books.

Simpson, P.L. (2000) *Psychopaths: Tracking the Serial Killer Through Contemporary American Film and Fiction*. SIU Press.

Sitford, M. (2000) *Addicted to Murder: The True Story of Dr Harold Shipman*. Virgin Books.

Skolnick, J.H. (2011) *Justice without Trial: Law Enforcement in Democratic Society*. Quid Pro Books.

Sky News – Courts (2023) Gunman who shot dead Olivia Pratt-Korbel, 9, jailed for at least 42 years, available at: https://www.youtube.com/watch?v=JbnBBhEhgzo (accessed 30 July 2025).

Slakoff, D.C. (2020) The representation of women and girls of color in United States crime news. *Sociology Compass*, 14(1), e127–e141.

Slakoff, D.C. and Duran, D. (2023) A new media frontier, or more of the same? A descriptive analysis of the 'missing white woman syndrome' in top true crime podcasts. *Race and Justice*. https://doi.org/10.1177/21533687231199271.

Smith, J. (2020) Laying bare the war: Responses to the My Lai Massacre and the trial of Lt William Calley in American public opinion. *The Ascendant Historian*, 7(1), pp 68–83.

Smith, J. (2013) *Misogynies*. Saqi.

Smith, O. and Raymen, T. (2016) Deviant leisure: A criminological perspective. *Theoretical Criminology*, 22(1), pp 163–82.

Solea, A.I. and Sugiura, L. (2023) Mainstreaming the Blackpill: Understanding the Incel commu nity on TikTok. *European Journal of Criminal Policy Research*, 29, pp 311–36.

Sontag, S. (1977) In Plato's cave, in S. Sontag (ed) *On Photography.* Farrar, Strauss, and Giroud, pp 3–24).

Sparks, R. (1992) *Television and the Drama of Crime: Moral Tales and the Place of Crime in Public Life.* Open University Press.

Spassov, O. (2021) The media in South East Europe after 1989, in M. Daskalova and H. Sitting (eds) *Three Decades Later.* Konrad-Adenauer-Stiftung, available at https://www.academia.edu/106053383/The_Media_in_South_East_Europe_after_1989_Media_and_Capitalism?rhid=29563222850&swp=rr-rw-wc-105708940 (accessed 12 August 2024).

Springhall, J. (1994) 'Pernicious reading?' 'The Penny Dreadful' as scapegoat for late-Victorian juvenile crime. *Victorian Periodicals Review*, 27(4), pp 326–49.

Stanko, E.A. (1993) The case of fearful women: Gender, personal safety and fear of crime. *Women & Criminal Justice*, 4(1), pp 117–35.

Steiker, C.S. and Steiker J.M. (2016) *Courting Death: The Supreme Court and Capital Punishment.* Belknap Press.

Storrs, E. (2004) 'Our scapegoat': An exploration of media representations of Myra Hindley and Rose West. *Theology & Sexuality*, 11(1) pp 9–28.

Strid, S. Walby, S. and Armstrong, J. (2013) Intersectionality and multiple inequalities: Visibility in British policy on violence against women. *Social Politics*, 20(4), pp 558–81.

Sullivan, K. (2019) *Ted Bundy's Murderous Mysteries: The Many Victims of America's Most Infamous Serial Killer.* Wild Blue Press.

Sullivan, K. (2020) *The Bundy Murders: A Comprehensive History.* McFarland.

Sweeting, A. (2000) In the land of plod, *The Guardian*, available at https://www.theguardian.com/media/2000/jan/27/tvandradio.television1 (accessed 27 August 2025).

Tabbert, U. (2012) Crime through a corpus: The linguistic construction of offenders in the British Press, in G. Gregoriou (ed) *Constructing Crime: Discourse and Cultural Representations of Crime and 'Deviance'.* Palgrave Macmillan, pp 130–44.

Telegraph and Argus (2003) Police re-examine 'Ripper's clothing', 10 March, available at www.thetelegraphandargus.co.uk/news/8016890.police-re-examine-rippers-clothing/ (accessed 19 June 2025)

Thompson, H. (2017) *Blood in the Water: The Attica Prison Uprising of 1971 and Its Legacy.* Pantheon.

Thompson, H.S. (2012) *Fear and Loathing on the Campaign Trail '72.* Simon & Schuster.

Thorne, H. (2022) From backlash to backtrack: How the supreme court reneged on the promise of 'Furman v Georgia'. *Law & History: Journal of the Australian and New Zealand Law and History Society*, 9(1), pp 158–87.

Thorpe, V. (2024) Why row over Baby Reindeer sleuths will change real-life drama forever, *The Guardian*, available at https://www.theguardian.com/tv-and-radio/2024/apr/28/baby-reindeer-sleuths-real-life-drama-netflix-debate-identities (accessed 19 July 2024).

Tompkins, P.K. (1966) In cold fact. *Esquire*, available at https://classic.esquire.com/article/1966/6/1/in-cold-fact (accessed 18 February 2024).

Topping, P. (1989) *Topping: The Autobiography of the Police Chief in the Moors Murder Case*. Angus & Robertson.

Touquet, H. and Schulz, P. (2021) Navigating vulnerabilities and masculinities: How gendered contexts shape the agency of male sexual violence survivors. *Security Dialogue*, 52(3), pp 213–30.

Toynbee, P. (2023) Faced with evil like Lucy Letby's we yearn for a rational explanation: Sometimes there is none, *The Guardian*, available at theguardian.com/comment-is-free/2023/Aug/18/Lucy-Letby-rational-explanation-inquiry (accessed 9 April 2024).

Trager, J. and Brewster, J. (2001) The effectiveness of psychological profiles. *Journal of Police and Criminal Psychology*, 16(1), pp 20–8.

Twitter (now X) (2018) Frans Timmermans post at 10:16pm, 7 October 2018, available at https://x.com/F__Timmermans/status/1049015690152300544, (accessed 12 October 2018).

Vicary, A.M. and Fraley, R.C. (2010) Captured by true crime: Why are women drawn to tales of rape, murder, and serial killers? *Social Psychological and Personality Science*, 1(1), pp 81–6.

Vitale, A.S. (2021) *The End of Policing*. Verso Books.

Voss, R.F. (2011) *Truman Capote and the Legacy of* In Cold Blood. University of Alabama Press.

Wacquant, L. (2001) Deadly symbiosis: When ghetto and prison meet and mesh. *Punishment & Society*, 3(1), pp 95–133.

Wacquant, L. (2002) From slavery to mass incarceration. *New Left Review*, 13(January–February), pp 41–60.

Wacquant, L. (2009a) *Prisons of Poverty*. UM Press.

Wacquant, L. (2009b) *Punishing the Poor: The Neoliberal Government of Social Insecurity*. Duke University Press.

Wacquant, L. (2010) Urban desolation and symbolic denigration in the hyperghetto. *Social Psychology Quarterly*, 20(2) (Summer 2010), pp 1–5.

Wacquant, L. (2012) Probing the meta-prison, in Preface to J.I. Ross (ed), *The Globalization of Supermax Prisons*. Rutgers University Press, pp 5–13.

Wakeman, S. (2013) 'No one wins. One side just loses more slowly': The Wire and drug policy. *Theoretical Criminology*, 18(2) pp 224–40.

Walby, S. (2023) Authoritarianism, violence, and varieties of gender regimes: Violence as an institutional domain. *Women's Studies International Forum*, 98(4), p 102677.

Walkowitz, J.R. (1982) Jack the Ripper and the myth of male violence. *Feminist Studies*, 8(3), pp 543–74.

Wattis, L. (2017) Revisiting the Yorkshire Ripper murders: Interrogating gender violence, sex work, and justice. *Feminist Criminology*, 12(1), pp 3–21.

Wattis, L. (2018) *Revisiting the Yorkshire Ripper Murders*. Springer International Publishing.

Wattis, L. (2020) Violence, emotion, and place: The case of five murders involving sex workers. *Crime, Media, Culture*, 16(2), pp 201–19.

Wattis, L. (2022) Analysing local newspaper coverage of murders involving street sex workers. *Feminist Media Studies*, 22(2), pp 425–40.

Wattis, L. (2023) The cultural scope and criminological potential of the 'hardman story'. *Crime, Media, Culture*, 19(1), pp 40–57.

Wattis, L. (2024a) Gender and true crime: Women, murder, feminism and therapy, in *Gender, True Crime and Criminology: Offenders, Victims and Ethics*. Emerald Publishing, pp 9–25.

Wattis, L. (2024b) Sexual violence and true crime: Exposing power and injustice in the longform docuseries, in *Gender, True Crime and Criminology: Offenders, Victims and Ethics*. Emerald Publishing, pp 61–76.

Wattis, L. (2024c) True crime, male audiences and the digital hardman, in *Gender, True Crime and Criminology: Offenders, Victims and Ethics*. Emerald Publishing, pp 27–43.

Wattis, L. (2024d) True crime's ethical dilemmas, in *Gender, True Crime and Criminology: Offenders, Victims and Ethics*. Emerald Publishing, pp 95-101).

West, H. and Sanders, T. (2003) *Transparency and Conspiracy: Ethnographies of Suspicion in the New World Order*. Duke University Press.

Wibberley, C. (2012) Getting to grips with bricolage qualitative inquiry: A personal account. *The Qualitative Report*, 17(50), pp 1–8.

Wilde, N. (2016) *The Monstering of Myra Hindley*. Waterside Press.

Williams, D.J. (2020) Is serial sexual homicide a compulsion, deviant leisure, or both? Revisiting the case of Ted Bundy. *Leisure Sciences*, 42(2), pp 205–23.

Williams, E. (1967) *Beyond Belief: A Chronicle of Murder and It's Detection*. Pan.

Wilson, D. (2007) *Serial Killers: Hunting Britons and their Victims 1960–2006*. Waterside.

Wilson, D. (2009) *A History of British Serial Killing: The Shocking Account of Jack the Ripper, Harold Shipman and Beyond*. Hachette UK.

Wilson, D. (2023) Lucy Letby confirms yet confounds our ideas of a serial killer. *The Guardian*, 20 August, available at www.theguardian.com/uuk-news/commentisfree/2023/aug.20/lucy-letby-confirms-yet-confounds-our-ideas-of-a-serial-killer (accessed 10 March 2025).

Wolf, D. (1993–present) *Law and Order*. Wolf Entertainment and Universal Television.

Wolfe, T. (1996) *The New Journalism*. Picador.

Wood, T. (2020) *Ted Bundy: Falling for a Killer*. Amazon Studios.

World Bank (2021) Bulgaria. Systemic country diagnostic. Report number: 166792-BG, International Bank for Reconstruction and Development / The World Bank, available at https://documents1.worldbank.org/curated/en/727791642521506054/pdf/Bulgaria-Systematic-Country-Diagnostic.pdf?_gl=1*lpwzgn*_gcl_au*MTI5ODA5ODc1MS4xNzI0MDU4MjY5, (accessed 10 August 2018).

Wood, M.A. (2018) 'I just wanna see someone get knocked the fuck out': Spectating affray on Facebook fight pages. *Crime, Media, Culture*, 14, pp 23–40.

Yallop, D. (1988) *Deliver Us from Evil*. Hachette UK.

Yardley, E. (2017) *Social Media Homicide Confessions: Stories of Killers and Their Victims*. Bristol University Press.

Yardley, E., Lynes, A.G.T., Wilson, D. and Kelly, E. (2018) What's the deal with 'websleuthing'? News media representations of amateur detectives in networked spaces. *Crime, Media, Culture*, 14(1), pp 81–109.

Yardley, E., Kelly, E. and Robinson-Edwards, S. (2019) Forever trapped in the imaginary of late capitalism? The serialised true crime podcast as a wakeup call in times of criminological slumber. *Crime Media Culture*, 15(3): pp 503–521.

Yardley, E. and Wilson, D. (2016) In search of the 'angels of death': Conceptualising the contemporary nurse healthcare serial killer. *Journal of Investigative Psychology and Offender Profiling*, 13, pp 39–55.

Young, J. (1998) Writing on the cusp of change: A new criminology for an age of late modernity, in *The New Criminology Revisited*. Palgrave Macmillan, pp 259–95.

Zarhy-Levo, Y. (2010) Looking back at the British New Wave. *Journal of British Cinema and Television*, 7, pp 232–47.

Index

A

Abbott, Jack Henry 60
activism 3
Adderley, E. 143
Alexander, M. 49
Allitt, Beverley 141, 144
American Civil Liberties Union (ACLU) 53, 56, 64
Anderson, Lindsay 69
Angry Young Man 69
artificial intelligence (AI) 16
Atkins, Susan 58
Atkinson, Kate 105
Atkinson, Patricia 94
Atkinson, R. 25
Attica Riot 41
autobiographies 13
Avery, Steven 33
Aviv, Rachel 147

B

Baldwin, James 54
Bandaya, Uphanda 94
Barker, Pat 105–6
Barkley, Elliot James 41
Barrett, Nicole Baker 56, 59, 60
Bates, Alan 74
Bauman, Z. 25, 67
Beale, V. 85
Becker, G. 44
Bennett, Keith 73, 75, 86
Bentham, A. 91
Bergdahl, Bowe 111
Berkowitz, David (Son of Sam) 16, 66, 109
Berlinger, J. 88, 89, 90, 91
biblical accounts 12
Bilton, Michael 97–8, 99, 101
binge watching 18, 26
biographies 13
Biressi, A. 18, 27, 35, 149
Birmingham Six 115–16, 117
Birnes, W.J. 87
Black communities 152
Black criminality 47

Black Lives Matter 48
Black masculinity 29, 43, 54
Black Panther 70–3
Black sexuality 48, 54
Blair, Tony 43
Bleksley, Peter 143
Boling, K.S. 111, 114
Bolter, J. 57
Bolton, Z. 140
Bonn, S. 66
Bourdieu, P. 38
Bowman, Margaret 84
Bowman, P. 33
Box, Dan 110
Brady, Ian 19, 21, 66, 73, 74–6, 85, 86, 139, 140, 141, 142, 150
Braverman, Suella 118
Brearey, Stephen 140, 145, 146
bricolage 5–6, 93, 103
British films and TV dramas 65–6, 67–8
  Black Panther 70–3, 79–80
  Des 76–9, 80
  documentary film 68
  Ealing Cinema 69
  New Wave 69–70, 73, 76, 80, 150
  See No Evil 73–6, 80
Bronte, Emily 75
Brooks, C 144
Browder, L. 27
Brown, S. 24–5, 37, 102
Browne, Tracey 94
Bruzzi, S. 33
Buford, Bill 59
Bulgaria
  accession to the EU 129–30
  corruption 121, 128, 129
  crime and the media 126–9
  fear of crime 128
  gender-based violence 132–3
  lack of media independence 126–7
  Mafia 128–9, 130, 131
  marginalized discourses 131–4
  political elites 127, 131
  post-communist transition 122, 123, 126, 127–8

INDEX

Roma community 131–2
shifting blame from individuals to institutions 125–6, 129–31, 134
social inequalities 124, 132, 134
Bulger, James 4
Bulley, Nicola 119, 156
Bundy, Ted 5, 27, 28, 34, 66, 81–4, 150, 151, 152–3
  Conversations with a Killer 88–9
  enduring fascination with 92
  execution 84, 89
  photographs of 91
  social status 90, 92
  The Stranger Beside Me 84–5, 86, 88
  trial 90, 91
  TV and film portrayals 86–9
Burn, Gordon 5, 21, 22, 29, 53, 101–3, 105, 106, 107, 150, 151
  Somebody's Husband, Somebody's Son 15, 93, 99, 103–4
Burns, Ken 48
Bush, George H.W. 43
Bushnell, Ben 56
Byford inquiry 96–7, 98

C

Cain, J.M. 14
Cameron, D. 151–2
Caparelli, Michael 109
capital punishment 58
  see also death penalty
Capote, Truman 1, 12, 14–16, 29, 63, 93, 103
Caputi, Jane 20, 95, 96, 105, 151
Carver, Raymond 59
Casey Review 101
Cashman, Thomas 110
catharsis 12
celebrity culture 2, 17, 18, 30, 66–7, 79, 91, 151
Chakrovarty, I. 145, 146
Chambers, Tony 140, 145, 146
Chapman, Annie 19, 20
Cheetham, Caroline 138
child pornography 25
Christian values 13
Christie, Agatha 116
Christie, John 67
cities 21–2
citizen detectives 17, 115–19
class bias 116
Claxton, Marcella 94, 101
Cleaver, Eldridge 60
Clift, Montgomery 19
Clinton, Bill 43
Colebrook, M. 103
Collier, A. 144
Collins, Wilkie 148

colonialism 110
combat sports 33
commercialization 2
commodification of crime 50, 53, 63, 85
conspiracy narratives 122, 123
consumer capitalism 35, 37
Costigan, George 75
Courtenay, Tom 74
Cowart, Edward 90
crack cocaine 46
crime dramas 12, 118
crime fiction 3, 12
  see also true crime genre
crime thrillers 65
Crimecon UK 11
Crimewatch 117
criminal justice system (CJS) 39, 45
critical criminology 4
cruelty 25
Cullen, Charles 141
cultural change 24
cultural criminology 35
Cummins, I. 16, 18, 19, 22, 27, 144

D

Da Ronch, Carol 83
Dahmer, Jeffrey 27, 82
Dalton, N. 143
Damiens, Robert-François 39
Das, Soham 143
Davies, Dan 102
De Angelo, Joseph James 108
De Rondo, M. 118
death penalty 44, 53, 56, 57–64, 89, 91
Demme, Jonathan 87
Dennehy, Joanna 136
Denzin, A.J. 6
Derrida, J. 58
detective fiction 14, 17, 39
deviant leisure perspective 35–6
Dickens, Charles 148
Didion, Joan 47–8, 60–1, 114, 115
digital culture 28–9, 150, 153–6
dirty realism 59
disorganized serial killers 81–2
disturbing content 24
DNA evidence 99
Doane, B. 153–4
Dobson, James 89
documentaries 12, 18–21, 30, 89–90
  British films and TV dramas 68
dog-whistle politics 43
domestic abuse 19
domestic violence 12
Downey, Lesley Ann 73, 75, 140
Downing, L. 151, 152
Du Vernay, Ava 49
Dukakis, Michael 43

187

Dunning, Eric 32
Dunning-Kruger effect 125
Duru, N.J. 48

E

Ealing Cinema 69
Eastwood, Clint 78
Eddowes, Catherine 20
Efron, Zac 86, 90
Egger, S.A. 18
elevator assault videos 28
empathy 25
Engley, R. 114
ethical questions 2–3, 4, 11, 24, 26, 35, 36
ethnicity 131–2
Evans, Dewi 144
Evans, Edward 73, 75
Everard, Sarah 44, 101
'execution sermons' 13
executions 14, 53

F

Fairstein, Linda 49
Fanning, S.E. 65
Ferrell, J. 66
fear of crime 40, 42–3
Federal Bureau of Investigation (FBI) 68
female victims 14
female vulnerability 31
femicide 20, 36, 104, 105, 106, 151–3
feminist critiques 30, 54, 94–5, 96, 151, 154
feminist-inspired content 34
Fernández-Morales, M. 31
fetishization 14
film noir 67
Finney, Albert 74
Flanders, J. 148
fly-on-the-wall documentaries 45
Foot, Paul 115
football violence 32, 33
forensic psychologists 22
Forman, Miles 55
Foster, Alan 98
Foucault, Michel 39, 40, 81
Fraley, R.C. 29
Fraser, Frankie 30
Frazer, E. 151–2
French cinema 70, 74
Friedman, M. 42
Froggett, Joanne 74

G

Gacy, John Wayne 66, 85
Gadd, Richard 156
Galizia, Daphne 121
gallows literature 89
gangster aesthetic 32
Garland, D. 39, 43, 44

Gavin, H. 142
Ghey, Brianna 111
Gilbey, Susan 140, 146
Gilchrist, K. 110
Gilmore, Leigh 31
Gilmore, Gary 5, 53, 55–7, 59–60, 61, 62, 63, 64, 150
Gilmore, Mikal 55, 57
glamour 13
Glass, Ira 112
gonzo journalism 113, 114, 120
Gordon Burn Prize 102
gothic escapism 14
Gothic fiction and drama 20–1, 92, 94
'governing through crime' 40
graphic content 24, 25, 26
Gray, Judd 14
Greer, C. 2, 65
Greer, Germaine 54
Grierson, John 68
Grover, G. 107
Grusin, R. 57
Guildford Four 115, 117
Guterres, António 122
Gutierrez, Maria Cristina 112

H

Haggerty, K. 2, 16, 67, 137, 138
Halbach, Theresa 33, 34
Hall, S. 40, 43
Hammett, Dashiel 14
Hancock, D. 114
Hanley, D. 68
Hansford Johnson, Pamela 139, 140
hardman genre 29, 30, 31–2, 154–5
Hardstark, Georgia 109
Harris, Thomas 28
Harrison, Joan 99
Harrison, Sean 74
Harvey, Ian 145
Hayek, Friedrich 42
health care serial killers 141
hedonistic killers 82
hegemony of science 24
Helliwell, Christopher 100
Hersey, J. 15
Hickey, E.W. 141
Hickock, Richard 15, 16
high-profile cases 4, 17, 27, 39, 41
Highsmith, Patricia 92, 104
Hill, Jacqueline 94
Hindley, Myra 19, 21, 66, 73, 74–6, 85, 86, 136, 138, 139, 141, 142, 150
    funeral 142–3
Hitchcock, Alfred 105
Hitchens, Peter 46
Hoare, Shauna 144
Hobbs, S. 30, 34

Hoffman, M. 30, 34
Holmes, R.M. 82
Holmes, S.T. 82
Holt, Sandi 88
homophobia 90
hooligan culture 29, 32–3
Horeck, T. 26, 28–9, 31, 35, 150, 153
Horton, William 43
Hull, K. 111, 114
Hull, Liz 138–9
Humble, John 107
hyper-real 24

I

imprisonment, use of 4
injustice narratives 33
institutional failures 4
Internet Movie Database (IMDb) 65

J

Jack the Ripper 16, 19–20, 65, 94, 105, 148
Jackson, Emily 94, 101
Jarvis, B. 65
Jayaram, Ravi 139, 145
Jena, S. 84
Jenkins, Phillip 28, 149
Jensen, Max 56
Jones, C. 43
Jones, Tommy Lee 57
Jordan, Jean 94, 98
journalists
 murder of and attacks on 121, 127
 World Press Freedom index 126
Jouve, N.W. 106

K

Kaplan, P. 11
Katz, Z. 66
Keenan, David 102
Kelleher, C.L. 141
Kelleher, M.D. 141
Kelly, Alison 145
Kelly, Mary Jane 20
Kemper, Ed 87–8
Keppel, R.D. 87
Kesey, K. 55
Kilbride, John 73
Kincheloe, J.L. 6
Kilgariff, Karen 109
King, M. 22
Kinnell, Hilary 95, 99
kitchen-sink dramas 5, 69, 73, 74, 80
Klaas, Polly 27
Kloepfer, Elizabeth 86–6
Koch, Ed 47
Koenig, Sarah 111, 112–14
Krasimirov, Severin 122, 124, 125, 126, 131–2, 135

Kray twins 29, 30, 66
Krustev, Ivan 134
Kuciak, Ján 121

L

LaChance, D. 11
Lang, Fritz 67
Larker, Walsh 30
Larsen, R.W. 86
law and order agenda 4, 14, 38, 39, 41, 42, 45
Law and Order series 11
Lawley, Sue 70
Leach, Barbara 94
Leach, Janet 100
Leach, Kimberly 84, 86, 91
Lederer, Elizabeth 49
Lee, Hae Min 108, 111–12, 114
Lee, C.A. 142
Lee, Harper 15
Leskewiecz, A. 138
Letby, Lucy 5, 17–18, 19, 110–11, 136–9, 151, 156, 157
 BBC *Panorama* documentary 139–41
 handwritten notes 143
 institutional responses 145–6
 photographs 138
 Thirlwell Inquiry 145, 146–7
Levi Strauss, C. 5
Levy, Lisa 84
Leyton, E. 18, 82
liberal elites 43, 58
libertarian tradition 42
Lincoln, Y. 5, 6
Linnemann, T. 149
Loach, Ken 76
Long, Maureen 94
longform murder narrative 148–1
Lorre, Pete 67
Louis XV 39

M

magazines 14
Maher, B. 147
Mailer, Norman 5, 29, 54–5, 93, 103, 150
 Eastern Voices 61–3
 (The) Executioner's Song 53, 55–8, 60, 62–3, 64
 Western Voices 59, 60, 63
Maksimov, Svilen 125, 126
male sexual violence 88
Mangan, L. 91
Manson, Charles 115
marginalized groups 22, 50, 82, 131–2
Marinova, Viktoria 121, 122, 123, 124, 125, 129, 130, 132, 133, 157
Martha's Rule 146
masculine ideal 30

mass media 2, 4, 17, 19
Masters, Brian 78–9
Mays, Daniel 77, 78
McCabe, R. 28, 34, 88, 92
McCabe, Wilma 88, 91, 92, 93–4
McClain, Asia 112
McDonald, Jayne 94, 95
McHale, Bernard 143
McKay, Neil 100
McMurtry, L. 114
McNamara, Michelle 29, 108, 155
McNulty, Matthew 74
McRobbie, A. 106
Me Too movement 30, 152, 154
media effects 24
media independence 126–7
mediatized murder 2, 65
  see also mass media
Meili, Trisha 47
memoirs 31
Menis, S. 35
Metropolitan Police Service (MPS) 101
Millward, Vera 94
Mina, Denise 102
miscarriage of justice 12, 38, 50, 117
  see also wrongful convictions
misogyny 20, 30, 92, 94, 95, 101, 103, 104, 106, 152
missionary serial killers 82
mixed martial arts (MMA) 33
Miyatovich, Dunya 122
monetization of crime 26, 50
Moore, Marilyn 94
Moors Murders 15, 16, 18, 19, 27, 73–6, 85, 91, 144, 149
  enduring fascination 107
moral panic 14, 90
Moritz, Judith 140, 141
Mormonism 58
motivation 1, 17, 82
Mounsey, Joe 75
mugshots 21
Mullin, Chris 115–16
murder narrative 26–8
Murley, J. 26–7, 149, 152
Murray, Chad Michael 87
Myers, Benjamin 102

N

narcissism 76, 79
Negra, D. 31
neoliberalism 38, 42, 134, 135
New Journalism 16, 54, 113
New Labour 43
New Wave 69–70, 73, 76, 80, 150
Newburn, T. 43
news coverage 12, 17
newspapers 13

Nichol, Annie 27
Nichols, Mary Ann 'Polly' 20
Nicholson, Jack 55
Nicholson, R. 34
Nicol, Brenda 56, 59
Neilson, Donald 70–3
Nilsen, Dennis 19, 76–9, 149
Nixon, Richard 114
Nordic Noir 65
nostalgia 21
notoriety 66–7
Nouvelle Vague 70, 74
Nozick, R. 42

O

O'Callaghan, C. 65
O'Hagan, A. 21, 22
Oldfield, George 96, 97, 100
online culture 150
Operation Hummingbird 140, 146
organized serial killers 81–2, 83
old-style true crime 36
Oswald, Lee Harvey 62–3

P

pamphlets 13
Pâquet, L. 34
patriarchy 20, 25, 36, 54, 89, 105
Patterson, J. 70, 71
Peace, David 22, 67, 70, 71, 102, 106–7
Peake, Maxine 74
Pearson, Yvonne 94
Peelo, M. 139, 140
penal policy 11, 40, 41, 42, 43, 44, 48, 49
penal populism 43–4, 118
Penfold-Mounce, R. 30, 66
'penny dreadfuls' 14, 22
photographs 21
podcasts 23, 154
  women-led 29, 30, 31
police officers 17, 118
  fly-on-the-wall documentaries 45
  'maverick' approaches to policing 46
  public confidence in 44–5
police procedural genre 67, 68, 75, 77, 80
Politkovskaya, Anna 121
Pope, Jeff 100
populism 3, 40, 43–4, 118
'pornoviolence' 25
Potter, Dennis 76
power–control killers 82
power dynamics 39
Pratt-Korbel, Olivia 110
Prejean, Helen 61–2
Presdee, Mike 36
prison system 48
probation officers 41
prostitutes see sex workers

psychological profiling 22, 81–2
psychopathic killers 27–8
public anxiety 2, 50
public executions 89
public fascination 19
punishment 38–9
  symbolism 39–44
  true crime and 44–6
punitive attitudes 44, 58
Punnett, I.C. 11
podcasts 12, 26, 108–11, 119–20
  Serial 108, 111, 119

R

racism 32, 38, 43, 58, 101, 110, 132
racist stereotypes 49, 54
Rackstraw, E. 45
radical criminology 118
Ramey, J. 14
Ramirez, Richard 91
rape myths 31
rape survivors 31
rational choice theory 44
Rawlings, P. 37
Raymen, T. 35
Reagan, Ronald 11
Reality TV 45, 118
Rector, Ricky Ray 64
Redhead, S. 32
Reade, Pauline 73, 75, 85
rehabilitation 40–1, 42, 44
Reisz, Karel 69
research methods 5–6
Ressler, R.K. 81–2
Reyes, Matías 47
Richardson, Kevin 47, 49
Richardson, Tony 69
right-wing extremism 32
ripper myth 104–7
Ripper tours 19–20
Ripperology 94–5, 148
Ritchie, June 74
Roberts, L. 6
Rokuljski, Anna 94
Rubenhold, H. 20, 94
Roma communities 131–2
Ruby, Jack 58
Rule, Ann 84–5

S

Salaam, Yusef 47, 49
Saltzman, R.H. 89
Santana, Raymond 47, 49
Savile, Jimmy 35
Schiller, Larry 58, 62, 63
Schmid, D. 91
Scottsboro Boys 48
Seal, L. 139, 140

Sears, J. 117
Seltzer, M. 2, 4, 11, 17, 27, 116, 123, 156
sensationalism 2, 14
serial killers 2, 4, 5, 16–18, 19, 20, 21
  British films and TV dramas 65–6, 67–8
    Black Panther 70–3, 79–80
    Des 76–9, 80
    documentary film 68
    Ealing Cinema 69
    New Wave 69–70, 73, 76, 80
    See No Evil 73–6, 80
  celebrity 17, 18, 66–7, 79, 81, 91
  cultural prominence 149
  fascination with 91–2
  female killers 142–5
  glorification 27–8
  health care workers 141
  myths 34
  outsider status 13
  psychological profiling 22, 81–2, 83
sex workers 20, 94, 95, 99–100, 105, 110
sexual abuse 31
sexual gratification 82
sexual violence 19–20
Shephard, Sam 57
Shipman, Harold 22, 94, 141, 144
Simon, J. 39, 40, 41, 42, 48
Simpson, O.J. 59
simulated violence 25
Sitford, M. 22
Smelt, Olive 94, 106
Smith, Christopher 99
Smith, David 74, 75
Smith, Joan 95, 96
Smith, Maureen 74
Smith, Michelle 144
Smith, O. 35
Smith, Perry Edward 15, 16
social, economic and political construction
  of crime 3
social learning theory 24
social media 2, 17, 89
Son of Sam 16, 66, 109
Sontag, S. 21
Soothill, K. 107
Sparks, R. 102
Spassov, O. 126
Special Air Service (SAS) 30
stereotyping 49, 54
Stop Mass Incarceration Network 48
Storrs, E. 142
stranger attacks 39
streaming 18, 23, 26
Stride, Elizabeth 20
Sumpter, Donald 71, 72
surveillance technology 28–9
survivor memoirs 31
survivor testimony 35

Sutcliffe, Peter 5, 20, 68, 70, 71, 93–6
  arrest 97
  death 97
  plea of diminished responsibility 95, 97
  see also Yorkshire Ripper
Sweeting, Adam 100
Syed, Adnan 108, 111–14
Sykes, Teresa 94
Synder, Ruth 14

T

Tabbert, U. 125
Tate, Sharon 58, 115
Taylor, Shaw 117
technological change 3, 24
Tennant, David 76, 78
Thatcher, Margaret 4
Thompson, Hunter 114
Thompson, Jim 14
Timmermans, Frans 121
titillation 139, 140
Tompkins, P.K. 1
Topping, P. 85
torture 82
toxic masculinity 33, 103
Toynbee, Polly 144
Tracy, Spencer 19
Trenchova, Daniela 124
true crime genre
  alternative justice spaces 37
  critical appetite for 50
  cultural impact 2
  cultural prominence 17
  distinguished from journalism 11
  ethical questions 2–3, 4, 11
  ethical shift 4
  expanding market 12
  exposing injustice 4
  focus on individual actors 3
  history 3–4, 12–14
  murder narrative 26–8
  newer genres 33–5
  old-style 36
  politics and 11
  popularity 1, 158
    with women 29
  public consumption 2
  subject matter 12
  technological developments 3
  template 1
  tropes 3
Trump, Donald 47, 49
TV documentaries see documentaries
TV news specials 17

U

urbanization 21
US penal system 48, 49

V

Vera Institute 48
Vicary, A.M. 29
victim advocacy 34
victim blaming 95
victim-centred documentaries 31, 37
victim hierarchies 36
victimisation 36
victims
  marginalization 17, 22, 26, 50, 82
  women 14, 19–20
Vietnam war 61
violent content 24, 25, 26, 35
visionary killers 82
visual content 26
voyeurism 3, 26, 36, 100, 138, 151

W

Wacquant, L. 38
Wakeman, S. 109
Walker-Craig, Colleen 110
Walkowitz, J.R. 152
Walls, Margaret 94
Walsh, Larke 32
Wattis, L. 2, 29, 32, 99, 100, 106, 107,
  149–50, 152, 154
Watts, Becky 144
welfare retrenchment 42
West, Fred 21–2, 27, 66, 100, 102–3,
  142, 149
West, Rosemary 21–2, 27, 66, 102–3, 136,
  142, 149
Western film genre 61
Whitechapel Murders see Jack
  the Ripper
Whittaker, Josephine 94
Whittle, Lesley 70, 71–3
Wibberley, C. 5
Wilde, N. 142
Williams, Alberta 110
Williams, Emelyn 15, 141
Wilson, David 16, 22, 137–8
Wise, Korey 47, 49
Wolfe, Tom 114
women, violence against 14, 19–20
women-led podcasts 29, 30, 31
women's rights 14
Wood, T. 33
working-class life 69
wound culture 116
Wright, Steve 100
wrongful convictions 33, 90,
  108, 115

Y

Yallop, D. 99, 100
Yardley, E. 109, 110, 116, 118, 156
Yorkshire noir 106–7

Yorkshire Ripper 5, 16, 20, 27, 68, 70, 71, 72, 85, 91, 93–7, 149, 152
  Byford inquiry 96–7, 98
  climate of fear 96
  cultural and media output 97–101
  enduring fascination 107
  feminist critiques of the case 94–5, 96, 100
  hoax tape and letters 96, 98, 99, 107
  'killing suit' 98–9
  misogyny associated with the crimes and police investigation 95
  police investigative failings 96–7, 98, 101
  ripper myth and 104–7
  sexualization of the Ripper narrative 98
  Somebody's Husband, Somebody's Son 15, 93, 99, 103–4
  timeline of murders and attacks 93–4
Young, M.L. 102

Z

Zodiac killer 66, 67
Zupansky, Dan 109

www.ingramcontent.com/pod-product-compliance
Lightning Source LLC
Chambersburg PA
CBHW070042040426
42333CB00041B/2133